**CHRIST CHURCH
COLLEGE
CANTERBURY**

Vision Critical Studies

General Editor: Anne Smith

George Crabbe

GEORGE CRABBE

Terence Bareham

VISION

Vision Press Limited
11–14 Stanhope Mews West
London SW7 5RD

ISBN 0 85478 084 X

© 1977 by Terence Bareham

Printed in Great Britain
by Clarke, Doble & Brendon Ltd
Plymouth and London
MCMLXXVII

Contents

Preface

The following texts are used throughout this book, and references to them are abbreviated as shown:

Ward: *Poems by George Crabbe*, edited by A. W. Ward in three volumes. Cambridge; 1905–1907.

Life: *The Life and Poetical Works of the Revd. George Crabbe*, edited by his son. John Murray; 1847. The son is referred to throughout this book as 'the biographer'.

New Poems: *New Poems by George Crabbe*, edited, with an introduction and notes by Arthur Pollard, Liverpool University Press; 1960.

Sermons: *The Posthumous Sermons of George Crabbe*, edited by J. D. Hastings. Hatchard; 1850.

Sources of manuscripts consulted, and relevant abbreviations in the text are as follows:

Bod.:   The Bodleian Library, Oxford.
B.L.:   The British Library.
Cran.: The Earl of Cranbrook's collection.
C.U.L.: Cambridge University Library.
Sheff.: Sheffield City Libraries, W(entworth) W(oodhouse) M(uniments) Bk. Papers.
Yale.: Yale University, Beinecke Rare Book and Manuscript Library.

For permission to quote from manuscripts I am grateful to the Librarians of all the above libraries, to The Earl Fitzwilliam and his Trustees; and to the Earl of Cranbrook who generously made photo-copies of all his Crabbe mss. available to me.

The editors of *Orbis Litterarum* have given permission for me to use material, in Chapter VI, which had previously appeared in a briefer form in Volume XXIV, no. 3, 1969.

My thanks are also due to Professor Arthur Pollard, of Hull University, who has given advice over a period of several years on both textual and critical matters. Professor Alastair Thomson, and Dr John McVeigh, of the New University of Ulster, read parts of the manuscript, and I am deeply indebted to them for guidance and encouragement. Jean Gow typed the manuscript, and my greatest debt of gratitude is to her.

Whatever errors or shortcomings of fact or opinion remain are entirely my own.

The reader who is not familiar with the detail of Crabbe's life may find helpful the following notes on his career, and on some of the people mentioned frequently in this book.

BURKE, Edmund (1729–1797). Whig statesman, and man of letters. Burke was at the summit of his political career in 1781 when Crabbe appealed to him for support. Burke was instrumental in getting his early work published, in introducing him to people like Samuel Johnson and Sir Joshua Reynolds, and in placing him as chaplain to the Duke of Rutland.

BOWLES, Rev. William (1762–1850). Became a close friend of Crabbe in his later years. Bowles was highly regarded as a poet in his day, and as editor of Pope. The posthumous *Life and Works* of Crabbe, published in 8 volumes in 1834, is dedicated to Bowles.

CARTWRIGHT, Rev. Edmund (1743–1823). Dean of Lincoln. Reviewer, poet and industrialist. Became friendly with Crabbe in about 1788, through having a neighbouring parish and common literary interests. Cartwright was the inventor of the power-loom.

FOX, Charles James (1749–1806). Leading whig politician. Met Crabbe through Burke. It was partly Fox's encouragement which induced Crabbe to publish *Poems* in 1807, though Fox was dead by then.

LEADBEATER, Mary (1758–1826). Quaker authoress of poetry and 'improving' stories. Her grandfather, Abraham Shackleton, had been Burke's first schoolmaster, and Mrs Leadbeater met Crabbe at Burke's house in 1784. Over twenty years later she wrote to remind the poet of their previous meeting, and a long correspondence began which supplies much detail on Crabbe's mind and art.

LONG, Charles. M.P. for Aldeburgh at the time when Crabbe was first trying to establish himself. One of the poet's principal champions and allies in his adversity.

NORTH, Dudley (1748–1829). Originally Dudley Long, the brother of Charles Long. Changed his name on inheriting an estate. Influential behind the scenes in whig politics, and another ally of Crabbe in the years before he became famous.

Chronological table of principal events in Crabbe's career

24 December	1754	Crabbe born at Aldeburgh.
age 14		1768	Apprenticed to a surgeon near Bury St Edmunds.
17		1771	Moved to Woodbridge, where he met Sarah Elmy, his future wife.
18		1772	First poems published in *The Lady's Magazine*.
21		1775	*Inebriety* published.
		1775	Returned home, on completion of surgical apprenticeship. Took temporary employment as a labourer on the quay at Slaughden.
	late	1775	Set up as apothecary at Aldeburgh.
22	late	1776	Visited London to acquire medical knowledge.
23		1777	Returned to practice in Aldeburgh.
25	December	1779	Resolved to abandon practice of medicine, and seek a literary fortune in London.

26	April	1780	Second trip to London, where he endured acute hardship and poverty.
	August	1780	*The Candidate* published.
27	Feb./Mar.	1781	Appealed, successfully, to Burke for assistance.
	July	1781	*The Library* published.
	December	1781	Ordained deacon. Went back to Aldeburgh as curate.
28	May	1782	Made chaplain to the Duke of Rutland.
	August	1782	Ordained priest.
29	May	1783	*The Village* published.
	December	1783	Married Sarah Elmy.
31	March	1785	*The Newspaper* published.
33	October	1787	Death of the Duke of Rutland.
35		1789	Became rector of the parish of Muston.
38	November	1792	Left his parish to reside in Suffolk.
51		1805	Forced to return to Muston by decree of his bishop.
53	September	1807	*Poems* published.
56	April	1810	*The Borough* published.
58	September	1812	*Tales in Verse* published.
59	October	1813	Death of Mrs Crabbe.
60	June	1814	Became rector of Trowbridge.
65	July	1819	*Tales of the Hall* published.
68	August	1822	Visited Sir Walter Scott in Edinburgh.
78	3 February	1832	Crabbe died.

Introduction

Crabbe enjoyed an immense popularity in his own day. The number of editions his work went through during his lifetime prove this beyond doubt: eight editions of *Poems* within as many years, six of *The Borough* within only four years, while *Tales* managed an average of more than one new edition each year for nearly a decade after its first appearance in 1812. Even if the print-runs were short for many of these ventures, it still indicates that a very sizeable part of the English reading public sought his work eagerly and regularly. Most of his contemporaries acknowledged his standing amongst Regency poets. Byron and Scott thought him in the very first rank of living authors: Wordsworth, though with reservations, declared that Crabbe's poems "will last from their combined merits as Poetry and Truth full as long as anything that has been expressed in verse since they first made their appearance." (Letter to the poet's son dated February 1834, quoted in *Life*, p. 117). His publishers seemed ready to back this popular feeling in the most handsome way. When the poet left the firm of Hatchard in 1818 to join the group of distinguished authors who wrote for John Murray, his new publisher paid him three thousand pounds for the rights of all his existing works, together with *Tales of the Hall*, then just about to appear. Though the market for poetry seems to have been particularly healthy during the first twenty years of the nineteenth century, such a sum would still place Crabbe among the best paid poets in the land.

Yet, within a further twenty years his stock began to decline. Though there continued to be a steady stream of reprints of his work, not only from Murray, his official publisher, but from many other houses too, and though some of the finest Victorian minds

—Newman, Tennyson, Rosetti, Landor, Clough, and Hardy—continued to proclaim his merits, he gradually lost his hold on "the general reader". It is difficult to see how a writer admired by such diverse minds as these could sink almost completely out of public recognition, yet by the last quarter of the century, Edward Fitzgerald (one of his most passionate admirers) had to admit that Crabbe was not now much read in England.

> Women and young people never will like him, I think: but I believe every thinking man will like him more as he grows older.
>
> (Letter to C. E. Norton, 1 Feb 1877.
> Cited in *The Letters and Literary Remains of Edward Fitzgerald*, 1889)

It is probably only among those engaged with English literature professionally, that any "revival" of interest in him has truly occurred, even today. "Who now, for instance, thinks of George Crabbe?", asks Somerset Maugham in *The Moon and Sixpence*. "He was a famous poet in his day . . . He had learned his craft at the school of Alexander Pope and he wrote moral stories in rhymed couplets. Then came the French Revolution and the Napoleonic Wars, and the poets sang new songs. Mr Crabbe continued to write moral stories in rhymed couplets . . ." (Penguin edition, p. 12).

Despite the inaccuracies in Maugham's account of things, the *fact* of Crabbe's continued lack of popularity is incontestable. Despite the luck he has had in commentators over the last thirty years, and the respect accorded to him as the man who created the story of Britten's opera *Peter Grimes*, he has remained firmly in an obscure corner between the "Augustans" and the "Romantics" where university syllabuses and the general reader alike can allow him a tiny mention in the history of English poetry without ever engaging in a serious attempt to explore the work. The very bulk of his writing may be daunting. A complete Crabbe is a hefty book: few poets who were as "occasional" in their writing can have written as much as Crabbe, and few are more different in substance from the reputation they have acquired. For most people he exists, if at all, as the gloomy and pessimistic author of *The Village* (which social historians use as evidence about the agrarian revolution), "Peter Grimes" (which is only known in the much transmuted operatic version), and, perhaps, "Sir Eustace Grey", which serves as a tentative reminder that he was not quite without awareness of the changing fashions in the literary world around him.

Such a view is wrong on every count. If we see him as a "Regency" poet, as an author intensely aware of the atmosphere, the problems, and the poetical trends of the years from 1780 to 1830, we must respect him, even if admiration comes more slowly in the train of respect. I have chosen to discuss him in this way in this book: I try to place him within the context of the church he served as an ordained minister for fifty years, of the political upheavals he witnessed—and, as serving magistrate, helped to alleviate—as a writer making a substantial contribution to the investigation of the human mind which so preoccupied his fellow authors in those years, and as "pure" artist as well. In this last category he can be his own worst advocate. Long-winded, quaint to the point of eccentricity, insistently moral, he can put up a daunting barrier to the willing reader. Yet despite these liabilities he offers a range and bulk of work which speaks skilfully, and often passionately, about the human predicament in terms which transcend the boundaries of time and place; which is as relevant today as it was in 1815, and which is shaped by an artist who was aware, sensitive, and adventurous in his employment of language.

I have not employed a strictly biographical approach, since this is not the most helpful way to view Crabbe's work. The first half of his life is usually presented as the archetypal struggle of aspiring talent to be recognised, and the latter years as the complacent drowsiness of satisfied ambition. Anyone who has read Crabbe's letters will know that this is an over-simplification. He took, as his son says, an "exquisite pleasure" in composing his verses, spent a great deal of time in revising and reworking them, and had a carefully considered attitude to both the morality and the technicality of poetry. There can be little doubt that it was only after he had found security in the church that he brought to fruition the talents which were latent in him, and only after his fortieth year that his imagination properly freed itself from the shackles of both form and content which he had inherited from the world of Johnson.

It is possible to get a glimpse of the man himself in old age through a letter sent by a young Irishman to his friends in a Quaker community just outside Dublin, in the year 1820. The addressee is Mary Leadbeater, herself a writer of both verse and novels, and for long the admiring friend of Crabbe. She had clearly advised her young protegé, James Lecky, to call on Crabbe if he should be passing near Trowbridge, and his account of the visit is still extant, though the manuscript is very difficult to read in places, and sadly deteriorated even over the last twenty years. In his enthusiasm, Lecky has "crossed" his letter—that is, has turned his paper and written over his own script: this makes even more difficult the task of deciphering his almost completely unpunctuated description of the visit to Crabbe. As far as I know, the letter has not been previously published, except in the fragmented and inaccurate version Mrs Leadbeater put into *The Leadbeater Papers*.

Calais November 21 1820.

My dear Mary Leadbeater,
The bustle of London and the attention of the many kind friends I met there prevented me writing to you before now which I intended doing as I was indebted to you for a great gratification in an introduction to George Crabbe I spent Tuesday [Thursday] the Twenty fourth of last month with him and his reception of me should show you the regard he has for Mrs Leadbeater—his gate opens into Trowbridge which is a dirty manufacturing town and his house stands in the middle of about two acres of ground surrounded with a high wall and is hid with trees so that standing at his hall door you see nothing of town and might fancy yourself far in the country when I first called he was in his study and I sent word by the servant that a gentleman wished to see him and [whilst] the servant in answer was telling me to walk up he himself was down after him to the hall with an eager look and manner that marks him on most occasions—he politely brought me up and while he was reading your letter he was also telling me what it was about. When he had done he shook hands heartily and bid me welcome because I was "a friend of dear Mrs Leadbeater" he then enquired eagerly how long since I had seen you—how you were—what health you enjoyed—how you lived—what were your habits—if you had reason to be happy on account of your family &c &c—and said he should be so glad to see you but ended "No I never shall". He said he intended making you a

present of his works and would have sent them by me if I [was] returning to Ireland. He will however write to you about them his appearance has nothing remarkable but [   ] and strong mind and energy his features are not [   ] so that his picture would give an idea of him but thought and activity are very visible in his countenance his mind seems to have all the energy of youth though his body is evidently losing it—his crown is balled and the few hairs he has on his temples and back of his head are [well] strewed with powder he talks fluently much more so than his letters would lead me to think—he likes to argue a point with you and he does it so well—so acutely and clearly that it is pleasant to argue with him—from his manner now I guess that amiability has been the character of his life every one about him seems anxious to serve him and his family appear thoroughly attached to him independent of duty—he told me he never liked children and I observed he took no notice of his little grandchildren after dinner tho' they had only come that day on a visit—a fine little boy and girl (the boy a noble one) George Crabbe and the hopes of the family. He told me he never had any ear for music No he said I never could know God Save the King from Rule Britannia but he has been made to like [Roy's wife] by its being played about twelve times for him—in answer to my surprise at this he laboured with much earnestness to convince me that an ear for music and a taste for harmonious verses were quite distinct and did not of necessity go together—be this as it may music gives him no pleasure He told me he was born at Aldborough a seaport village on the coast of Suffolk he remained there till he was three or four and twenty he was then introduced to his patrons who were the means of bringing him forward in the world and by their means about this time got a living near Belvoir Castle in Leicestershire where he remained till about six years ago when he removed to the living of Trowbridge—from the time he first left Aldborough he never visited it till this summer and [from] the way he spoke of it I am sure that the scene of his birth and youth "had its attraction still" it has lately from being a poor village become the resort of visitors at watering season and he said he found it like an old friend in a new coat. he told me it was from his residence in this town that he had his knowledge of seafaring men and manners He said writing had paid him very well and money was a great inducement to him to write yes—said he—And fame too but—he added—"the nearer we get to that state where money will be of no use the less it is to be regarded"—he regretted in strong terms that Milton and

15

Dryden should have been so badly paid and seemed to think this was owing to the times they lived in—He said Tales of The Hall deserve and have had a greater popularity than any of his works— that the Smugglers and poachers was an imaginary tale and was suggested to him by a conversation with Sir Samuel Romilly in which Sir Samuel reprobated the evils which arise from the law as it now stands on these points—he said he intended moving for some amendment and thought a popular writer might found a story with a good moral in the mischief of these practices. here again it is to be regretted—as far as we can see—that death has deprived us of the services of that useful man—Lady Barbara and the Ghost he has told just as he heard it—he told me he is oftener at a loss for incidents than for characters. that few of his stories are real nor are they entirely made out but that he has been in the habit of putting parts of different stories and incidents together till he makes out what pleases him—he seldom takes anything from books but all from what he sees and hears—Now—I was not so impertinent as to ask him all these questions but when I was alone with him in his study he told me most of what I have written without my asking him—his good nature led him to tell me unasked what he knew I had curiosity to hear—I was greatly struck with his unassuming manner—he will hear you with as much attention and shew as great defference to what you say as if he was your inferior—He goes to bed at twelve rises at nine and from breakfast till four—his dinner hour—he is alone in his study from that till twelve he devotes to intercourse with his famly &c—tho' his second son John Crabbe is his curate yet he himself preaches every Sunday the church is just at his gate—a fine old gothick building—built— as he told me—when labor was a penny a day . . . Crabbe is writing another work he sais he will write while he lives for writing is now the business of his life . . .   (B.L. ms. Eg. 3709.b.)

If a re-assessment of Crabbe's art began only with the contents of Lecky's letter, it would show us a fuller, more complex and more devoted poet than we often assume him to be. There are other grounds for a revaluation, however, and it is these, together with hints and suggestions taken from letters by and about Crabbe, which have made another book on him seem worth while. Since René Huchon's study *Un Poète Réaliste Anglais*, which was translated by Frederick Clarke as *George Crabbe and his Times* in 1907, most of the books on Crabbe have done justice to aspects of the man's interests and avocations, but few have concentrated as much as I wish to do upon his political and religious thinking or his investigations of the unconscious mind. What emerges, I hope, is that while Crabbe remains one of the greatest individualisers of experience—and to this extent my account of him must re-tread ground it shares with earlier studies—yet the degree to which he was in the main-stream of a current of sane, rational, reliable English thought and custom, and the extent to which he was regarded as the proper spokesman of that point of view, may not have been put before in quite the way that this book hopes to present it.

1

Crabbe's Church

Had I been more intimate with . . . Crabbe . . . I should have
ventured to touch upon his office as a minister of the Gospel,
and how far his heart and soul were in it so as to make him a
zealous and diligent labourer: in poetry, though he wrote much,
as we all know, he was not so.

(Wordsworth, *Works*, ed. Dowden, 1893, Vol. V. p. 360)

I

Most accounts of Crabbe take note of him as a writer, and then,
incidentally, as a clergyman. Following a tendency initiated by the
less charitable of his parishioners, some critics have gone so far
as to suggest that he crept into the haven of the Church for purely
mercenary reasons. Here, they argue, lay sanctuary for the indigent country lad with a taste for letters and for luxury. It is
maintained that to Crabbe, holy orders meant little more than a
release from the humiliation, the near starvation, in which Burke
found him.

Such an attitude suggests moral obtuseness on Crabbe's part,
and indifference to it on Burke's. In the end this might not matter:
it is not the moral character of the author with which this book
is primarily concerned, but with poetic integrity. Yet there is a
direct link between the two, and only through an investigation of
the Church Crabbe served, and his responses to it, shall we gain a
complete picture of him as a poet. Such a composite view will,
of course, involve us with the consideration of Crabbe as a moral
poet. There is a tendency, in recent criticism particularly, to avoid
this issue. Morals do not furnish an immediately congenial area

19

of discussion for the twentieth-century literary critic. Yet Crabbe is a moral poet, and to read him as any other kind of writer is to select unwarrantably, or to misconstrue.

On many counts, therefore, it is profitable to see Crabbe as a parson who wrote verses, rather than as a poet who happened, for very worldly reasons, to have become a parson. Thus we put Crabbe's moral emphasis back where it belongs, as the clarifying and defining focus of his ideas, the radical impetus behind virtually all his mature work. I hasten to add that, far from making him a uniformly dull, gloomy or humourless writer, it is only through an understanding of his real religious motivation, that we can grasp the nature and effect of the trenchant wit, as well as the appalled sadness he so often encompasses.

It is an old failing to cry, "amuse me, amuse me, but for God's sake don't let me see that you are *teaching* me anything"—particularly if the teaching tends to take the form of an unpalatable truth, such as the value of restraint and continence. Such truths, *because* they are self-evident, may render their author "suspect". Hence a great deal of the bewilderment Crabbe's poetry has always inspired may be explicable if we accept that he was a parson of the Church of England at the end of the eighteenth and commencement of the nineteenth centuries; the difficulty may disappear if we understand aright the climate and circumstances of the church he served. Not that I wish to make him a simple writer. The time span of his life, and the social and ecclesiastical background to that life make simplicity an unlikely attribute. Though it is a tiresome truism to speak of an "age of change", as we do when we write of Chaucer, of Shakespeare, or, for that matter, of Wilfred Owen, yet by common consent the century from 1750 to 1850 probably effected more rapid changes upon the face of England and her people than any other one hundred years.

The church of which Crabbe was a servant shared in that change. At his birth it may have been at its nadir, both as a social organisation and in its philosophical and theological speculation. It is *this* church, we must remember, that Macaulay is calling up in the third chapter of his *History* where the contempt pours from his pen; this church that Fielding and Hogarth depict. The Church of England, during the years of Crabbe's ministry had a pretty unsavoury public image. Fielding, Smollett, Hogarth,

Macaulay, from the outside give a grim picture of the rampant simony, worldliness, corruption, or moral torpor. The clerics themselves in real life sometimes seem to be trying to step back into the pages of *Joseph Andrews* or *Humphrey Clinker*. Sydney Smith, a member of the church himself, seemed to sum it up when he wryly commented to Mr Gladstone, in 1835: "Whenever you meet a clergyman of my age, you may be sure he is a bad clergyman". Crabbe tends to be placed within this embarrassingly latitudinarian fold, after which it can be virtually forgotten that his living, for fifty years, was earned in the Church, and that only a small handful of his poems were written before he committed himself to this life.

II

To begin with, the Church had become a political institution. This will only be properly understood by casting back as far as the Restoration, and then on to the "Glorious Revolution". The uneasy years in which Englishmen watched their newly re-instated monarchs flirting with Catholicism, cast a shadow forward for well over a hundred and fifty years: they take us past Pope's chagrin at being denied the laureateship because he was a Catholic, past Locke's exclusion of the Romish from his definition of civil toleration, past the absurd but frightening popular outburst of the Gordon riots with their cry of "No Popery", and well beyond the Reform Bill, before there was sufficient forgiveness and forgetfulness in the English to allow Catholics anything like an equal share of the common democratic rights. Though one may now feel that nothing can really justify this, it is only by trying to understand, that we shall begin to comprehend the factors which make the Augustan and Regency church so worldly, so venal, so political. James II gave many people cause to fear that he actively supported the cause of Catholicism, to the point where he would wish to direct the government of secular institutions by a religious principle which was at odds with the will of the majority of his subjects. It was against such despotic government by the monarch that the nation had formerly rebelled, and which had driven it to the desperate, and uncharacteristic, step of regicide. Not only the memory of mis-government, but the guilt of the national

21

crime which brought it to an end haunted the English conscience for a long time to come.

In the eighteenth century simple issues of allegiance were clouded by the influence and personality of Robert Walpole, for thirty years first minister of the kingdom. Opponents of the Walpole ministry were ready to attribute all the nation's moral and social ills to the personal character of this extraordinary man. It was his misfortune to have nearly all the best writers lined up against him; Swift, Gay, Fielding. Such literary opposition tended to stratify society even further, so that the traditional rivalries of City and Court, or Court and Country, which had been the bases of earlier political behaviour, were superceded by the Whig faction that comprised the Walpole supporters in office, opposed by the discomfited Tories in opposition. It was during the eighteenth century that England became a political nation, in the modern sense, and it is unfortunate that it was during the same period that writers in opposition were so insistent that it was becoming an immoral nation. Walpole kept a mistress and governed by a system of bribes and jobbery. It is doubtful whether this public face of corruption represented anything radically different from earlier abuses of office. But when Fielding or Swift is presenting the case to us, it is difficult to keep a balanced and open mind. It was into the immediate aftermath of this literary war that Crabbe was born.

He inherited a world in which the novelty of the strife and the very old tendency to compromise were at war with each other. For compromise, the doctrine of "let well alone" runs deep through the century, making itself felt in literary as well as in political judgements. From the accession of William III, Englishmen had become tacitly convinced that they had had enough of civil war and regicide, and that any price was worth paying to avoid a repetition of the events of the first half of the seventeenth century. There were few enough Englishmen in 1715 who seriously wanted a Stuart restoration by force of arms; there were precious few by 1745. To Fielding, though he opposed the Walpole regime most bitterly, the Young Pretender's army was merely "the banditti". Whatever ironies may lurk behind the quizzical surface as he describes Tom Jones' meeting with the military, the passage epitomises the feelings of the average Englishman.

The serjeant had informed Mr Jones that they were marching
against the rebels, and expected to be commanded by the glorious
Duke of Cumberland. By which the reader may perceive . . . that
this was the very time when the late rebellion was at the highest;
and indeed the banditti were now marching into England, intending, as it was thought, to fight the king's forces . . . Jones had
some heroic ingredients in his composition, and was a hearty well-
wisher to the glorious cause of liberty, and of the Protestant
religion.

(Penguin edition, p. 336)

The Church was, through the middle years of the eighteenth
century, intensely whiggish in its higher echelons, latitudinarian
in its tenets, and worldly in its outlook. There was an undertow
of toryism amongst the country parsons. One cause of this was
that the benefice often lay in the gift of the local squire, who,
being of the conservative, landed, opposition party, as like as not,
would seek out an incumbent of like mind. Though Crabbe's "The
Squire and the Priest" (*Tales*, XV) is about a dogmatic rather
than a political difference, it shows an awareness of the troubles
that arose when squire and parson were at odds, just as the
obvious sympathy of George, the squire in *Tales of the Hall*, makes
the duties of Jacques, the vicar, easier to perform. In all prob-
ability the natural inclinations of many of the country clergy made
them conservative in politics. For their position was anomalous.
The vast majority were men educated at the universities, where
the long and expensive course gave them a professional status,
and should have bequeathed some social recognition too. Yet
throughout the century we read of the economic and social plight
of the curates in particular. After taking a degree at Oxford or
Cambridge, the aspirant for employment in the Church was
admitted to deacon's orders. This permitted him to preach, but
not to officiate at communion. Nor did it guarantee him a pulpit
or a stipend. He had to look either to his college for a fellowship, to a patron to find him a place, or to his own initiative and
fortune to offer himself as curate to an absentee vicar. There was
a sideways path into the household of some wealthy family, as
chaplain. This, of course, was the means by which Crabbe entered
the Church.

Usually, the newly-ordained deacon sought a pulpit in some

parish where the rector was not present to fulfil his duties. Over half the parishes in the land were of this kind, for often the value of the living was so small that it could not, alone, support an incumbent. A rector would then hold more than one living, reside upon the more profitable, and hire in a curate to tend the needs of the parishioners of his smaller living. Curates often lived a most miserable and penurious life, some never actually progressing to the dignity of having their own cure of souls. The livings were in the hands of various wealthy parties. Crabbe's first presentation—to two tiny parishes in Dorsetshire—was made by the Lord Chancellor, and we find local Member of Parliament friends trying to manipulate an exchange for him, and the Prime Minister himself being involved in the business. Livings, then, were to be given away or sold by whoever owned the rights to them. Higher offices in the Church were distributed in a like manner, bishoprics being exchanged for votes in the House of Lords, and perquisites like Deaneries and prebends were used like railway tickets to make as long and profitable a journey towards the top as was possible within the sphere of influence of the traveller concerned. Thus it was a Church structured on intensely hierarchical lines.

III

The Church was divided into sections almost sealed off from each other. The bishops were political appointments—on one famous occasion it was their vote in the House of Lords which saved Walpole's administration—made by the Crown under pressure from the Ministry of the day. Since, for forty years through the middle of the eighteenth century this ministry was whig, it is not surprising that the bench was of like political opinion, almost to a man. Many bishops had no particular religious inclination; the church, at this level, offered a respectable and often profitable career to the younger sons of the aristocracy. It was almost a matter of course for the eldest son to inherit the estate, the second to be found a convenient see, and the third to enter the army or the navy. Many of the bishops were non-resident: indeed, even the most conscientious of them had to be for at least half the year, since their presence was required in London during the annual sittings of parliament from October to May.

There was a notorious difference in the value of the bishoprics. The poorest was worth only about five hundred pounds a year, which meant that it was not regarded as tenable without other emoluments. These came in the form of the "pluralities"—other benefices and church offices, which increased the value of the living, though often not adding to the burden of the duties required of the holder. Bishop Watson, who held Llandaff for thirty-four years without ever residing there, is perhaps the most famous of all the eighteenth-century pluralist bishops. He also held the professorship of chemistry at Cambridge, which he later exchanged for the chair of divinity, that latter office being the more remunerative: Watson had the stipend raised from three hundred and thirty to one thousand pounds. His appointment to Llandaff should have been the stepping-stone to better church preferments. That was what Llandaff was for. Few men stayed there many years. Unfortunately Watson was an outspoken and independent man, and he remained in his tiny see because he was unpredictable in his vote in the House of Lords. It was rather his political than his religious conscience which was active, but the effect of the one upon the other was immediate as far as preferment was concerned. No administration could trust him to "toe the line"; he sympathised with the American rebels, he advocated the repeal of the Test Act, (which forbad Catholics to hold office), and he agitated for church reform, ironic as this latter cause may seem in such a man. Clearly then, he was "unsafe" to the government and his failure to proceed beyond Llandaff is eloquent testimony to the necessity of obeying political pressures in the eighteenth-century church. Given the heavy expenses, even of non-residency, it is not surprising that Watson had to be a pluralist. Beyond his Cambridge posts, where he was again frequently non-resident, he held sixteen separate church benefices. His scale of priorities is revealed in his own words:

> . . . my time . . . has been spent, partly in supporting the religion and constitution of the country by seasonable publications; and principally in building farm-houses, blasting rocks, enclosing wastes, in making bad land good, in planting larches, and in planting in the hearts of my children principles of piety, of benevolence, and of self-government. By such occupations I have recovered my health, entirely preserved my independence, set an example of

spiritual husbandry to the county, and honourably provided for my family. *(Anecdotes of the Life of Bishop Watson, 1817, p. 240)*

Watson had befriended Crabbe when they met at Belvoir in 1782.

An even more interesting example is the Bishop of Lincoln, Tomline—or Pretyman, as he later called himself. We meet Pretyman in the pages of the *Life of Crabbe*, written by the poet's son who was himself a clergyman. Crabbe, who had been living away from his parish, was ordered by Bishop Pretyman (or Prettyman as the biographer calls him) to return to his flock at Muston, where various curates had served in the poet's absence. As Bishop of Lincoln, Pretyman had two thousand pounds a year from his revenues within the see. This put it about half way up the list of bishoprics. He also held the deanery of St Paul's, however, which was worth as much again, making him a wealthy man.

That the duties of these two busy posts should have made joint tenure quite impossible seems never to have entered the Bishop's head. The implicit acceptance of all this by Crabbe, and by his son in the biography, is interesting. It reveals the state of mind of the clergy towards not only their superiors, but to the ecclesiastical system as a whole. Pretyman had come up by one of the customary paths to power: he had been tutor to the younger Pitt, and was swept into a bishopric on the Prime Minister's political coat-tails, almost into the Primacy. His case became something of a *cause célèbre* when George III dug in his heels and, for once, refused to accede to the advice which his political leader gave on an ecclesiastical appointment. This is not quite the end of him, for he had also come into a private fortune. An eccentric gentleman who had met him only once, had offered to leave him a vast sum if he would change his name to that of his benefactor. (Rather acidly, a contemporary remarked that had his benefactor met him *twice*, it would never have happened!) Thus it is that he crops up as both Tomline (his own name) and as Pretyman, which he accepted with his inheritance. Yet neither Crabbe nor his son seemed to have found anything anomalous or offensive in the instruction by the Bishop with his sixteen incomes and his two names, that one of his clergymen must not hold two benefices.

With Frederick Harvey, the Earl Bishop of Londonderry, even his contemporaries recognised a total lack of religious interest or commitment. He represents the *social* status of the eighteenth-century church, pure and simple. Neither his uncertain sanity nor morals impeded his elevation to the see of Londonderry. There is a comment on Harvey in the diary of the Reverend William Jones, who is himself a typical Anglican priest of the later eighteenth century. His diary, which I shall be quoting again later, gives a fair picture of what parish life was like at the time. Jones' financial lot, and his moral outlook, offer a strong contrast with the lives of people like the Bishop of Derry, yet one feels that professional disgust rather than personal envy motivates Jones to write thus:

> The Bishop of Londonderry . . . realised an income of £5,000 a year, by leases of lands, independent of the profits of the see, which are computed at £10,000 a year. I wish his lordships conduct authorised me to say that equal attention had been payed to his spiritual duties.
> (*Diary of the Reverend William Jones*, ed. O. F. Christie, 1929, p. 161)

IV

There were bishoprics of business and bishoprics of ease—the terms are those actually used in the eighteenth century. It would be quite wrong either to assume that all the bishops were merely venal hacks, or that even the "bishops of ease" were quite without feeling for their office. It is easy to exaggerate the torpor and the worldliness of the church of Crabbe's day. Where a bishop took his office seriously, it could be an extremely onerous one. His diocesan visitations had to be crowded into the months when parliament was not sitting, and the state of the roads made travel over long distances dangerous as well as wearisome, hence the administrative duties of a large diocese far removed from London must have been intensely burdensome. Carlisle was apparently one of the most tiresome.

Under such circumstances the business of confirmation was conducted on a huge scale; there are records of up to three thousand persons being confirmed on one day. Ordinations were difficult to arrange. In theory, any aspirant for orders had to present himself to the bishop in his see for the ritual to be undertaken, or to make the long and expensive visit to the capital. There were ways round this; Letters Dimissory allowed absentee bishops to direct intending ordinands to other sees. Unfortunately this allowed some singular abuses. There were several cases of imposters who had never been ordained being in possession of a curacy. It became almost a regular practice to claim a degree from Trinity College, Dublin, the details of which had been conveniently lost in transit across the water.

In addition to ordination and confirmation, and his visitations, the bishop had general responsibility for the administration of his see, though this often devolved on the arch-deacon. Though there are notorious cases of abuse of office, one is struck rather by the examples of conscientious practice than by a picture of universal neglect. To some extent the tide was turning by this time: the Methodist upsurge helped to galvanise the Established Church into renewed activity—Crabbe experienced the effects of it in his parish at Muston, as we shall see. The evangelical movement within the Church itself signalled a renewed spiritual vigour, growing during the period of Crabbe's ministry. He was the servant, in other words, of a still predominantly worldly church, whose interests were in courts and camps as well as in cloisters, but a church more careful and diligent in attending its spiritual functions than we sometimes allow.

The lifetime of Crabbe saw few of the dynamic forward-looking divines of the decades before or after. He lived within the flat period between Law, Butler, and Berkeley, on the one side, and Pusey and Newman on the other—a period designated by Leslie Stephen as that in which the traditional link between philosophy and religion finally broke asunder. Post-Cartesian scepticism drove the wedge in deep, and political nepotism may have bred complacency. It is certainly true that if a comparatively humble parish priest like Crabbe was lacking in a dynamic or creative attitude to theology, if he failed to evolve and articulate a coherent and consistent creed which was not simply a redaction of the truisms of the past fifty years, he shared this fault with the most eminent divines of his day. Contentiousness, and change itself, were regarded with suspicion. Such activities, in the recent past, had led towards deism. Since that bogey had so recently been laid, it may have seemed better to leave the obscure places dark rather than start another spirit of the same ilk. And Leslie Stephen is probably right in sensing within the Church a shift to speculative indifference or atrophy in the years from 1760 to 1830:

> The most conspicuous literary phenomenon in the latter half of the eighteenth century in England is the strange decline in speculative energy. Theology was paralysed. The deist railed no longer; and the orthodox lapsed into drowsy indifference . . . England, the land of philosophers and freethinkers, no longer gave birth to iconoclasts or to serious investigators. Another set of topics was coming to the front in contemporary literature. Political discussions absorbed the energy of the keenest intellects.
>
> (*History of English Thought in the 18th Century*, 1962, Vol. 1, p. 316)

This was the generation to which Crabbe belonged. Despite the blandness or flaccidity in the fibre of the religious thinking he inherited and practised, he was a capable and respected pastor, and as a poet, arguably drew his strengths from exactly where his polemical and spiritual weakness may appear to lie.

V

The road to priesthood trodden by most country vicars, and the daily round of their pastoral care, has been recorded by William Jones, James Woodforde, and William Cole in the diaries they left. In the private records of these men we can recapture something of the spirit of their times. None of them wrote with an eye for posterity, and the picture they give of honest, committed labour, of earnest desire to serve their communities and to receive only their fair and due tithes in return, goes a long way to helping us understand the attitudes of George Crabbe, who is their contemporary and who shared their commitment to public service. The most profitable way of understanding Crabbe's poetry is as a document furthering this end. *The Parish Register* has a great deal in common with the diaries of Jones, Cole, and Woodforde. The sense of identity comes across very clearly in the following:

> The year seems to me to revolve more rapidly now than at any former period of my life. Death has been of late, and still is, unusually busy in my parish . . .   (*Jones, op. cit.*, p. 146)

> The year revolves, and I again explore
> The simple annals of my parish poor:

What infant-members in my flock appear;
What pairs I bless'd in the departed year;
And who, of old or young, or nymphs or swains,
Are lost to life, its pleasures and its pains.
(The Parish Register, "Baptisms", lines 1–6)

Crabbe's poem is as much about the priest as it is about the flock, just as though a diarist is recording both his own and other people's affairs. He prepares the ground by stating that he scarcely needs a "Muse" for this purpose, since it is his professional responsibility to know such subject matter. In "Marriages", he adopts a rigorously paternalistic attitude, pleading with his flock to take care before they plunge into wedlock, and "Burials" opens with a definition of the relationship between priest and parishioners which should obtain but all too seldom does. Interestingly, this little social and moral disquisition ends with "the diarist" recognising that he gives a permanence to these transitory lives:

Who are the dead, how died they, I relate,
And snatch some portion of their acts from fate.
(The Parish Register, "Burials", lines 73–4)

But the last line is an echo of Pope—"Oh snatch some portion of these acts from Fate, Celestial Muse! and to our world relate." Since Crabbe began his poem by disclaiming the Muse, we can see what a *structured* journey he has led us through his annals. This sense of control and discipline in *The Parish Register* is not generally enough recognised. The poem is criticised for falling apart into separate little thumb-nail sketches. But read properly, as the work of a parish priest within a tradition both social and literary, it takes on a new authority and sense of control.

The life of a country vicar was not an easy one. Samuel Johnson saw its difficulties very clearly:

Sir, the life of a parson, of a conscientious clergyman is not easy. I have always considered a clergyman as the father of a larger family than he is able to maintain. I would rather have Chancery suits upon my hands than the cure of souls. No, sir, I do not envy a clergyman's life as an easy life, nor do I envy the clergyman who makes it an easy life.
(Boswell's Life of Johnson, ed. A. Birrell, 1896, Vol. 5, p. 6)

30

Just how varied the conditions were, and how differently the incumbent could take them, emerges from a welter of often apparently contradictory information. Goldsmith's rector at Auburn was "passing rich on forty pounds a year" (while Bishop Watson was impoverished upon five hundred pounds); Fielding's parson Adams seemed to subsist on even less, while his colleague Trulliber enhanced his living by farming—a regular enough way of augmenting the stipend of a small living. Indeed, so many of the country parishes fell below Goldsmith's standard forty pounds, that pluralism among the rank and file clergy was an absolute necessity, whatever its rights and wrongs among the higher echelons of the church. Some livings were worth less than twenty pounds, which goes a long way to explaining why the *Extraordinary Black Book* can cite, in 1827, that three-fifths of the clergy of the Established Church were non-resident.

To attain this often inadequate remuneration the humblest of the curates had, or was supposed to have taken his B.A., and if he could possibly afford it, an M.A. thereafter. Even at the very beginning of the century an intensely frugal student at Oxford had to spend something like forty pounds a year to read for his first degree. Since the law forbade the ordination to a deaconship of anyone under twenty-three, it was possible for a poor man to obtain his qualifications (entry to the universities at seventeen being not uncommon), and still find himself with an intolerable wait before he could be ordained. Unless lucky enough to be elected to a college fellowship, the deacon then began the search for his first curacy, entering upon a vicious circle which ran, "no orders, so no curacy, no curacy so no orders". Even if he were lucky enough to be the lowest bidder to a non-resident vicar, the curate's worries were by no means over. Many cures did not boast a vicarage, or a recognised dwelling place of any sort for the incumbent. It is this which explains the almost nomadic life which Fielding's and Smollett's curates seem to live.

The profession was dreadfully over-subscribed. Nonetheless it remained for many poor but intelligent men a desirable step up the social and intellectual ladders. Men like William Jones who began as schoolmasters in these days when pedagogues and warehouse-keepers were on a par—Crabbe's father had been both—felt that the church was an "improvement" on school-teaching.

31

The laxness and unwieldiness of the ordination system meant that no effectual check could be kept upon the number of ordained curates.

This suggests a world where the worst of conditions obtain: too many aspirants for too few positions, which will yield too little subsistence, and too little scope for conscientious work. It is really more remarkable that the Georgian church did not collapse, than that it was marked by blemishes in its practice. These blemishes were well enough documented, and have remained to give the over-riding impression of parish priests in the period: the vicar of Ax-bridge was "intoxicated about six times a week" and was often prevented from conducting services by "the black eyes, honestly earned in fighting" (*Memoirs of the Life of Mrs Hannah More,* ed. W. Roberts, 1835, Vol. 1, p. 452). One remembers Square, Trulliber, and an army of similar disgraces to the cloth. It is too easy to forget the hundreds, the thousands of decent honourable men who, for a pittance, supplied both moral and physical counsel to their parish, who tended the sick, encouraged the talented, and comforted the bereaved. Of these were Woodforde, Jones, Cole, Crabbe, and his two sons.

The Rev. Jones exclaims on the trials of a busy parish, "What constant, solicitous care attends a large, extensive Parish . . ." (*op. cit.* p. 89). It may help to fill in some corners of the picture of Crabbe's art, to look at these cares. During the eighteenth century, services, which had been frequent during the week, especially upon saints days, became gradually curtailed to Sundays and a few holy days. Communion might become a quarterly affair, though taken with great earnestness by devout souls like Johnson. Despite the apparent laxness suggested by only one Sunday service, the parson might well be intensely busy on that day, since, if he held neighbouring cures, he would be expected to minister at each in turn. There are some hair-raising accounts of cross-country gallops from church to church!

Crabbe knew something of the poverty which could afflict the parish priest, even in his own benefice, let alone as curate to another:

Not one living in fifty enabled the incumbent to bring up a family comfortably. As children multiplied and grew, the household of the priest became more and more beggarly. Holes appeared more and more plainly in the thatch of his parsonage and in his single cassock. Often it was only by toiling on his glebe, by feeding swine, and by loading dungcarts, that he could obtain daily bread; nor did his utmost exertions always prevent the bailiffs from taking his concordance and his inkstand in execution. It was a white day on which he was admitted to the kitchen of a great house, and regaled by the servants with cold meat and ale. His children were brought up like the children of the neighbouring peasantry. His boys followed the plough; and his girls were out to service. Study he found impossible . . .   (Macaulay, *History of England*, 1953, pp. 247–8)

While these chapters on Crabbe and the Church are concerned, for the main part, with his *message* as this is affected by his status as a minister, there will also be insights into his technique, his attitude to literature, and indeed, into the sudden slump in his reputation after he died in 1832. On this last point Leslie Stephen's remark that "he lost his popularity with the present generation" (*Hours in a Library*, 1909, Vol. 2, p. 60), for instance, takes on a new cogency when one realises that to Stephen, "the present generation" is the post-Tractarian period, on the eve of which Crabbe himself died. A *theological* barrier between the latitudinarian of the old school, and the more aesthetic taste of the next generation, goes a long way to explaining what otherwise continues to be one of literature's minor mysteries—the decline in Crabbe's standing from being for Byron (and for most readers of the 1810s) an acknowledged master of English verse, to almost total neglect by the end of the century. One has only to read George Crabbe junior's memoir of his father to sense the change. It is not just that the poet was a more gentle man than *his* own father, the saltmaster, had been. The Biographer, himself a clergyman, a Cambridge graduate, and, incidentally, an author in a minor way, lives, breathes, and writes a different atmosphere from that which the poet emanates. The self-defensiveness, the rawness of the social questioning, have been shed in the Biographer's generation. He can assume automatically that it is not only *good* to be a parish priest, but that it is respectable, it will not cause him to be slighted or viewed askance.

VI

There is no simple linear development by which we can trace this advance in the standing of the ministers of the church from 1750 to 1830. To say that the poet ministered to a "Georgian" congregation, the Biographer to a Victorian one, gives a broad sweep of the change; it sketches in an effect, but leaves the causes unexplained. Even as late as 1803 we can catch the genuine whiff and savour of Swift's or of Smollett's church, through the reflections of the Rev. William Jones:

Surely the life of a clergyman, if his mind be properly disposed, and attuned, and his outward circumstances at all competent, is of all lives the most happy! But how do I pity the poor unfortunate, who enters into an office so solemn, as a mere profession, or business! What up-hill drudgery and how tedious must the several services appear, when not the *heart* but the *lips* only are engaged! It is to be feared that there are too many of this unhappy sort. Some unwary youths aspire to the profession, as what is styled "a genteel one". To others their friends and relations dictate this, strongly seconding their cruelly unkind suggestions with the immediate possession of "handsome preferment" from family, or friendly patronage. These are your "master-men", who do their duty by proxy, haggling with poor curates, till they can find those who will starve with fewest symptoms of discontent.

As to the fine gentlemen themselves, they are far more anxious to attain the fame of being "excellent shots", giving the "view-halloo", . . . than raising their voices in the desk or pulpit, or feeding the flock whom they are eager to fleece . . . A journeyman in almost any trade or business, even a bricklayer's labourer, or the turner of a razor-grinder's wheel, all circumstances considered, is generally better paid than a stipendiary curate . . ."

(Jones, *op. cit.*, pp. 147–9)

There can be little doubt that a traveller through England in 1803 would have met as varied a collection of clerics as did Joseph Andrews sixty-one years earlier. But the proportions would have changed: there would have been fewer Trullibers and fewer Thwackems. It is worth reminding ourselves that could this traveller have compassed time as well as space, within this same sixty years he could have met Gilbert White, Laurence Sterne, Crabbe,

Sydney Smith, John Wesley, Malthus, and Cartwright, the inventor of the power loom. Clearly, not all the members of this moribund institution were hacks or time-servers. The diaries which have survived, the unpremeditated testimony of the ordinary ministers who, having no literary aspirations, had no interest in presenting an untrue face to admiring posterity, tell of quiet devotion, of parochial care and of service, willingly given and gratefully received. William Jones states, without any particular pride, that he served his parish for nineteen years with no more than two Sundays' absence in all that time. For the last thirty years of his life Crabbe suffered from facial neuralgia, for which increasingly large doses of opium were prescribed. Yet Crabbe's younger son, who acted as curate to the poet at Trowbridge, writes thus of his father's sense of duty:

> . . . he did not omit the duty on one Sunday for nearly forty years —it would have been distressing to him to have ceased to officiate; but the pain to which he was subject, was frequently very severe; and when attacked during the service, he was obliged to stop and press his hand hard to his face . . . Under these paroxysms . . . he often hesitated whether he had not better give it up altogether . . . (but) he continued to officiate till the last two Sundays before his decease. (*Life*, p. 86)

The notorious cases, such as those of Watson and Harvey, may persuade us that there existed a schism between the humble parish priests and the prelates above them:

> Bishops live in high places with high people, or with little people who depend upon them. They walk delicately, like Agag. They hear only one sort of conversation, and avoid bold reckless men as a lady veils herself from rough breezes . . . What bishops like best in their clergy is a dropping-down-deadness of manner . . . It would be just as rational to give a frog or a rabbit, upon which the physician is just about to experiment, an appeal to the Zoological Society, as to give a country curate an appeal to the Archbishop against his purple oppressor.
>
> (Hesketh Pearson, *The Smith of Smiths*, 1934, p. 280)

So speaks Sydney Smith, himself a fascinating mixture of contradictions; wit, raconteur, socialite, avowedly unhappy with many of the functions of his office, yet, by his lights a faithful and useful member of the clergy.

What is clear, even from the thumbnail pictures presented thus far, is that a young man of humble origins, without benefit of powerful family or university connections, would have been mad to expect that this avocation would yield an easy living. The words of William Jones ring all too true:

> An increasing family and a decreasing income—What is to be done? . . . It struck a damp on my spirits yesterday, when, on casting up my accounts I found that the expenses of the last quarter exceed £36 which sum is almost double my income for the same quarter.　　　　　　　　　　　　　　(Jones, *op. cit.*, p. 94)

Nor would it have been primarily for the honour of the station that a man entered the Church amongst its junior ranks. Jones again, at Easter 1802:

> Mr Jones has the pleasure of waiting on his worthy friends and parishioners, to solicit the offerings usual at this season of the year, which constitute the chief value of his Vicarage, together with an equivalent for the tenths of gardens, etc. He hardly needs to suggest to his friends that the liberality of many individuals, which cannot impoverish them, will, (if it does not enrich), at least conduce to furnish him and his numerous family with a cheerful competence, which is all that he desires,—not for his own sake only, but that, after twenty-one years' residence here already, he may be able to attend to the solemn and very important duties of his ministerial office.　　　　　　　　　　　　　　(*op. cit.*, 135–6)

Thus was a parish priest obliged to solicit the tithes, legally his due, upon which his wellbeing depended. Had Crabbe suffered any illusions on this score, he was speedily disabused. A fair proportion of his voluminous correspondence is taken up by irritated or downright outraged letters to laymen and to other clerics about the financial rights and duties inhering in the parish organisation.

VII

The story of Crabbe's ordination and preferment, because it is so typical, offers a good introduction to the manners and conduct of the Church he was striving to join, and I will trace the course of his career in my next chapter. Venality, simony, pluralism, torpor, indifference: these are the charges frequently brought against the Church of England in the eighteenth century. While it is impossible to deny their substance *in toto*, it is none the less quite inaccurate to see these maladies as characterising all branches of the church, as being uniformly prevalent, or as being unnoticed and unreproved. By the end of Crabbe's life, in 1832, the tone and temper of the Church was very different from that which had prevailed at his ordination in 1781. The worst was past even by then, though the old customs of non-residence and politicking died hard. In Trollope's Barchester one sees signs of the old habits still; in preferment, in personnel, in structure, in the very ethos of the church, worldly influence dominates.

It is as a son of this Church, in all its aspects, that I wish to consider Crabbe: as venal pluralist and as devoted curator of souls, as poet who will "preach his hour", and as anatomist with the scalpel. There can be few poets, not only who arouse such diverse feelings, but whose allies themselves are so opposed to each other on why they wish to champion his cause. To me, the reconciling and the governing factor is his adherence to and his practice within the eighteenth-century Anglican Church.

By looking at Crabbe the parson one comes much closer to the heart of what bewilders many of his commentators—his moral stance. An extraordinarily small part of his output is overtly and specifically the work of a member of the Anglican Church, speaking *cum privilegio* from his pulpit. He is a teacher, not a preacher, and if this seems semantic juggling, the works themselves are there to clarify the point. He does not touch the mysteries of faith as Donne or Hopkins may do. He lacks the clear grave note of conversation with which Herbert addresses his personal God. Crabbe's religion emerges by indirect ways and at one remove. It could be argued that much of it might equally well have been the work of a lawyer or a gentleman farmer. Like Jacques in *Tales of the Hall*, Crabbe is "a moral teacher". At the end of the eighteenth century this was a very specific term of denigration. Crabbe presented a challenge to the critics of his faith by accepting for the character in his poem and for himself, this contentious title. Part of the trouble is that his moral is so simple; it can be grasped by anyone (which is more than can be said for many moral or religious systems), yet it is followed by almost no-one—"I preach for ever; but I preach in vain!" (*Parish Register*, "Marriages", line 130). It is often the frustration implied in these stories where the catastrophe could so easily have been avoided that makes Crabbe seem pessimistic or ill-humoured. On occasion, in his parochial work, he must have felt these sentiments himself. It must be frustrating to have so clear a view of what makes sin successful, what makes vice so prevalent, and yet fail to communicate the simple message whereby remedy can be achieved. It can be reduced to this: there are no passports to bliss, there is no guaranteed security. Sin steals upon our secure hour; indeed, the danger really begins when we become aware of apparent security. Only a constant exercise of the trained and disciplined will can help us avoid the pitfalls. Do good, and some happiness *may* ensue; do evil, and misery *certainly* will.

This "may" and "will" go to the heart of Crabbe's so-called pessimism. Put thus it can equally be called a sad, realistic recognition of the course of life. Even in his most strictly and inexorably moral tales, Crabbe does not cheat though. He does not stand as puppet-master manipulating the strings in order to lead naturally innocent people to a pre-determinedly vicious end. Perhaps many of his tales fail to be *tragic* because they show people getting just what they deserve. On occasion however, he can rise to genuine heights, to join the remarkably small band of English writers who have written pure tragedy. "The Parting Hour" (*Tales*, II) is of this kind, as is "The Mother" (*Tales*, VIII). In neither can Crabbe be accused of manipulating events, for both are based on strict fact, events which the poet himself witnessed or was told of. I deal elsewhere with "The Mother", from the aspect of the ill-treated daughter. What I would call attention to in this chapter is the discretion with which Crabbe hints the punishment which the mother herself receives for her heartless and utterly inhuman conduct. Very briefly the situation of this poem is that Dorothea, who as a child always had her own way, grows to expect her family to obey her whims implicitly. Her elder daughter is just like the mother, but Lucy, the younger, is of an entirely finer temper. An important society wedding is arranged for this elder daughter, and Lucy—although in love with a humble curate, can only marry him once her sister is settled. The elder sister dies, and the mother "warns off" the poor curate so that the younger daughter can fulfil the aristocratic match. Her lover leaves in despair, and Lucy gradually pines away, though the mother seems totally oblivious of behaving vilely, and continues to preen herself and socialise whilst her daughter goes mad before her very eyes. The grotesque, posturing shadow which Dorothea is, the mirror-life when reality is fading, convinces us not only that the mother is more mad than Lucy, but that she is passing through a living death which is the utter negation of all she strove for, all for which she wantonly destroyed other people. The poet manages to leave us uncertain whether Dorothea *knows* what she has done, and is acting out a self-defensive role, or whether she is unaware of her own in-humanity. Thus he makes us empathetic witnesses to the distress in the poem. From Lucy's point of view it is all totally unfair; she has done nothing to deserve the treatment she receives.

This tale is of a completely different kind from those where a just "cum-uppance" befalls the embodiment of pride ("The Parish Clerk", *The Borough*, Letter XIX), greed ("The Struggles of Con-science", *Tales*, XIV), or ingratitude ("The Brothers", *Tales*, XX). Nor are his moral outcomes trite, for Crabbe can make the interior punishment so severe that any external sanction against the offender is superfluous; the ending of "The Brothers" shows this. A sailor, having entrusted all his wealth to his landsman brother in return for hospitality when he is ashore, finds ingratitude and contempt. He is rejected, ostracised, finally denied even the company of his favourite nephew, and he dies of a broken heart. The successful brother is left, apparently unpunished and unmolested, but the poet knows better:

> He takes no joy in office, honours, gain;
> They make him humble, nay, they give him pain;
> "These from my heart," he cries, "all feeling drove;
> "They made me cold to nature, dead to love."
> He takes no joy in home, but, sighing, sees
> A son in sorrow, and a wife at ease;
> He takes no joy in office—see him now,
> And Burgess Steel has but a passing bow;
> Of one sad train of gloomy thoughts possess'd,
> He takes no joy in friends, in food, in rest—
> Dark are the evil days, and void of peace the best.
> And thus he lives, if living be to sigh,
> And from all comforts of the world to fly,
> Without a hope in life—without a wish to die.
>
> ("The Brothers", *Tales*, XX, lines 398–411)

It is that last half line which gives the final turn of the screw, revealing, as it does, the degree of moral torpor and attrition which Isaac has brought upon himself.

The purpose of this moral teaching, based for the main part upon instances from life which the poet has observed for himself, is to demonstrate that we are most often fallible through what we regard as our strengths. Where there arises a co-incidental fusion of temptation and the blind-spot of pride, we shall fall. It is our own fault, usually, for we have neglected in our spiritual gymnastics, exactly the one exercise which would have identified and conquered this pride. Crabbe's skill is in showing the infinite diversity of methods by which the individual deludes himself: "The Parish Clerk" is the perfect example. In passing, it is worth noting that this may explain why those who know Crabbe best, still feel that "Peter Grimes" is one of his most noteworthy productions. To those who know little of him except this poem, it may appear his norm. It is far from being so, and the more frightening for its unusualness. Grimes is a natural phenomenon, rather than a fallible, weak, or silly man. There seems to be an original sin in Grimes which, for all his "strictness", Crabbe seldom suggests that man is cursed with.

2

Portrait of a Man Promoted

"Unskilful he, to fawn, or seek for power"
(Goldsmith, *The Deserted Village*)

I

No man entered a profession as tiresome and exhausting as that
I have described unless he had either the positive chance of rapid
advancement, or a very real sense of dedication. At the outset of
his career in the church, Crabbe did not have the former; we must
therefore assume that he did enjoy a sense of vocation, and without giving him credit for it, we cannot understand the motive
springs of his life or of his poetry. The story which emerges is a
curiously trammelled one. With Crabbe's devotion to the church
there is a curious admixture of shrewdness, sheer cupidity, and
social malaise. He often behaved badly by standards other than
those of his own generation. Yet all the elements—the reprehen-
sible with the meritorious—must be caught in any assessment of
the man and his work which hopes ever to commence doing
justice to the ambivalence, the contradictions, and the range of
experience he writes about. The evidence is clear before us on both
sides—the ambiguity of the life, and the earnestness of the man
himself. The Biographer tells us that his father composed sermons
and devotions at a period considerably prior to that at which
Burke effected an entry for him to the ministry, and the London
Journals bear blunt witness to his distress at the crisis in his
affairs, and to the devout spirit in which Crabbe faced that crisis
during his long months in the wilderness, with one coat, and no
prospect of his next meal before him:

41

My God, my God, I put my trust in thee; my troubles increase, my soul is dismayed, I am heavy and in distress; all day long I call upon thee: O be thou my helper in the needful time of trouble. Why art thou so far from me, O my Lord? Why hidest thou thy face? I am cast down, I am in poverty and in affliction: be thou with me, O my God; let me not be wholly forsaken, O my Redeemer! Behold I trust in thee, blessed Lord. Guide me, and govern me unto the end. O Lord, my salvation, be thou ever with me. Amen. *(Life, p. 25)*

This was the period at which Crabbe left home, desperately unhappy, and with a slim volume of indifferent verses in his pocket, and headed for London to make for himself a literary reputation. The story of those months is told most movingly in the *Life*. There can be no doubt of the deep sense of faith which sustained him at this time, and which made him an entirely proper candidate for holy orders, even though there is a sense of opportunism about the timing of the decision, and a suggestion of worldly ambition behind it all. Yet these private devotions ring with conviction.

It is not much to the credit of Edmund Burke, to suggest that he enabled Crabbe to enter the ministry whilst lacking all proper motivation. The Biographer's testimony is quite explicit about the circumspection with which Burke acted:

It was in the course of one of their walks . . . that Burke, after some conversation on general literature, suggested by a passage of the Georgics . . . passed to a more minute inquiry into my father's early days in Suffolk . . . and drew from him the avowal that . . . he felt a strong partiality for the church, "It is most fortunate", said Mr Burke, "that your father exerted himself to send you to that second school; without a little Latin we should have made nothing of you: now I think we shall succeed . . . Having gone through the form—for it was surely little more—of making proper inquiries as to the impression left of Mr Crabbe's character in his native place—Mr Burke, though well aware of the difficulties of obtaining holy orders for any person not regularly educated, exerted himself to procure the assent, in this instance, of Dr Yonge, the then Bishop of Norwich: and in this, backed by the favourable representations of Mr. Dudley North and Mr. Charles Long, he was eventually successful. *(Life, pp. 27–8)*

Burke was a man of devout and sincere mind, and though the above account is almost over-eager to justify the moral propriety of Crabbe's clerical ambitions, it seems quite unnecessary to question the motivation on either side. The account given in the *Life* is too bland, it slides over dates, times, and motivations, but it is essentially true. All the available private correspondence confirms the rectitude with which both Burke and Crabbe proceeded. It is important to establish this point, since any claim that Crabbe is to be read as a religious poet will clearly be suspect if his convictions themselves are open to doubt. The human-ness of the man emerges from this story too. He was, after all, a grace-and-favour entrant to orders by the back door of Burke's power and influence. He became a pluralist who for thirteen years left his parish in the charge of a succession of curates; a trafficker in benefices, and a tenacious insister upon the last farthing of his clerical rights and tithes. A footpath driven across his glebeland can raise as much ire in him as the sight of the Bristol or the Gordon riots. This side of him, so often overlooked, or not known to critics who have not looked at the poet's letters, helps one to understand the curious tone of his poetry, where at one moment, a parish priest may seem to be lecturing us, whilst at another, a whimsical critic of society is relishing his private jest. We do not set the boundaries of his art far enough apart. Behind the bland wall of couplet verse, the moods and inflexions alter subtly.

Crabbe was a very human and in many ways, a very simple man. Perhaps he was soured in temper by early humiliations. He certainly found it difficult to return as a curate to the town where his drunken father still tyrannised the family. The blessing of security which fate bestowed on him with one hand seemed immediately trammelled or cancelled by other factors. It is precisely this mixed view of the world which informs much of his writing. Yet we are dealing with a man who, in later years, could be scarcely let out of the house by his family, for fear he would be dunned of all the money in his pockets by the first mendicant to cross his path. The humiliation of living the entire middle part of his life with a wife so near derangement that any social life was impossible, cannot have increased his optimism of temper. His wife came from a class above that of his own family, and she waited faithfully—and prudently—for years whilst her poetical lover made good against all odds and predictions: "Yet happiness was not granted", as he wrote on one of her letters after her death (*Huchon*, p. 193). It is remarkable not that this son of the dull Suffolk marshes should have been a poet of monotones, but rather that he can so often rise above and beyond them, can be a powerfully emotive writer as well as an accurate documenter.

II

Some account of Crabbe's preferment to the church is important. It begins rather obscurely. His first declared preference had been for medicine. (The critics have been ready enough to seize on this: he is a "gloomy anatomist", a "wielder of a remorseless scalpel", a "dissector of dead morsels".) The temerity, the vast ambition of a village lad in nursing such aspirations suggests both courage and ignorance. In any case, the medical career seemed doomed from an early date. Though Crabbe had a temperamental inclination towards amateur scientific pursuits, becoming a competent botanist and geologist, nobody seems to have found any traces of specifically clinical or surgical skill in him. There is an almost pathetic neatness and methodicalness about the voluminous notebooks in which he recorded his scientific data, as though tidiness had to compensate for lack of innate skill. (One sometimes wishes he had kept his poetical notebooks with anything like the same care and neatness!) The scientific notebooks are still extant, in the University Library of Cambridge. Labourious transcriptions of Linnaeus, verbatim, class by class, bear witness to Crabbe's diligence, and to a strange tenacity which helps to explain how he could go on writing his reams of verse, ploughing his own relentless furrow, regardless of the tastes of the world outside, and presupposing in his audience a stamina equal to his own.

Clearly, a Suffolk lad with little formal education would not progress in medicine unless he could broaden his experience. Village 'pothecary was the best Crabbe could expect of a provincial training, and so he went, late in 1776, to walk the wards and "pick up a little surgical knowledge as cheap as he could" (*Life*, p. 9). This venture ended with the rapid exhausting of his funds, but without much addition to his stock of knowledge. One admires the courage with which he could face the prospect of a second

London visit, in 1780—this time with even less likelihood of career-making, and with that hideous liability, a pocket full of poems. Perhaps it was not surprising that his landlord "often warned him of the fate of Chatterton".

It is true that in all this time we hear nothing, either in his own letters, or in the *Life*, of an aspiration to enter the church—indeed the only considerable poem written by this time, *Inebriety*, is scathing in its presentation of clerics—but the numerous devotions and prayers in his Journal bear witness to a genuine piety. During his second London visit he was a regular attender at St Dunstan's, and his idea of a letter home to "Mira" (his pet name for Sarah Elmy, his wife-to-be) was to transcribe a short extract of a sermon which had particularly attracted him. Its subject was "For many are called, but few are chosen": perhaps the applicability of the text to his own fortunes assisted the attention he paid to the Rev. Winstanley's oratory!

The story of his indigence, his near starvation, and poetical disappointment, is well enough known. These miseries were brought to an end by the famous appeal to Burke, early in 1781. Crabbe's last resources were exhausted, he had appealed to every source he could think of (the Prime Minister and the Lord Chancellor included!), and had placed his poetry with the publishers. All had been to no avail. The only mystery is that it took him so long to try Burke, or at least, the almost immediate success of this last appeal gives one cause to wonder. For, with his last few pence in his pocket, and the bailiffs close on his heels, he wrote to Burke and at last found a sympathetic ear.

There followed a period of complex manœuvering. Even a man as eminent as Burke took a little time to work miracles. The transformation of an unassuming Suffolk caterpillar into a rare but genuine butterfly was, however, under way. Once the aspirant's credentials had been verified, Burke could set in motion the complicated machinery which would eventually yield to the half-educated village boy a comfortable living within the established church. Crabbe's son gives a rather simplified account of the long months of negotiation. From Crabbe's letters at the time, we can see how diffidently he dropped his hook into the hopeful waters.

He hints—no more—that Burke might consider sending him to Oxford, where presumably he could get a degree and enter the church by the regular method. The letter is worth quoting in full in that it throws some light on the circumstances surrounding *The Library* in addition to what it tells us about the poet's clerical ambitions. As with so much of the poetry, the tone of this letter is worth noting. Tone is a quality in Crabbe too often ignored or misapprehended by his critics. He can have a curiously oblique way of writing, hiding a strong motivating force behind a diffident, deferential front. Often his mordant humour serves the function of a mask in this way. In the early letters to Burke, a note of almost obsequious deference conceals the vigour of Crabbe's hopes and intentions. It cannot have been easy for him to find a tone acceptably placed between crawling and demanding. The statesman seems to have treated his protégé with a nicely judged ease of manner. This very affability may have made Crabbe's role the more difficult to play, while his natural propensity to fall into old-fashioned modes which smack of subservience, makes his tone appear even more unnatural. The "curiosity" of tone in his poetry is often akin to this. I shall discuss it more fully in a later chapter.

Once Burke was convinced of Crabbe's *bona fides*, the delicate process of insinuating him into the church could begin. Such a procedure may, today, strike us as rather ludicrous, if not distasteful, like the courting-dance of a pigeon, as he circles round his would-be mate. Certainly the Biographer's description slides over the laboursome and dubious process which came to a head on 27 March 1781. Crabbe writes thus:

Sir,

I have ventured to trouble you once more by sending you a copy of my poem in its former state, and that which (if it has merit enough to deserve your correction), I will endeavour to get printed as expeditiously as possible: I am afraid my frequent applications will induce you to repent of your kindness to me; but I must intreat you Sr. to remember that I am yet uncertain of my fate, and in fear of feeling again the evils I have experienced: you have saved me from sinking and supported me on shore, but I am still unable to help myself: bear with me Sir a little longer and I will walk alone as far as I can—I find my friends will take off about 200 of my poem. If you think it right this Impression shall extend no further, but I will endeavour to sell the copy; if it gets me but a trifling sum, that is entire profit, and I am afraid it has not merit enough for me to venture a large impression, or if it has the sale would be too slow, and the expense of printing too great for me to expect any benefit from it at the time it is most wanted.

I will apply myself diligently to the study of the Greek and Latin languages. My great inclination to the church and your late hints to me on this subject give me perhaps too fair a prospect of success, but I am ignorant of the difficulty, and you will pardon me if I hope too much. I have a friend in Suffolk on whom I can depend for every little help that can be afforded, by a person who has no superfluous income. There I can reside at any time when it would be expensive and not necessary for me to be elsewhere. There is also a family in Oxford, who in this way would be of service to me, should my good fortune ever lead me there—I in the strict sense of the words know not what I ask when I hint these things and only do it with a firm confidence that you Sir will feel for my circumstances in which I hope much and have much to fear.

If this poem should not be ill received perhaps a small collection carefully revised and published, would bring me in something to support the expenses of a College; but when it may be convenient I will intreat you to think for me.

If the line wherein the Duke of Rutland is indirectly mentioned, be such as would offend his Grace or if you disapprove it, it is almost unnecessary I hope to say, it shall be immediately altered.

I will again do myself the honour of seeing you, and am Sir with ye highest respect and the most lively Gratitude

Yr very hbl Servant
Geo Crabbe

B. Street Mar 27 (Sheff. 1/1431)

It was not, in fact, until *The Borough* in 1810 that Crabbe finally confessed himself free of the desire to take radical advice on his work. The letter quoted above is from the pen of the poet who, within a very few years, was to be recognised as one of the most original and independent writers England had produced, yet he seems to have been the last to recognise this side of himself. Any attempt to understand his art must comprehend both the independence and the reliance upon order, system, and established custom. The tone, with regard to his clerical advancement particularly, may be more comprehensible by the end of this chapter, which will try to show how wise, how necessary, and how proper it was to sue thus gently and formally. That any author can promise to alter or trammel his work to suit the taste of a patron or the public may seem distasteful. Yet it was common practice and com-

mon sense; it does not really matter, except that it may be construed as a reflection upon the poet's integrity. Crabbe has to be
understood by his own needs and standards before we judge him
by those we presuppose to be the "proper" ones, for he seems
to have had a curiously ambivalent attitude to poetry, as the subsequent course of his career will show. Here is an author who
achieved some early fame, had the majestic approval of Johnson
himself, and with every encouragement from the reviewers to write
more, retired into a silence for twenty-two years, only to emerge
when university expenses needed to be paid for his eldest son.

III

With his hook baited and dangled into the stream of preferment, Crabbe was obliged to await the pleasure of the large fish
he had cast for. To say, as the Biographer does, "He went into Mr
Burke's room, a poor young adventurer, spurned by the opulent,
and rejected by the publishers, his last shilling gone, and all but
his last hope with it: he came out virtually secure of almost all
the good fortune that, by successive steps, afterwards fell to his
lot . . ." is to simplify a process which was uncertain and often
embarrassing, and which lasted several months—though this is in
the light of letters to which the poet's son had no access. They
were months of continuing anxiety and stress, and they left a per-
manent scar.

Almost five months after the last letter to Burke, we find that
Dudley Long has been active with the Bishop of Norwich on
Crabbe's behalf. Crabbe seems to have been lucky in his allies and
champions. Dudley Long (later Long North) was a friend of Fox
and Samuel Johnson. He had lent Crabbe five pounds to make that
second journey to London. Presumably he saw real talent in the
young poet, though he never tried to pet or patronise his "find"
as Capell Lofft did with Bloomfield, for instance, or John Taylor
with Clare. The work of both these men is permanently marked
by the interference of their patrons: for all his deference, Crabbe's
is not. Dudley Long's negotiations seem to have been promising,
in that, later the same year, Crabbe is far enough on with his
business to express doubts about serving as curate at Aldeburgh,
where he has to face not only neighbours who knew him in his in-

digence, but also his father; a prospect which he views with more
realism than filial piety:

> . . . It happens a little unfortunately that the place my friends
> have chose for me is Aldbro'. and in this interval of suspense I con-
> sider it more than a little so: but there it is most convenient on
> account of two neighbouring half curacies to which Mr Long and
> his friends will procure me a title;—I cannot say to them that I
> have no peace there: that I was very miserable and miserably treated
> and *cannot* esteem a great part of the Inhabitants who must be
> [con]scious that they did not use me well—It is [not] everyone,
> it is hardly any one can make [   ] delicate allowances for pre-
> judices in favour [   ] which you do nor for those against
> them and I determine to bear this inconvenience as a small one, nor
> would have mentioned it but the better view afforded me in your
> letter forced me on the comparison and that gives me a dissatis-
> faction which I hope will be but temporary. In this subject I may
> further say (though perhaps it is not a proper place for it) that my
> affection and my duty to my father leads me to avoid him.—It is
> only to you Sir that I can say these things—My father and I are
> in perfect agreement; we parted with every appearance of it and I
> am persuaded there was deceit in none: but if I live in the same
> place I know that it is impossible to please him and others or my-
> self: to separate our interests without making him angry or unite
> them without making myself miserable: his employments, his in-
> clinations, his connections and mode of living are so different from
> my own that there is no way to preserve that harmony there is and
> should be between us, but by our separation . . . I love my father,
> but I have other duties and stronger affection and cannot give up
> these tho' I could many things to his pleasure. this and every
> other consideration make me wish to avoid a place where however
> if I be situated I will endeavour to be satisfied and to give satisfac-
> tion: but these things will I hope be my excuse to my friends there
> for my readyness to depart whenever an opportunity offers.
>
> (Sheff. 1/1472)

This letter, from which a few words have disappeared due to
tears in the manuscript, is dated 9 October 1781. Where the truth
of Crabbe's relationship with his father really lay, it is now hard
to discern. The *Life*, as one might expect, presents a gentler
picture:

> His father had the candour to admit, that he had underrated his
> poetical abilities, and that he had acted judiciously in trusting to

the bent of nature, rather than persevering in an occupation for which he was, from the outset, particularly disqualified. The old man now gloried in the boldness of his adventure, and was proud of its success: he fondly transcribed *The Library* with his own hand; and in short, reaped the reward of his own early exertions to give his son a better education than his circumstances could well afford.

(Life, p. 29)

As far as the poetry is concerned, it is difficult to think of anywhere in Crabbe's enormous output where he describes a totally successful father/son relationship, though there are plenty of examples of unhappy ones. How far his own experiences account for this would be difficult to say, though the sentiments of his letter to Burke make it tempting to draw conclusions.

At any rate, the young aspirant for deacon's orders felt the paternal skeleton might rattle too loudly in the Aldeburgh cupboard, and was only too eager to serve there for as short a time as possible.

He was ordained as deacon on 21 December 1781, three days short of his twenty-seventh birthday, and took up those two half-curacies he had been promised. A brief letter to Burke in April 1782 speaks of an intended trip to town:

> Having procured a successor to my curacies I expect to be in Town within a few Days and for a few: I shall then hope once more to see you. (Dated from Beccles)
> (Sheff. 1/1599)

A month later he was writing to Burke, from Belvoir Castle, to announce his appointment as Ducal Chaplain to the Duke of Rutland:

> Sir,
> It is my duty to inform you that His Grace appointed me his domestic Chaplain on Sunday last, and to thank you for this as well as every other advantage I have obtained since I had the happiness to know you. I hope so to conduct myself that you may never repent your recommendation ...
> May 15 1782. (Sheff. 1/1653)

Here, one might feel, was the station to which he had aspired. The recipient of a chaplaincy in a ducal household was a particularly privileged person, such office being frequently reserved for younger sons of the nobility themselves. Further preferment to a comfortable and lucrative benefice was almost automatic. And yet Crabbe does not seem to have been happy or comfortable in his chaplaincy. Such disappointments, real or imaginary as their causes may have been, characterise the "success-story" which Crabbe's life outwardly appears to be. Whether a naturally gloomy temper turned even good fortune sour, or whether his lot was a consistently unfortunate one, the effect on his writing is clear, though most people who knew him speak of his affability and sweetness of temper in ordinary intercourse.

<h3 style="text-align:center">IV</h3>

His clerical career continued on the surface almost as though it had been calculated to afford a perfect example of the steps by which promotion could come in the church of his day, but there is an undertow of discontent. We know that Crabbe's chaplaincy was an unhappy one. The *Life* indicates the obvious and acceptable reasons why, despite the personal condescension of the Duke and Duchess of Rutland, he was not at ease, either socially or professionally:

> . . . the situation he filled at Belvoir was attended with many painful circumstances, and productive in his mind of some of the acutest sensations of wounded pride that have ever been traced by any pen.
>
> (*Life*, p. 32)

"Wounded pride" is a major theme in his mature work. Occasions when the Duke would seek out his chaplain to "converse on literary topics, quote verses, and criticise plays", were outweighed by the formal occasions when the chaplain's manners at dinner seemed to have caused comment, or when his whiggish politics obliged him to drink a glass of salt water rather than respond to the tory toasts of the ducal table. The most notable outcome of this, poetically, was the fifth of Crabbe's *Tales*, "The Patron". Had there been no other outcome, it would have been a fruitful episode, for "The Patron" is one of Crabbe's most assured and sustained poems. It reveals at once the personal animus which had stayed with him all the intervening years—("The Patron" was probably not written much before 1808)—and, at the same time, it shows the distancing effect Crabbe always sought to introduce between the real life on which his poems were based, and the people and events within the fabric of the poem itself.

The story is as transparent as his fables usually are. A young poetaster, son of the local bailiff, having written a satire which favoured the cause of the neighbouring lord at election time, is "taken up" and made much of at the Hall. Despite a lengthy letter of counsel from his father, the success goes to his head, he imagines a mutual passion between himself and the Lord's sister, and lives in a dream world of expectation where, every next day, Lord Frederick will make his fortune. But when he pursues the nobleman to town, he is "denied" in the classic manner, and left to die of disappointment and humiliation. Lord North, the Prime Minister, had caused Crabbe to be "denied" during the poet's period of distress, so there is no lack of personal vigour or insight in the writing. Yet it is far enough from Belvoir and Rutland neither to cause personal feelings not to interrupt or vitiate the poet's necessary distance from his subject. "Necessary" because it is a point of personal honour as well as a matter of artistic probity with Crabbe not to let his own life directly into his works. This seems to make him a drastically "unromantic" author, though in later chapters I shall contest this presupposition.

"The Patron" is disturbing because of the dispassionate and remote manner in which the narrator, an anonymous and quite impassive voice, delivers his cruel story. As is usual when Crabbe is at his best, tone is skilfully varied. The opening is neutral, verging almost towards the jocose. It describes the harmless folly of young John's poetic taste. Sent to reside with an elderly pair in the country, he had imbibed the simple ballad-literature which they enjoyed. This is very similar to the description the Biographer gives of Crabbe's own literary background, of course:

> Such were the fruits of John's poetic toil—
> Weeds, but still proof of vigour in the soil.
> He nothing purposed but with vast delight,
> Let Fancy loose, and wonder'd at her flight . . .
> Till, spurr'd by glory, to a reading friend
> He kindly show'd the sonnets he had penn'd . . .
> This heard the father, and with some alarm;
> "The boy", said he, "will neither trade nor farm;

"He for both law and physic is unfit;
"Wit he may have, but cannot live on wit: . . ."
("The Patron", *Tales*, V, lines 35–55 *passim*)

A good deal of Crabbe's unassuming but judicious narrative art is concealed even in a low-keyed exposition such as this. Throughout the poem a contrast is to be drawn between nature—the proper and unassuming way of life—and artifice—the insincere world of the Hall. Hence the almost agricultural simile of the first two lines initiates a train of ideas which run right through the poem and bind its substantial length into a close-knit unity. John's magazine successes with "Fanciful" sonnets echo rather ruefully the early career of Crabbe himself in *The Lady's Magazine*, and the father's word are uncomfortably close to the sentiments of George Crabbe senior: "That boy must be a *fool*. John, and Bob, and Will, are all of some use about a boat; but what will that *thing* ever be good for?" (*Life*, p. 4). Despite a college education, John has drifted into a dream-world, where he flinches from the external realities around him. This is a constant theme with Crabbe. Fancy, enthusiasm, personal indulgence, are suspect to him, as priest and as poet. Time and again he has to present the battle between them not only in terms of an overt struggle as here between John and his father, but within himself.

John's inner world is designated by images suggesting warmth, (the over-heated fancy), whilst the external world is characterised by the often repeated adjective, "cool". There is an almost claustrophobic aptness in this, for the voice using these descriptions, which are in themselves so subjective and private, is the voice of the disinterested narrator. I do not think that any commentator has noticed the use of subjective and objective voices in this poem. *The Borough* is entirely structured upon such a removal of immediate commitment by the narrator, for Crabbe goes to considerable lengths to prove that it is not *he* who is providing the narrative, but rather an imaginary correspondent. This is an aspect of the same circumspection which the Smith brothers represent in *Rejected Addresses*, and which can be linked directly with the poet's moral attitude to satire as an art form.

In "The Patron", by a trenchant irony, it is a "cool" poem of the "warm" John which draws him to His Lordship's attention:

He read the satire, and he saw the use
That such cool insult, and such keen abuse,
Might on the wavering minds of voting men produce.

(lines 111–13)

So John is invited to the Hall. It is high summer (the warmest time of the year), and his foolish passion for the Lady Emma runs riot. With the autumn comes a letter from his father, its tone cool by contrast with the mock-Spenserian excesses of John's dream-life at the Hall. The father's tone is beautifully done; the mercantile imagery, far from offending, seems full of honest, worldly sense:

"John, thou'rt a genius; thou hast some pretence,
"I think, to wit, but hast thou sterling sense?
"That which, like gold, may through the world go forth,
"And always pass for what 'tis truly worth?
"Whereas this genius, like a bill, must take
"Only the value our opinions make".

(lines 221–6)

There is a forthright no-nonsense ring about the prosody here, in the timbre and inflection of the father's tone of voice. Let the "Pope in worsted stockings" brigade assimilate the innate manliness of this passage, of this poem as a whole, and ever more be silent! The following, again from the father's counsel, is neatly done, with the voice of reason and worldly sense apeing the fops and the sycophants with whom John is associating:

"Prudence, my boy, forbids thee to commend
"The cause or party of thy noble friend;
"What are his praises worth, who must be known
"To take a patron's maxims for his own?
"When ladies sing, or in thy presence play,
"Do not, dear John, in rapture melt away;
" 'Tis not thy part, there will be list'ners round,
"To cry '*divine*!' and dote upon the sound;
"Remember too, that though the poor have ears,
"They take not in the music of the spheres;
"They must not feel the warble and the thrill,
"Or be dissolved in ecstacy at will;
"Beside, 'tis freedom in a youth like thee
"To drop his awe, and deal in ecstacy!

(lines 337–50)

Here is Crabbe at the height of his special and peculiar powers, writing with force and concentration, even down to the minute but utterly telling detail where, in the father's vocabulary, the word "freedom" clearly implies unwarranted licence whereas, to the son, it has been shown to represent a desirable shedding of social shackles.

The worldly advice, of course, falls on deaf ears. John is totally wrapped up in his self-deluding world of romance and wish-fulfillment. The passage in which Crabbe describes the departure for town of His Lordship—the abandoning of John, as it is to turn out—is most haunting:

> Cold grew the foggy morn; the day was brief;
> Loose on the cherry hung the crimson leaf;
> The dew dwelt ever on the herb; the woods
> Roar'd with strong blasts, with mighty showers the floods;
> All green was vanish'd, save of pine and yew,
> That still display'd their melancholy hue;
> Save the green holly with its berries red,
> And the green moss that o'er the gravel spread.
>
> (lines 426–33)

This is effective, evocative, mood-poetry, and yet for all its mist-shrouded atmosphere it is narratively functional. It demonstrates Crabbe's ability to amass his couplets into a paragraph unit, to cross the restricting bounds of the end-stopped heroic lines and run the sense, actively and discreetly, on to a larger unit. Like Pope and Dryden he is a fine poet to read aloud—the surest way of separating the first from the second rate composer of heroic couplets.

John is abandoned, though cruelly summoned to town by a "cool" letter from Lord Frederick. He is dealt one last humiliation, in a passage which is itself a calculated echo of the lines describing the departure for town:

> Alone our hero sate; the news in hand,
> Which, though he read, he could not understand.
> Cold was the day; in days as cold as these
> There needs a fire, where minds and bodies freeze;
> The vast and echoing room, the polish'd grate,
> The crimson chairs, the sideboard with its plate;

> The splendid sofa, which, though made for rest,
> He then had thought it freedom to have press'd;
> The shining tables, curiously inlaid,
> Were all in comfortless proud style display'd;
> And to the troubled feelings terror gave,
> That made the once-dear friend the sick'ning slave . . .
>
> . . . There was something in that still, cold place,
> That seem'd to threaten and portend disgrace.
>
> (lines 524–47 *passim*)

Mr Dombey would have been proud of such a waiting room! Time and time again one notices Crabbe's instinctive skill in making the dress, the trappings and the furniture speak for the people who own them. In his poetry inanimate objects take on a pregnant metaphysical life. Nowhere is this better illustrated than in "The Patron".

One last shrewd insight into John's psyche, its derangement, and its apparent cure, is revealed by the poet's discreet choice of imagery—"apparent" cure, for though frenzy is not the symptom of John's final decline, yet there is a slow painful attrition of his will to live which is as fatal as hysteria could ever be, and far more powerful in its narrative force. Crabbe gathers in all the skeins of his imagery and employs them one last time in a minor key, as the poem moves to its close. He is describing the last days of the melancholic and disappointed John:

> . . . quiet, love, and care,
> Strove with the gloom, and broke on the despair.
> Yet slow their progress; and, as vapours move
> Dense and reluctant from the wintry grove;
> All is confusion till the morning light
> Gives the dim scene obscurely to the sight;
> More and yet more defined the trunks appear,
> Till the wild prospect stands distinct and clear—
> So the dark mind of our young poet grew
> Clear and sedate; the dreadful mist withdrew;
> And he resembled that bleak wintry scene,
> Sad, though unclouded; dismal, though serene.
>
> (lines 642–53)

The metaphorical mist is now the same as the physical one evoked earlier. The contrast-structure is again emphasised by the *physical* description which follows this metaphorical one, for internal and external, subjective and objective, blur in the last phase of the poem:

> His frame was languid, and the hectic heat
> Flush'd on his pallid face, and countless beat
> The quick'ning pulse . . .
>
> (lines 666–8)

And the last irony:

> My lord, to whom the poet's fate was told,
> Was much affected, for a man so cold . . .
>
> (lines 704–5)

—from which point the story folds rapidly to its almost otiose conclusion. "The Patron" is a powerful testimony to the effect which the system exerted on the mind of Crabbe, despite the fact that he owed his success entirely to the influence of Burke and his friends. If Crabbe is "old-fashioned" in being virtually the last English poet of substance to come up through this system, he is entirely modern in his response to it, as is the poetical capital he can draw from its ills and anomalies. "The Patron" is by no means the only tilt he took at this bogey: "The Squire and the Priest" and "Squire Thomas" both present us with people who try to patronise others—it seems to have been one of the social sins which Crabbe found particularly hard to forgive. Often he presents it in such a way that we are persuaded it is more than venal.

v

The memories of those months in London and at Belvoir scarred him ineradicably; right through to his subconscious mind and across the later years of plenty and fame. The nightly visitations during his successful London visit of 1817 seem clearly to hark back to the Belvoir days and the labours on Slaughden Quay:

> . . . I was incommoded by dreams such as would cure vanity for a time in any mind where they could gain admission . . . Awake, I had been with the high, the apparently happy . . . Asleep, all was

57

misery and degradation, not my own only, but of those who had been.—That horrid image of servility and baseness—that mercenary and commercial manner . . .   (*Life*, p. 71)

He seems here as close as he ever came to an admission that there had been a social tension, not only about his own relationship with the Belvoir ménage, but with his wife and her family too; Sarah Elmy was, of course, connected with the minor squirarchy, whilst Crabbe, younger than her, to make matters worse, was of declining stock. The "commercial manner" might well be a term of opprobrium. One can, I think, sense this social sensitivity in a lot of his writing. The relationship with his wife's family yields poetic capital time and again. Sarah's aunt, old Mrs Tovell, "becomes" the Widow Goe of *The Parish Register* and probably the aunt in "Delay has Danger". But it goes deeper than that. The poetry is full of sardonically observed families which are presenting one face to the world outside and quite another to themselves—"The Family of Love" and "The Widow's Tale" are two such, and there are other thumb-nail sketches through the works that one recognises as the *alter et idem* of the Tovell household. Squire Asgill from *The Borough*, Letter XVI, seems to be a very close recollection, with all his virtues and limitations, of old Mr Tovell of Parham Hall:

> "He bravely thought it best became his rank,
> "That all his tenants and his tradesmen drank;
> "He was delighted from his favourite room
> "To see them 'cross the park go daily home,
> "Praising aloud the liquor and the host,
> "And striving who should venerate him most.
> "No pride had he, and there was difference small
> "Between the master's and the servants' hall;
> "And here or there the guests were welcome all.
> "Of Heaven's free gifts he took no special care;
> "He never quarrel'd for a simple hare;
> "But sought, by giving sport, a sportsman's name,
> "Himself a poacher, though at other game.
> "He never planted nor inclosed—his trees
> "Grew like himself, untroubled and at ease;
> "Bounds of all kinds he hated, and had felt
> "Choked and imprison'd in a modern belt,

"Which some rare genius now has twined about
"The good old house, to keep old neighbours out; . . .
    "His worship ever was a churchman true,
"He held in scorn the methodistic crew;
" 'May God defend the Church and save the King,'
"He'd pray devoutly and divinely sing.
                (*The Borough*, Letter XVI, lines 67–99, *passim*)

The humour lies in the fact that this description is given by a
character of whom Crabbe basically disapproves. He is able at
once to praise such of old man Tovell's qualities as he does admire,
whilst setting the whole picture in an ironic frame which controls
and regulates the tone. The more we read of the blazing logs, the
brimming bumpers, and all the trappings of bonhomie, the more
clearly does a critical moral purpose come through the verse.

VI

The chaplaincy at Belvoir aroused the response one might expect
in this sensitive, prickly, socially uneasy man. It continued to be
something of a burden to Crabbe throughout his tenure. Fortune
continued to smile on him with that tight-lipped half grimace
which seemed to be the nearest he ever got to her open favours.
Chancellor Thurlow, who had already been shamed into an
acknowledgement of Crabbe's potential merits, at last made him
the presentation of two small livings—Frome St Quentin, and
Evershot, in Dorsetshire, miles from Belvoir. Unfortunately they
were both of small value, and scarcely likely to make the fortunes
of an impecunious curate, just on the point of matrimony. Though,
as we shall see, there were alternative ones offered which were
worth less, they were still in the Ducal eye. Equally, Crabbe's
hankering after the Eastern Counties could be indulged from
Leicestershire, but scarcely from Dorset. Much as he writes with
distaste of the Suffolk coast and people, his imagination was
never totally free of them, and a power gradually leaches from his
writing as he settles in Trowbridge later in life, and the pulse of
the tides grows slacker in his veins. Again the Burke correspondence enables us to be rather more accurate than the Biographer
chooses to be about the course of events surrounding Crabbe's
ordination and preferment. The impression is of a series of ma-
nipulations:

... I am compelled to supplicate still—To avoid this as long as I could I wrote about six weeks since to Mr Fox, telling him, (after apologising as well as I was able for the liberty I had allowed myself in writing) "that it was an object of much consequence with me to obtain leave of Lord Loughborough to exchange a living in Dorsetshire given me by the late Chancellor for one in the Diocese of Lincoln, and begging his interest for that purpose." I know that my not hearing from Mr Fox is by no means proof that he declines my business, but as there may be other reasons why he does not chuse to interfere, I am afraid sir I must ultimately depend upon you: thus far I mean depend, that if you can with propriety assist me, I rest assured that you will.—The particulars of the case are these: the living of Frome with Evershot which I now hold, is £190 a year and I verily believe honestly improvable that which the Duke of Rutland intends for me is but £130 and I do not know that it can be improved; I can therefore safely affirm that if I be not permitted to change my present living I shall keep it, as I have no prospect of anything that will tempt me to make such a resignation. Though the Duke's living is not yet fallen, yet the present possessor is so very old and so ill that his death is continually expected, and as I shall probably find both difficulty and delay, I should be happy to have this point settled soon ...

The poet's real reasons for this unprofitable looking exchange emerge a little later in the same letter, which is dated 28 October 1783:

As soon as I found the value of my living, I declared to the Duke of Rutland my intire satisfaction, and thanking him for the protection he had hitherto afforded me, I submitted it to his determination whether I should go and reside there, or in what manner I might dispose of myself to his satisfaction. His Grace told me, by residing near him and that he had designed a provision for me, recommending it to me by any means I could think of, to part with my living for one tenable with that he meant for me ...

(Sheff. 1/1844)

It really reads more like a young investor consulting his broker than a clergyman trying to settle a cure of souls, but it is only through an understanding of the temper of the age, and that of the man himself, that one comes to a complete appreciation of the poetry written by this strange personality with its mixture of the shrewd and the innocent, the worldly and the altruistic.

In the midst of the ecclesiastical shuffling he was causing at this time, Crabbe was awarded the honorary degree of LL.B., and he had assumed the curacy at Stathern by June 1784, though there are letters still dated from Belvoir as late as 1786. The poet often spoke of these years as the happiest of his life, yet the poetic outcome was small: since *The Library* and *The Village*, which had really been presented as his credentials to Burke, he had written almost nothing. *The Newspaper* appeared in 1785, but it fails to carry even the fire of *Inebriety*, let alone the sombre, brooding authority of *The Library* or the contentious provocation of *The Village*. Chamberlain is right when he calls it "Crabbe's dullest production" (R. L. Chamberlain, *George Crabbe*, 1956, p. 53): as though happiness and composition went ill together, or that he simply had no need of publishing his muse while the world went well with him. The work which makes up *Poems*, his next publication, was written mainly after the turn of the century, during the stress of his wife's increasing derangement and the irritations of being called back to his parish from Suffolk.

The death of the Duke of Rutland in 1787 led indirectly to the advancement Crabbe had angled for. After further protracted dealings with the irascible Thurlow, Crabbe was inducted into the rectorship of Muston early in 1789, with the living of West Allington added. At last the impoverished village lad had made good, for this was, after the initial acceptance into deacon's orders, the most important step towards real security. A man could wait half a lifetime for this: it took William Jones nineteen years to move from curate to rector of his parish.

It is at this stage that Crabbe's propriety, his commitment to the pastoral cares of his profession, were tested, and found wanting. In 1792 the death of old Mr Tovell, his wife's uncle, left Sarah Elmy with an interest in Parham Hall. The temptation to get back to Suffolk and to play the squire was too much for Crabbe, and, hiring a curate to look after Muston, he set off for his native county:

> The beginning was ominous. As we were slowly quitting the place, preceded by our furniture, a stranger, though one who knew my father's circumstances, called out in an impressive tone, "You are wrong, you are wrong." The sound he said found an echo in his own conscience. (*Life*, p. 42)

Though he found much scope for close character observation and social comedy at Parham Hall, Crabbe found little there of the domestic peace and dignity which he sought. Something troublesome in his own conscience went on furnishing a major theme for his poetry to the end of his life. *This* is where the change in his work comes. Everything up to 1785 is essentially genre work: *The Library, The Village, The Newspaper,* belong to the same world as *The Dispensary, The Hopgarden,* and *The Chase.* Then, after the turn of the century, begins to emerge this new, probing, analysing poet who, though he can still turn off a disquisition on schools, pubs, or elections, is groping towards an understanding of people rather than general phenomena—who is trying to see the soul, not the surface. The change must have come from within, and one likely contributary cause seems to have been his struggle with his private convictions on the one side, and his parishioners and their needs on the other. As Leslie Stephen said, "With him sin is not punished by being found out, but by disintegrating the character and blunting the higher sensibilities. He shows . . . the lacerations inflicted by wounded self-respect" (*Hours in a Library,* p. 53). My next chapter is entirely devoted to the subjective responses which the eighteenth-century church elicited from Crabbe. The foundations of such a scrutiny can only be laid by a preliminary, external account of his own career in the church.

VII

The loss of a son—her third—at the age of six, seems to have precipitated Mrs Crabbe's mental decline, and the family moved to yet another curacy. The face of plurality must here be shown at its worst; a man who, to gratify his squirarchal tastes has hired in a curate to tend his own flock, now takes on the curacy of another parish to supplement his income, for in October 1796, the family moved to Great Glemham Hall, which the thrifty biographer is pleased to tell us they had "at a greatly reduced rent". So passed another four or five years.

About this time the bishops began very properly to urge all non-resident incumbents to return to their livings; and Mr Dudley North, willing to retain my father in his neighbourhood, took the trouble to call upon the Bishop of Lincoln, Dr Prettyman, and to request that Mr Crabbe might remain in Suffolk; adding, as an argument in favour of the solicited indulgence, his kindness and attention to his present parishioners. But his Lordship would not yield—observing that they of Muston and Allington had a prior claim. "Now", said Mr North, when he reported his failure, "we must try and obtain you an incumbency here;" and one in his own gift becoming vacant, he very obligingly offered it to my father. This living was, however, too small to be held singly, and he prepared ultimately (having obtained an additional furlough of four years) to return to his own parishes. His strong partiality to Suffolk was not the only motive for desiring to remain in that county, and near to all our relatives on both sides; he would have sacrificed mere personal inclination without hesitation, but he was looking to the interests of his children. (*Life*, p.47)

I doubt it! Whatever the rights and wrongs of the situation, Crabbe moved to yet another curacy, at Rendham, for the four remaining years of his Suffolk furlough. The Bishop of Lincoln who, in this narrative, seems to behave with such rectitude, was, as we have seen, a notorious pluralist and political climber.

There were still two moves to come. The unpalatable command to return to his sheep was obeyed in 1805. The circumstances would belong to one of his own ironic tales, were they not so real and immediate. In the long years of absence the Methodists, who were at least ready to demonstrate a local and immediate response to the pastoral needs of Muston, had virtually stolen Crabbe's congregation from him. *Malus, peior, pessimus*: a Huntingtonian had cashed in on the absence of the Establishment too. This extremist sect of the non-conforming church was particular anathema to Crabbe:

The *social* and *moral* effects of that new mission were well calculated to excite not only regret, but indignation; and, among other distressing incidents, was the departure from his own household of two servants, a woman and a man, one of whom had been employed by him for twenty years. The man, a conceited ploughman, set up for a Huntingtonian preacher himself; and the woman, whose moral character had been sadly deteriorated since her adoption of the new lights, was at last obliged to be dismissed, in consequence of intolerable insolence. I mention these things, because they may throw light on some passages in my father's later poetry. (*Life*, p. 51)

This is one of the few occasions when the admirable Biographer allows personal animus to creep into his narrative. The wound seems to have gone nearly as deep as it did in the poet himself—(George junior was, by this time, an undergraduate at Cambridge, and reading for Orders himself). Whatever the rights and wrongs of the case, Crabbe's verse thereafter never fails to swell and warm when the wretched Methodists can be brought into the line of attack. The "Letter on Sects" in *The Borough* is the most extended of these attacks, but throughout *Tales* and *Tales of the Hall*, to be a Methodist is to be on the side of the losers, the obtuse, the hypocrites, or the political scoundrels of the extreme left.

VIII

One more move was yet to be made in Crabbe's otherwise superficially uneventful later years. In 1815 he left Muston for Trowbridge. The familiar ritual of barter and trading went on again. The Duke of Rutland wanted Muston back, for presentation to someone else—in fact, to a relative of Byron. Crabbe was offered the living at Trowbridge in exchange for Muston, which was fine as far as it went. But the poet's other living, that of West Allington, had been served by his son George, which meant that the family was deriving the benefit of two sets of tithes. When news got out that Crabbe was to leave Lincolnshire, the Duke was lobbied to re-bestow West Allington elsewhere. This deprived Crabbe of part of his income, and he expressed considerable indignation. (One must remember that this was a period of galloping inflation. It was not so much greed as protection of his living standards which motivated Crabbe's protests.) The Duke, however, shuffling through his pack of ecclesiastical cards, was able to offer the Crabbes the living of Croxton in lieu of Allington, though only after the prior offer of a much smaller card from the pack—the vicarage of Granby. This suggestion drew from Crabbe the following letter to the Dean of Lincoln:

Now, my dear Sir, if my *translation* depend upon my son's taking Granby or my taking it, it will never be accomplished, and this I can but conceive His Grace must, if he deigned to think, have thought of himself; he must surely know of a village so very near him, that it is the poorest benefice in his gift; that it long stood at £80, but may now be at £100, that the house is an Hovel no decent labourer would live in, and in short that if my son resided he must live in misery . . . and that if he did not . . . the curacy would . . . take all the income   (Bod. ms. Don d. 16)

This is a long way from the tone of the supplicating letters which accompanied Crabbe's initial struggles to enter the church. Reading Cobbett's *Rural Rides* one constantly meets scathing comments on non-resident vicars who have allowed the vicarage to fall into decay, and looking at statistics of clerical incomes during that period, it is difficult to share Crabbe's utter horror at the hundred pounds benefice in part exchange for what he held. There would have been plenty of poor souls, squeezed by the agricultural depression or back from the war with no prospect of employment, who would have been grateful enough for a hundred pounds and this hovel!

When he went back to Muston he was fifty-one. He was still to publish, and for the main part write, the works on which his fame should principally rest: *Poems* (1807), *The Borough* (1810), *Tales* (1812), and *Tales of the Hall* (1819). Quantitatively this means that, at the age of fifty, well over half of his output was still unwritten: qualitatively, the proportion is even higher. Through the years when the young men of the next generation were growing hectic, pale, and dropping from the branches like leaves in autumn, the robust old vicar continued to go from strength to strength. He was not oblivious to changing tastes, for he had read Coleridge, Clare, Bloomfield, Hogg, Maturin and Mary Shelley. With Wordsworth he was on terms of uneasy affability, and for Scott he had an intensely warm personal affection. Yet the life within seems to have sustained his idiosyncratic muse, without need of constant changing fashions. The catalogue of his books, in the Cambridge University Library, reflects a much wider and more "modern" appetite in Crabbe than we might expect however.

At the age of sixty, he transplanted himself to Trowbridge, that "dirty manufacturing town" where we have already met him in his study, through the words of John James Lecky. There are in these last years, fewer signs outwardly of tension and malaise. After the initial hesitancy, caused by his own reticent character and the advanced age at which he made the move, he seems to have taken to Trowbridge, at least as a convenient base for the jauntings to Bath and to London which characterise his mainly serene and sociable last years. Life at Trowbridge was not all tranquillity. There are dozens of letters from this period which show how niggling and punctilious Crabbe could be about money matters. Murray paid him three thousand pounds in 1818 for the rights on all his works, which represented something like twenty-five years' worth of income for a clergyman in a modest benefice. Hence financial security was assured. It is impossible to say whether this, or increasing old age, or the physical shift from Muston to Trowbridge, was the cause of the changing tone of his later poetry. There certainly *is* a change to be reckoned with.

As tranquillity and old age come with the move to Trowbridge, perhaps some of the fire, the vigour and indignation, does leach away from his stories. At the same time, it has been noticed often enough, that they become more middle-class. To a degree it is moral resignation that dictates the benignity of *Tales of the Hall*, as much as personal affluence. The old fire will flash forth occasionally, but we are now in the parish ruled by Jacques the moral teacher and George the tory squire, and there are, naturally, less occasions and less causes of passion. The crises tend to be those which happened in the past, not those of a present tense narrator: "Smugglers and Poachers" (*Tales of the Hall*, XXI) concerns events in the past, and is a powerfully tragic tale. "William Bailey" (*Tales of the Hall*, XIX) is social comedy, and the narrator brings his story right up to the present moment. The "Farewell and Return" series of *Posthumous Poems*, by its very *schema* of a double past, carries this tendency to its logical conclusion.

3

A Duty to Devotion

"He must make a most miserable choice who would not be religious"

(Sermon at Swefling, 14 July, 1805)

I

To unfold Crabbe's own fortunes as chaplain, curate and rector over a period of fifty years is not, in itself, enough. The story may appear to be one of a very venal, unspiritual life, with more care of tithes than of souls. I have tried to present this side of Crabbe but I also want to show the careful spiritual counsellor, the thoughtful and sympathetic shepherd behind the poet. Only the composite picture does justice to the range of his work, to the apparent contradictions which may well be seen in it as well as in his life. He lived in an age of contradictions and gave embodiment to many of them. His professional life and its relationship to his art is the proper and inevitable place to start if we are going to understand these contradictions. The entire first part of this book is concerned with the moral rather than with the technical Crabbe although, as I hope my analyses of the poems will show, there is an irrefrangible link between the two. Jeffrey seemed to feel this about Crabbe:

Considering Mr Crabbe as, on the whole, the most original writer that has ever come before us . . . we have directed our remarks rather to the *moral* than the literary qualities of his works—to his genius, at least, rather than his taste—and to his thoughts rather than his figures of speech. By far the most remarkable thing in his writings is the prodigious mass of original observations and reflections they everywhere exhibit, and that extraordinary power of conceiving and representing an imaginary object, whether physical or intellectual, with such a rich and complete accompaniment of circumstances and details as few ordinary observers either perceive or remember in realities—a power which must for ever entitle him to the very first rank among descriptive poets, and, when directed to worthy objects, to a rank inferior to none in the highest departments.   (*Edinburgh Review*, 1812, Vol. XX, pp. 277–305)

This puts the case very clearly; Crabbe is a moral poet, his morality is the quality which enables him to discern, describe, and discriminate with unique clarity, and all else is of secondary importance to this in understanding his art. This in no way prevents me from believing that the art itself has been seriously undervalued, or from attempting to demonstrate the proposition that Crabbe is a careful and conscientious craftsman, and that his technical range and variety is considerable. Nor should a preoccupation with his moral stance persuade the reader that he is a montonous or gloomy poet:

> The peculiar humour which gives brilliancy to his writings . . . [tended] . . . to excite pleasurable feelings, by affording indulgence to harmless curiosity by a peep behind the scenes of human nature . . .   (*Life*, p. 85)

was how one acquaintance tried to sum up this essential quality of the man.

Crabbe's pastoral duties were manifold. If the bishops were too busy at Westminster to engage in deep theological speculation, most of their conscientious clergy were certainly too preoccupied with pastoral duties to supply any deficiency in novelty of dogma thus created. Hence, we shall find in Crabbe's religious thought a great deal of the commonly accepted, a great deal of the downright commonplace, and more than a leavening of secular common sense. It may not be such a bad mixture on which to run a parish as his detractors would have us believe. To describe his religion as Huchon does as "a colourless reproduction of that of his contemporary Paley" (*op. cit.*, p. 211) is rather an unfair way of stating Crabbe's position. His muse is, to a certain extent, a "utilitarian" one; it has often enough been seen as rational and matter of fact; but just as the practice of the parish priest throws humanising warmth over this kind of description, so does a powerful, idiosyncratic, and deeply humane imagination give to the best of his verse something which preserved it from the lack of colour which Huchon describes.

II

The figures of the sometimes dark social comedy which life in the church afforded often appear in Crabbe's poetry. The Vicar and the Curate in *The Borough* may be better understood and appreciated once their background, both in general terms and as a manifestation of the author's experience, has been grasped. The Vicar is "an admirable sketch of what must be very difficult to draw; a good, easy man, with no character at all. His little, humble vanity; his constant care to offend no one; his mawkish and feeble gallantry, indolent good-nature, and love of gossiping and trifling —are all very exactly delineated" (Jeffrey, in the *Edinburgh Review*, *Life*, p. 184). It is a picture, very honestly and shrewdly written, of one side of Crabbe himself.

> ... to the end
> His constant care was, no man to offend;
> No haughty virtues stirr'd his peaceful mind,
> Nor urged the priest to leave the flock behind;
> He was his Master's soldier, but not one
> To lead an army of his martyrs on:
> *(The Borough,* Letter III, lines 15–20)

Even here a good deal of Crabbe's quiet art is at work: the word "peaceful" manages to be an overt praise and a covert criticism of the vicar's attitudes at one and the same time. The capital letters, suggesting the terminology of evangelicalism or methodism, give a peculiar savour to the praise/blame syndrome on which the character commentary is based. I am taken by surprise by the flexibility of rhythm which I find in the quotations I have used throughout the book so far. Later I shall give detailed consideration to Crabbe as artist. Here we are considering him in other aspects but the artistry is still apparent: this man is not only a shrewd psychologist, but an innately accomplished craftsman. He has listened to Pope, even more to Dryden, he has assimilated their timbre and their rhythms, and he has also demonstrated his individuality, his right to be numbered among the original contributors to the course of English prosody. No wonder Byron admired him despite his coarse subject matter, for Byron saw the downfall of English poetry in the wilful neglect of Pope, and Crabbe demonstrates in this, his normative style, the benefits which could still be reaped by a sensitive ear which did not neglect the great tradition of the eighteenth century.

Not all the picture of Crabbe's vicar is thus blandly innocuous; the tone can sharpen:

> Fiddling and fishing were his arts; at times
> He alter'd sermons, and he aim'd at rhymes;
> And his fair friends, not yet intent on cards,
> Oft he amused with riddles and charades.
>   Mild were his doctrines, and not one discourse
> But gain'd in softness what it lost in force:
> Kind his opinions; he would not receive
> An ill report, nor evil act believe;
> "If true, 'twas wrong; but blemish great or small
> "Have all mankind; yea, sinners are we all."
>   If ever fretful thought disturb'd his breast,
> If aught of gloom that cheerful mind oppress'd,
> It sprang from innovation; . . .
>
> *(ibid.*, lines 102–14)

If one were to quote no further, and quoted without consciousness of the self-scrutinising irony of this portrait, it would go some way to justifying latitudinarianism. The kind of pastor here delineated is more good than bad. Yet, though he may be latitudinarian, even venal, Crabbe can see, and can give scalpel-sharp analysis of where such toleration and broadness fails. One needs to look at the passage *in extenso*—as one normally looks at Crabbe. He will not condense, abbreviate, or even anthologise. He has his boundaries, they are broad ones, and we must adhere to them to see him with anything like proper respect for his craftsmanship. Consider, however, the passage with which he rounds off his critique of the vicar:

> The rich approved—of them in awe he stood;
> The poor admired—they all believed him good;
> The old and serious of his habits spoke;
> The frank and youthful loved his pleasant joke;

Mothers approved a safe contented guest,
And daughters one who back'd each small request:
In him his flock found nothing to condemn;
Him sectaries liked—he never troubled them;
No trifles fail'd his yielding mind to please,
And all his passions sunk in early ease;
Nor one so old has left this world of sin,
More like the being that he enter'd in.

(*ibid.*, lines 154–65)

How easily this flows off the page; how little hard work the artistry seems to involve. Yet it is a passage of much rhetorical skill, one of those technically accomplished things for which Crabbe never got enough credit, precisely because the art of hiding art has been so deftly accomplished. The first two lines have a nice ambiguity in them: did the rich approve *because* the vicar stood in awe of them? One suspects so, but the line does not actually say so. It may equally be read as an inconsequential comment that the vicar was in awe of the rich, quite ancillary to the fact of their approval. Was he a syncophant or an independent-minded innocent, in fact? Likewise, it is creditable that the poor admired him, but how far was that admiration consciously sought, how far was it the adulation of a blind ignorance which is itself criticised, and how far is the belief in the vicar's goodness actually justified? Two lines could not be asked to work harder than these, yet their shape, their proper form itself, is neatly chiselled and complete. The passage is working through pseudo-Popean antitheses—one can see and relish where the music has come from, but the *alter* is more important than the *idem*. The last two lines sharpen the tone, leaving the character analysis perfectly achieved, yet the judgement is made in the mind of the reader: time and time again we shall see in Crabbe this *fairness* of mind at work. He can give colouring, viewpoint, comment upon a situation, yet he seldom (until his very last years) leads us by the nose to where he would have us go, irrespective of humanity or justice. Many of his best portraits of errant mortals are those where he bends over backwards to explain and justify the reasons for sinning, though he has no doubt that to sin is a serious failing in personal responsibility, and that there will be a punishment for it. It seems very wrong, however, to see this as incorrigibly gloomy, or in any way mechanical. In this he is like Shakespeare; even his villains are suffering humans, whom we recognise and understand, since the bases of their crimes are those we share with them.

III

The curate presents us with another aspect of Crabbe's art; here the attack is much more direct, much more pungent in its immediate intention. Crabbe composed this piece for the Literary Society, where it was recited at the annual dinner in 1809. The immediate effect was that the Society agreed to extend the range of its charitable ventures thereafter, to include "a learned and officiating clergyman in distress, or an officiating clergyman, reduced and rendered incapable of duty, by age or infirmity" (*Life*, p. 185).

The skill with which this impoverished priest is contrasted with the vicar gives the last twist of bitterness to the portrait, as though Crabbe has been able to divide his own mind into separate parts and see the sybarite and the ascetic in himself, the self-indulgent pampered chaplain, and the hard-working and underpaid surrogate. This is exactly the dichotomy which Trollope presents in *Framley Parsonage*, of course. A good number of Crabbe's poems are constructed around this personal ambivalence—we shall meet it again when we look at his treatment of madness. The language used of the curate is simple, direct, without artifice:

> . . . one whom all believe
> Pious and just, and for whose fate they grieve;
> All see him poor, but ev'n the vulgar know
> He merits love, and their respect bestow.
> A man so learn'd you shall but seldom see,
> Nor one so honour'd so aggrieved as he—
> Not grieved by years alone; though his appear
> Dark and more dark, severer on severe:
> Not in his need,—and yet we all must grant
> How painful 'tis for feeling age to want;
> Nor in his body's sufferings—yet we know
> Where time has plough'd, there misery loves to sow:
> But in the wearied mind, that all in vain
> Wars with distress, and struggles with its pain.
>
> (*ibid.*, lines 184–97)

72

Such, indeed, might all too often be the lot of the curates of the church Crabbe served. What a splendid line is the twelfth one quoted above: "Where time has ploughed, there misery loves to sow." It makes a genuine compression of grand abstractions into a pregnant, moving, almost metaphysical vision of the human lot. The ability to handle "upper case emotions" is not always evident in his work, but on this occasion he has succeeded.

IV

The figure of the curator of souls recurs frequently in Crabbe's work. Jacques, the "moral teacher" of *Tales of the Hall* will occupy us at length later. "Flaminius", the "easy chaplain of an atheist lord", is selected as an example of venality, of appetite conquering conscience, in the very early *Inebriety*. The type, extended and sophisticated, is characteristic of Crabbe's mature work: it is interesting to meet him in embryonic form in this early poem—certainly prior to Crabbe's own ordination. At slightly fuller length the portrait is repainted in *The Village*, where the parish priest is summoned to the workhouse to hear the last confession of a dying pauper:

> And doth not he, the pious man, appear,
> He, "passing rich with forty pounds a year"?
> Ah! no; a shepherd of a different stock,
> And far unlike him, feeds this little flock:
> A jovial youth, who thinks his Sunday's task
> As much as God or man can fairly ask;
> The rest he gives to loves and labours light,
> To fields the morning, and to feasts the night;
> None better skill'd the noisy pack to guide,
> To urge their chase, to cheer them or to chide;
> A sportsman keen, he shoots through half the day,
> And, skill'd at whist, devotes the night to play.
> Then, while such honours bloom around his head,
> Shall he sit sadly by the sick man's bed,
> To raise the hope he feels not, or with zeal
> To combat fears that e'en the pious feel?
> (*The Village*, lines 302–17)

This figurine, the personality subjected to self indulgence, we will meet time and time again in Crabbe. Here "jovial" has an

73

inappropriateness which genuinely shocks as descriptive of a priest. "To fields the morning and to feasts the night" manages a Popeian tightness, and the couplet about his hunting and card-playing is a model of what the epigrammatic style can achieve in terseness and suggestiveness at once. "Shoots" is precisely the right word, connoting not only the physical activity of slaughtering the game but suggesting a slippery, facile, mindless progress from morning to night—a rapid succession of aimless pastimes which reflect a severe moral judgement on the priest. And "honours" becomes a deft and apposite pun on success at cards and in society, which are thus equated.

The conduct of the parish priest called for considerable self-restraint and self-sacrifice, particularly in neighbourhoods where convivial company might tempt the apparently under-occupied inhabitant of the rectory. It is true that comparatively well-to-do vicars, such as Crabbe was in his later years, could afford, by bringing in a curate, to lead a leisured life. From Trowbridge, Crabbe made very frequent trips to London, to Bath, and else-where. His son, John, was his curate; an admirable arrangement for an author-rector. Even so we should beware of assuming that it must have been easy to combine verses and sermons in the daily round of a country parsonage. For all that Fitzgerald called Crabbe "a careless old fellow" in the composition and correction of his poetry, the manuscripts bear witness to a conscious and arduous struggle to achieve a finish in his work.

Crabbe was, nonetheless, an occasional and an amateur poet: that gap of twenty-two years between *The Newspaper* (1785) and *Poems* (1807) must be unique in English poetry. He seemed to care little for publication. The intervening years were divided be-tween his writing, his botanising, and his parochial cares. And the latter, taken earnestly, were not slight in themselves. Adding to them, as Crabbe sometimes did in his earlier years at least, the task of unofficial doctor, the insights into human nature afforded to him were those of a most privileged spectator. As physician he was the recipient of every intimate secret, while as pastor he saw both sides of the bland and sociable front which people could put upon their troubles. The critics' references to his physician's eye, to his "scalpel", to his tendency to "dissect" his subjects and their problems, are recognitions of this. Perhaps the other side, the sympathy, the implicit didactic aid which is being offered to errant mankind, is not enough stressed. To say Crabbe has "palpable designs upon us" is true enough; to many people no more may be said, for didatic poetry has come *ipso facto* to mean bad poetry. It may be when the physician in Crabbe is thoroughly aroused to diagnose, to probe, to make tests, that his stories take off towards success, but it is when the priest takes over that they are brought to their most satisfactory artistic conclusion. The suggestion that he is merely a conveyor of slightly distasteful reality—the school of criticism which Hazlitt so forcefully exemplified—bases itself on very partial evidence, most of it from the earliest and most "programmatic" part of Crabbe's work, and it does great injustice to the sympathy, the sudden quirks of laughter around the corners of the mouth, and the earnest desire to help people, which are the real bases of Crabbe's poetry. Perhaps Wilson, in his review of *Tales of the Hall* allowed himself a little too much emotion when he put it thus: ". . . in the midst of all his skill—all his art—we always see the tenderness of the man's heart; and we hear him, with a broken and melancholy voice, mourning over . . . woe and wickedness" (*Life*, p. 378). I shall investigate this relationship between *dulce* and *utile*, sentiment and satire, instruction and entertainment in a later chapter. The problems of striking a balance between them arise everywhere. The poet was not deluded about the importance or likely success of his "mission":

> Little I am afraid can be effected by the Muse of most moral and even seraphic endowments . . . Creating in the reader a general sobriety and some elevation of mind is all that I think can be expected or that will be found to arise from the perusal of the more serious and sublime poetry . . . I endeavour to take up the burden that fits my shoulders and I fear that under one of more weighty and precious kind, I should stumble and fall.
>
> Letter to Hatchard, 11 Nov 1819
> (Broadley & Jerrold: *The Romance of an Elderly Poet*, 1913, p. 242)

"I preach for ever, but I preach in vain," he had complained, a decade earlier, in *The Parish Register*. Like most of his contemporaries, Crabbe literally preached the same message time and again. Many of the manuscripts of his Sunday effusions are marked with four or five dates and places at which they were delivered, and where there was only one church to serve, there were usually two services a day, though often only the morning one boasted a sermon. It is strange that, with our picture of the eighteenth-century parson preaching his hour to a torpid flock and then turning the glass and continuing, one finds repeatedly that congregations complained about being deprived of their sermon at evensong. The sermon was the real centre of the service: it implies a listening and a reading public with tastes markedly different from ours, and to read Crabbe aright we must make the effort to understand the minds of people who liked being addressed at length on moral issues, who regarded this as a normal and proper intellectual activity. Interestingly, many of Crabbe's tales are of much the same length as his sermons; *Tales* of 1812 actually takes secular "texts"—quotations from Shakespeare—and, sermon-like, weaves illustrative variations upon the themes implicit in those texts. Unless we can understand that world where sermons were entertaining as well as instructive, we might as well not read Crabbe.

v

The services themselves changed over the period of Crabbe's ministry. Hymnody replaced psalmody gradually—the century gave us some of our greatest hymn-writers: Charles Wesley, Cowper, Newton, make the hymn into fine poetry. The few attempts Crabbe made at hymn writing fall below Cowper's best, and significantly, they all belong to his very early years, but they are by no means despicable examples of the genre. They are personal rather than public utterances, that is—they do not prescribe conduct, or offer guidelines towards a communal religious response (as, for instance, does a hymn like *How Sweet the Name of Jesus Sounds*, one of Newton's contributions to English hymnody). This unexplored bye-way of Crabbe's mind and art shows him in an interesting light, as a more "personal" poet than we usually assume to be the case, and as a more competent lyricist too. The poem entitled "Hymn" dates from 1778; that is, while he was still training for medicine, before the trauma of his London visit, and a good three years before Burke suggested the church to him as a career. Yet even here we can see the poet debating the secular and the spiritual points of view on life, and choosing to dedicate himself to the latter:

> OH, Thou! who taught my infant eye
> To pierce the air, and view the sky,
> To see my God in earth and seas,
> To hear him in the vernal breeze,
> To know him midnight thoughts among,
> O guide my soul, and aid my song!
> Spirit of Light! do thou impart
> Majestic truths, and teach my heart;
> Teach me to know how weak I am,
> How vain my powers, how poor my frame;
> Teach me celestial paths untrod—
> The ways of glory and of God.
>
> No more let me, in vain surprise,
> To heathen art give up my eyes—
> To piles laborious science rear'd
> For heroes brave, or tyrants fear'd;
> But quit Philosophy, and see
> The fountain of her works in Thee.
>
> Fond Man! yon glassy mirror eye—
> Go, pierce the flood, and there descry
> The miracles that float between
> The rainy leaves of wat'ry green;
> Old Ocean's hoary treasures scan;
> See nations swimming round a span.
>
> Then wilt thou say—and rear no more
> Thy monuments in mystic lore—
> My God! I quit my vain design,
> And drop my work to gaze on Thine:
> Henceforth I'll frame myself to be,
> Oh, Lord! a monument of Thee.

(Ward, Vol. 1, p. 39)

Through that conventional language which is a proper part of the eighteenth-century hymn, there come interesting suggestions. Crabbe, in his mid-twenties, a largely self-trained apprentice surgeon, has had some inkling of the anguish which was to haunt men's minds sixty years later. The "problem of science" has been apprehended here, though his answer (as it was ultimately to be,

indeed) is that of faith. To Crabbe, there is no innate schism between science and God: he must have seen enough, as surgeon,
as botanist, and geologist, to have some awareness of nature as
a machine as well as manifesting God's handiwork, yet simple
faith can bridge the gap. One sees the same kind of shift towards
total commitment to the Christian attitude in his re-working of
The Library just a few years later. It is all too readily assumed that
when he revised the poem, after it had been a prime part of the
evidence upon which Burke accepted him as a worthy protégé, his
shifting of emphasis from philosophy to divinity as the "light and
guide of mortals through their mental night" was no more than
politic. It is possible, however, to see both poems as illustrating a religious awareness to which Crabbe was growing in these
years.

The lyrics which have survived from this period and their relationship with the general trend of evangelical hymnody are
worth a passing glance. They will help to lay one foundation stone
upon which my later consideration of Crabbe's art will be based,
namely the conscious channelling of his lyrical power into the
couplet form, for better or worse. The hymn called "The Sacrament" is certainly the most sing-able of all Crabbe's minor pieces,
and, had it appeared earlier than the Appendix to the 1834 *Works*,
must have stood a good chance of inclusion somewhere among
the collections of sacred songs which proliferated around the last
decades of the eighteenth century. In addition to a lyrical light-
ness of touch and a metre which has music whilst retaining a
proper "tightness", the poem conducts an argument very neatly
to that point where we can see how it justifies its title. Its neat
reconciliation of the "dear" with the "tremendous" God, its
acceptance of the facts of the mystery of Christ's ministry, make
one regret that Crabbe wrote so little in this style. These early
hymns are far superior to the non-religious verse of the same
period. It is possible to see that the author of "Hymn", of "The
Resurrection", and "The Sacrament", has the spark of talent in
him; it is doubtful if we could honestly say the same of the
mawkish poet's-corner pieces like "Mira" or "Ye Gentle Gales".
One further piece from these early poems may be apposite here,
since it seems to lay down the ideals by which, eventually, we are
to understand Crabbe's intention, by whose criteria we should

78

test his success. "The Wish", dated from Aldeburgh in 1778, is virtually a plea for inspiration towards a useful and moral art:

> Give me, ye Powers that rule in gentle hearts,
> The full design, complete in all its parts,
> Th'enthusiastic glow, that swells the soul—
> When swell'd too much, the judgement to control—
> The happy ear that feels the flowing force
> Of the smooth line's uninterrupted course;
> Give me, oh give, if not in vain the prayer,
> That sacred wealth, poetic worth, to share—
> Be it my boast to please and to improve,
> To warm the soul to virtue and to love;
> To paint the passions, and to teach mankind
> Our greatest pleasures are the most refined;
> The cheerful tale with fancy to rehearse,
> And guild the moral with the charm of verse.
>
> (*Ward*, Vol. 1, p. 40)

The last six lines of this patchy but interesting programme piece really say everything about Crabbe's art as it will be from *Poems* onwards, which Jeffrey and Wilson expand in their critiques of him, but to which, substantially, they can add little. It is an accurate prediction by the poet about the direction his muse will ultimately take.

Curiously, in spite of these minor successes in hymnody, Crabbe, like many of the more conservative people of his day, was not altogether approving of the place hymn-singing was coming to occupy in church services. The replacement of the old book of psalms in the metrical version of Sternhold by that of Brady and Hopkins, was quite sufficient for many. Yet Crabbe himself seems to have retained a taste for the Sternhold version, despite Wesley's castigation of it as "miserable scandalous doggerel". In *The Borough* Crabbe writes half approvingly, though in the persona of the late vicar whom we have already met,

> "Mistaken choirs refuse the solemn strain
> "Of ancient Sternhold, which from ours amain
> "[Comes] flying forth, from aile to aile about,
> "Sweet links of harmony and long drawn out."
>
> (*The Borough*, Letter III, lines 130–3)

Crabbe's ear for music was, by his own confession, utterly

defective, as several of his contemporaries noted with great surprise. This may explain the narrow compass of the verse-music he is content to work within during most of his mature work. It conceals, however, the rhythmic and vocalic subtleties he can effect within this compass. At a slightly later date we find him solicited for contributions to a book of hymns. He wrote to Walter Scott asking about the credentials of an Edinburgh clergyman who had requested some pieces for inclusion in a forthcoming volume. Nothing came of the invitation: diffidence, and preoccupation with other tasks made it necessary for Crabbe to refuse. We find no trace of devotional writing as such anywhere in his later manuscript notebooks. It seems to have been a phase of activity which he felt the verse tales and his weekly sermon had superannuated.

With or without its hymns, the Sunday service was the focal point of the week for parson and congregation alike—more so than it needs to be today, for social, political, and scandalous news was distributed at this, the one regular gathering of the rural community. Through his pulpit the priest of such a flock could exercise considerable influence. However lowly the social status of the incumbent may have been—or may have been made by the snobbery or prejudice of the influential laity—yet the parson did occupy a natural function as teacher, arbiter and judge, in most villages and small towns. His position must have given him a constantly replenishable supply of characters and situations from which to shape his quasi-fictitious accounts of life around him. Beyond these obvious pastoral duties lay the multifarious offices which a conscientious pastor performed in the miniature welfare-state which a well-run parish could be. Though he is writing of a Scottish setting and giving the colour of fiction to his account, we see in John Galt's *Annals of the Parish* just how diverse and complicated was the business of being the parish spiritual guide. The diaries of men like Woodforde and Jones corroborate such a view. Perhaps no person in society was so well placed to become a student of human nature as the vicar of such a community, and of course, he had the literary training and, usually, the leisure to document his thoughts. The parson-poet is a common enough phenomenon. Cartwright and Bowles, both clerical friends of Crabbe, were much respected as poets in the early years of the nineteenth century.

VI

It was Blackstone, the famous legalist, who remarked that in visiting the London churches of his day he found it impossible to discern in what was actually delivered from the pulpit, whether the preacher was a disciple of Confucius, Mahomet, or Christ. Though he would have been horrified to fall under such a stigma in his own public preaching and practice, there is no doubt that Crabbe belonged to the latitudinarian wing of the Church which, at its worst, could become no more than a sounding-board for general prescriptions of social conduct. He confessed the breadth of his sympathies in a letter to his son, George: "Are you of this or that Church is a matter of no great importance. Are you a Christian is one of the most important" (Huchon, p. 212, 15 August 1831). What was it, then, to be a Christian in Crabbe's eyes, and how did the practice or neglect of Christianity affect a man morally, intellectually, and socially? How far did his own Christianity—whatever that may be—influence Crabbe's attitudes as a poet? At worst it might make him a prig or a moral bore. Let it be said immediately that he avoids these pitfalls to a remarkable degree. Precisely because he is interested in people rather than ideas, his work retains a sense of practical, earthy, tactile, horse-sense, even when it is dealing with complex and abstract notions.

We shall not find in Crabbe's work any deeply personalised scheme for the redemption of the world. He lived to be a contemporary of Shelley, whose proper function this was, and no two poets could be more dissimilar. We shall not find the intimate relationship between one man and his God that Herbert before or Hopkins after him created for us. Nor does Crabbe erect a theistic scheme which will correlate nature with the creating hand. To him God is in man, and indeed this is then a proper study *for* man. But he lacks the grandiloquent shaping mind which can utter such a tenet in capitalised generalisations and which can rise to the sonorities of Pope:

> The proper study of Mankind is Man.
> Plac'd on this isthmus of a middle state,
> A being darkly wise, and rudely great . . .

81

The more heavily upper case Crabbe's page becomes, the weaker the effect is likely to be: this may well be why he gave up the genre of the verse essay. Topics like *The Library, The Village,* and *The Newspaper* lead one away from individual studies of small men at work, and towards the rhetoric of abstractions.

Yet, to any poet of Crabbe's generation, the alternative was not easy to perceive. Seen through our diminishing telescope, the whirligig of taste might appear to have been at work during Crabbe's lifetime attacking the "gaudy and inane phraseology" of the old school. The Regency, however, still admired and expected such stuff. It admired Bowles before Keats, Campbell before Clare, whilst Wordsworth himself felt his way back from *Lyrical Ballads* to the custom-sanctioned comfort of his Miltonic grand manner—often as otiose and circumlocutory as anything he appeared to be campaigning against. If we are attempting to understand the problems Crabbe faced in presenting to an audience his idiosyncratic view of the world and its moral laws, we must make the effort to see from a contemporary viewpoint how priest and poet could cope. The craftsmanship is important, but is not more so than the urgency of getting Crabbe's moral viewpoint in perspective. This entails a consideration of his theories, such as they were, of his personal convictions, and of the obligations to society which he felt in shaping his ideas for public scrutiny. He was always most earnest to get this right, yet he was constantly falling foul of those reviewers who adopted an *a priori* religious line:

> In the pages of Mr Crabbe, Christianity itself—we say it with pain —seems to us degraded from its high and priveleged authority; and the pure and undefiled religion of Jesus Christ, more than once unfeelingly confounded with the most horrid and polluted mixtures, is almost at all times exposed as a totally insufficient antidote either to the ills or the vices of mankind.
>
> (*Christian Observer,* Vol. XVIII, Oct. 1819, pp. 650–68)

If it were so, it was a grievous fault . . .! Yet this same man was hailed by many as "the first moral poet of the age".

The controversy between "enthusiasm" and "worldliness" affects views of the nature and function of religion throughout Crabbe's lifetime. Samuel Horsley, Bishop of St Asaph, exemplifies one point of view at the beginning of the century:

He dreaded the teaching prevalent in some quarters, that practical religion and morality are one and the same thing, and that moral duties constitute the whole, or by far the better part, of practical Christianity. This he regarded as reducing practical Christianity to heathen virtue. Sermons that inculcated only moral duties were not sermons, but mere moral essays divested of the genuine spirit and savour of the ministry of the Word.

(Overton and Relton, *The English Church from the Accession of George I to the end of the 18th Century*, 1906, p. 257)

This represents the High Church ideal; it implies an emphasis on something mysterious which is of the spirit alone, untrammelled by the world or the flesh. At its best it may save faith from becoming rule of thumb dogma: it is difficult to have Horsley's "spirit and savour" and to be a pharisee or a Grundy, both of which become prevalent complaints during the last years of the Augustan period. It is from this side of the debate that evangelicalism sprang and from which it derived its missionary fervour. Yet fervour itself may be suspect—Crabbe, Sydney Smith, and Peacock were deeply suspicious, as Johnson and Smollett had been a generation earlier

At its worst, the emphasis on faith could lead to a zealous overplus. It could take off into numinous flights of introspected and indulgent excitement which raised righteous indignation in the minds of those not intoxicated with the heady essence. Yet equally it could produce a Wilberforce or a Cowper. William Jones demonstrates the blurring of simple boundaries between different kinds of religious mind. His diary tells how he was ashamed to have been seen in conversation with a methodist minister, lest he be assumed to have caught the infectious disease of enthusiasm; yet he has scathing contempt for the socialising, un-spiritual members of his own church who would have condemned his converse with a methodist:

What a pity that so many . . . drones are admitted into the Church, for instead of attempting to be useful, painstaking parish-priests, some of them are finical *Jemmy-Jessamies*, while others are keen sportsmen, sharp shooters, and mighty-hunting Nimrods of the cloth, . . . For the accommodation of the latter class of these Reverends daily advertisements appear for the sale of next presentations to valuable livings, rendered much more valuable, as being "situated in fine sporting countries"—"plenty of game"— . . . These men are, of course, rare, charming preachers . . . When these worthy first-rates think proper to preach, the name of Christ is scarce ever heard, nor any of the characteristic doctrines of His holy religion. The watch-word, or *catch-word* . . . is "Morality"—and even on this subject meagre, Heathen virtue is substituted in the room of substantial, Christian morality.   (Jones, *op. cit.*, p. 159)

This emphasises how Crabbe was nailing his colours to the mast with some bravery when he let himself be seen to approve of the "moral" rector, Jacques:

> . . . who with decent force,
> But not of action, aided his discourse:
> "A moral teacher!" some, contemptuous, cried;
> He smiled, but nothing of the fact denied,
> Nor, save by his fair life, to charge so strong replied.
> Still, though he bade them not on aught rely
> That was their own, but all their worthy deny,
> They call'd his pure advice his cold morality;
> And though he felt that earnestness and zeal,
> That made some portion of his hearers feel,
> Nay, though he loved the minds of men to lead
> To the great points that form the Christian's creed,
> Still he offended; for he would discuss
> Points that to him seem'd requisite for us,
> And urge his flock to virtue, though he knew
> The very heathen taught the virtues too.
> Nor was this moral minister afraid
> To ask of inspiration's self the aid
> Of truths by him so sturdily maintain'd,
> That some confusion in the parish reign'd.
> "Heathens," they said, "can tell us right from wrong,
> "But to a Christian higher points belong."
> Yet Jacques proceeded, void of fear and shame,
> In his old method, and obtain'd the name
> Of *Moral Preacher*—yet they all agreed,
> Whatever error had defiled his creed,
> His life was pure, and him they could commend,
> Not as their guide, indeed, but as their friend;
> Truth, justice, pity, and a love of peace,
> Were his—but there must approbation cease;

He either did not, or he would not see,
That, if he meant a favourite priest to be,
He must not show, but learn of them, the way
To truth—he must not dictate, but obey.
They wish'd him not to bring them further light,
But to convince them that they now were right,
And to assert that justice will condemn
All who presumed to disagree with them.
In this he fail'd, and his the greater blame,
For he persisted, void of fear or shame.

(*Tales of the Hall*, XIV, lines 3–42)

If this is read in conjunction with the lengthy note which the Biographer appends to it, one will get a good idea of the kind of clergyman Crabbe was, of where he stood on this great, divisive issue of the Enthusiast versus the Moralist, and why. Such an understanding is essential to any reading of his work, as well as to an understanding of the particular tenets of his declared faith. The issue is clouded by a change of heart which the Biographer would have us believe Crabbe experienced in his last years. He gives us a moving account of the principles in which Crabbe was brought up, and implies that they "excuse" his rather unintellectual, unspiritual approach to doctrine and duties, but notes a shift towards more "fashionable" and up-to-date attitudes in the later years at Trowbridge:

> Mr Crabbe's early religious impressions were, no doubt, strongly influenced by those of his mother; and she was, as I have already said, a deeply devout woman; but her seriousness was not of the kind that now almost exclusively receives that designation . . . I am bound to add that, at a later period in life, and more especially during the last ten years of it, he became more conscious of the importance of dwelling on the doctrine as well as the practice of Christianity, than he had been when he first took orders . . .
>
> (*Life*, pp. 30–1)

Any such shift is too subtle for the modern eye, perusing Crabbe's rather barren published sermons, to identify with clarity. By and large the terminology and the ideas of the early sermons, which still lie in manuscript, are indistinguishable from those published after his death. Some of the sermons from his Stathern days were still doing service at Trowbridge thirty years later: the poet cannot have felt his ground to have shifted all that much. It will, none-the-less, be interesting to contrast the poetry of the last period with the earlier work; here one can see a shift, even though not quite that which the son would imply. The old man seems to have become more tolerant, more benevolent, less concerned with emphasising the grey, the sordid, and the depressing. At the end of a story in *Posthumous Tales*, where, for once, the punishment does seem to outrun the failings which caused it, Crabbe can lead us not to where The President of The Immortals had finished his sport, but to a stoical acceptance:

> Yet Resignation in the house is seen,
> Subdued Affliction, Piety serene,
> And Hope, for ever striving to instil
> The balm for grief—"It is the Heavenly will."
> And in that will our duty bids us rest,
> For all that Heaven ordains is good, is best;
> We sin and suffer—this alone we know,
> Grief is our portion, is our part below;
> But we shall rise, that world of bliss to see,
> Where sin and suffering never more shall be.
> (*Posthumous Tales*, XVIII, "The Boat Race",
> lines 299–308)

VII

It will be convenient to begin an investigation of Crabbe's religion with a look at his attitude to outward forms, and to other sects, and his idea of the norm from which deviations may spring. Though it is a curious, bleak, and not totally successful tale, "Jane" (*Posthumous Tales*, IX), shows how pure orthodoxy may provide a prop for the believer, though nothing can prevent the darts of misfortune from stinging. The poem is almost painfully honest in its refusal to use religious faith as a panacea for secular disappointment: it is this uncompromising truth which gives Crabbe the reputation of a pessimist. The story, such as it is, comprises the relationship between a calm, dignified girl, and the man with whom she falls in love, only to find him already contracted to another woman who has been taken in by his specious rhetoric just as Jane herself is. It is denuded of atmosphere, and of furniture, save that which concentrates our attention exclusively

upon the intellectual nature of both the problem and its solution.
We are given a good deal of information about Jane's beliefs—the
entire poem is only 180 lines long and about 60 of these concentrate upon her intellectual life:

> . . . hers the mild good sense
> That wins its way by making no pretence.

> . . . the maid is kind to all—
> Is pious too, and that without a call.
> Not that she doubts of calls that Heav'n has sent—
> Calls to believe, or warnings to repent:
> But that she rests upon the Word divine,
> Without presuming on a dubious sign—
> A sudden light, the momentary zeal
> Of those who rashly hope and warmly feel;
> These she rejects not, nor on these relies,
> And neither feels the influence nor denies.
> Upon the sure and written Word she trusts,
> And by the Law Divine her life adjusts;
> She blames not her who other creed prefers,
> And all she asks is charity for hers.
> Her great example is her gracious Lord,
> Her hope his promise, and her guide his Word;
> Her quiet alms are known to God alone,
> Her left hand knows not what her right has done;
> Her talents, not the few, she well improves,
> And puts to use in labour that she loves.
>
> (*Posthumous Tales*, IX, lines 5–30 *passim*)

The emphasis upon "the Word" is one we find continually in
Crabbe's religious pronouncements; this was characteristic of
many of the clergy of his day, a direct outcome of their lothness
or inability to engage in abstruse speculation upon points of religious philosophy. Bishop Watson's conduct as Professor of
Divinity at Cambridge epitomises the attitude which Crabbe
shares: Watson was "unconcerned about the opinions of Councils,
Fathers, Churches, bishops and other men, as little inspired as
(himself). When students came to him with theological difficulties
he held out to them a Bible, with the words *"En Sacrum codicem"*, and the implication that they would find there the answer
to all questions."

87

The rather grotesque poem, "Lady Barbara, or The Ghost" (*Tales of the Hall*, XVI) offers this same emphasis upon scriptural authority—and in this poem the words are spoken by a ghost which has come back to warn Lady Barbara against a foolish second marriage. It is a curious case for parson Crabbe to put himself in: the ghost is that of Lady Barbara's brother, who, though brought up in a deistic household, dies a good and respected man. Hence, wherever he is coming back from, one is supposed to have credence in his words. He doesn't tell very much, however, except to repeat the old, familiar, instruction:

> " 'First let all doubts of thy religion end—
> " 'The word reveal'd is true: inquire no more;
> " 'Believe in meekness, and with thanks adore;
> " 'Thy priest attend, but not in all rely,
> " 'And to objectors seek for no reply:
> " 'Truth, doubt, and error, will be mix'd below—
> " 'Be thou content the greater truths to know,
> " 'And in obedience rest thee—
>
> (*Tales of the Hall*, XVI, lines 599–606)

Despite the odd, the almost embarrassing poem in which it occurs, this ghostly advice seems a fair summary of what Crabbe himself believed. Many a good eighteenth-century parson would ask to believe no more than this. It is easy to see how the holder of so simple a creed comes to have an uncompromising attitude to human behaviour. It is not possible to fabricate mysteries and spiritual enigmas which will offer a reconciliation of the misery and misfortune one sees in life; with this simple reliance upon the *sacrum codicem* as sole guide, it is clear that acceptance, resignation, and dogged faith, are all the sufferer can be offered:

> To the plain words and sense of sacred writ,
> With all my heart I reverently submit;
> But, where it leaves me doubtful, I'm afraid
> To call conjecture to my reason's aid;
> Thy thoughts, thy ways, great God! are not as mine,
> And to thy mercy I my soul resign.
>
> (*The Borough*, Letter IV, lines 204–9)

Crabbe is deeply suspicious of any religious sect which tries either to create a mystery out of "the Word" or which strives to build an esoteric or cabbalistic creed. This attitude to scriptural authority carries over, in a most pragmatic manner, into his attitude to words themselves as the tools of his poetic craft. His use of antithetic and quibbling lines is always effected with a self-conscious nudge of the reader's attention, as though that quirk of laughter at the corner of his mouth were betraying his sense of relish at a minor linguistic impropriety which he is allowing himself to indulge in. For the main part his words are intensely honest, plain, hardworking ones, quite without attempt at the nuances and resonances of more "atmospheric" poetic styles.

He abhorred wrangling and chop-logic in his religion, not only because it was a perversion of common-sense, but because it was a perversion of words themselves. In looking round his ideal library, his eye fell upon the shelves of Divinity, and upon the numbers of contentious and polemical works:

> Methinks, I see, and sicken at the sight,
> Spirits of spleen from yonder pile alight:
> Spirits who prompted every damning page,
> With pontiff pride and still-increasing rage.
> Lo! how they stretch their gloomy wings around,
> And lash with furious strokes the trembling ground!
> They pray, they fight, they murder, and they weep—
> Wolves in their vengeance, in their manners sheep;
> Too well they act the prophet's fatal part,
> Denouncing evil with a zealous heart;
> And each, like Jonas, is displeased, if God
> Repent his anger, or withhold his rod . . .
> Against her foes Religion well defends
> Her sacred truths, but often fears her friends;
> If learn'd, their pride, if weak, their zeal she dreads,
> And their hearts' weakness, who have soundest heads.
> But most she fears the controversial pen,
> The holy strife of disputatious men;
> Who the bless'd Gospel's peaceful page explore,
> Only to fight against its precepts more.
>
> (*The Library*, lines 223–56 *passim*)

Crabbe's annotations of this vigorous passage are revealing. He quotes his friend Bishop Watson with approval: "it is not the reading many books which makes a man divine, but the reading a few of the best books often over, and with attention." A list of what comprises these "best" works is offered to the reader of the poem; very high on that list is Paley's *Evidences of Christianity*. Perhaps it was from this that René Huchon drew his conclusion that Crabbe's religion owed much to Paley: "utilitarian, rational and matter of fact, Crabbe's theology is only a colourless reproduction of that of his contemporary, Paley" (*Huchon*, p. 211). He enjoyed a considerable vogue during the early years of Crabbe's ministry, and there is a temperamental affinity. Though Huchon calls him matter of fact with a rather down-the-nose glance, he has also been described as "a man of strong common sense", and it was this side of him which would have attracted the generation to which Crabbe belonged.

The limitations of Paley's methods are, typically, those of the years 1785 to 1810. Johnson lived just long enough to taste it, and called it the era of "Old Bailey Theology". Much of it was an investigation of the authenticity and credibility of the documentary remains upon which the New Testament was based, "when the Twelve Apostles were arraigned and acquitted of lying and forgery". The whole business was rather arid, and not nearly as scientific as was believed, but without paying some heed to it we miss an aspect of Crabbe's mind which is important to an understanding of his poetry, where similarly pragmatic and systematic approaches are made to the analysis and investigation of human psychology. He is a Paley-ite in his verse as well as in his pulpit. It is the quality in him which has always made his critics love or loathe him, which can make him ludicrously factual and mundane, or reassuringly concrete and assimilable. It is the more remarkable that underneath this bland accepting surface there ran those currents of doubt and instinct which Crabbe's investigations of derangement attempt to explore. Leslie Stephen, who is rather contemptuous of Paley, gives a succinct, if partial, statement of his beliefs and objectives in his *History of English Thought in the Eighteenth Century*. Paley cannot believe in a deity whose interference in men's lives is capricious; we have already seen that Crabbe's stories of human vicissitude rigorously eschew such an attitude too. But, says Stephen, Paley finds it equally difficult to credit "a deity of whom nature is the living raiment". The sometimes colourless or unenthusiastic treatment which nature is accorded in Crabbe's poetry is consistent with this. The purpose of the Christian religion, for the divines of this school, was "to establish the proof of the future state of rewards and punishments". Furthermore, morality becomes a system of rules for promoting public happiness, which allows us to calculate the effect of any action, as we judge it by the rules of that morality, and to predict the outcome. This seems to be what Crabbe told his flock at Swefling on 14 July 1805:

> He must make a most miserable choice who would not be religious even if there was no more than a chance, and that a very slight chance, of living again; and how much greater his folly and how much deeper his sin, who, with our evidence of the truth of Christianity, continues in neglect of its duties and is careless of its rewards! As the comforts of a pious mind greatly overbalance the restraints our duties lay upon us, and the disappointments and stings of our evil passions are more than a balance also for their enjoyments, it follows that even in this world the more prudent, and they who enjoy most of the good and avoid most of the evil must take the side of religion and virtue.
>
> (Sir John Murray's ms. collection)

It is easy to see why a creed of this kind might cause adventurous or imaginative minds to baulk. It can become almost calculating and cynical. What surprises me is the warmth Crabbe manages to give such ideas as he embodies them in the flesh and blood of the best of his tales. It is certainly *not* surprising that he found sectarianism and bigotry so hard to stomach.

VIII

The *locus classicus* of his attack on the Methodists, is in *The Borough*, though many of the tales are built around protagonists whose religion is of prime importance to the unfolding of character; "David Morris" and "Poins" (*New Poems*) both show the insidious effects which hypocritical non-conformity may have on innate moral fibre. In "The Convert" (*Tales*, XIX) we have an interesting insight into Crabbe's attitudes to methodism, to the "self-sufficiency" school in religion, and also to his control of tone within a poem. The story is a very simple one, and as so often, is based mainly upon truth. In 1791 James Lackington, the successful London bookseller, had published *The Memoirs of the*

91

Forty Five First Years of James Lackington . . . Lackington had been converted to Wesleyism, and, after a relapse, was gathered back into the fold in old age. Despite his "wicked" period, his business had been enormously prosperous; he was able to leave over three thousand pounds for the building of a chapel on his death, with one hundred and fifty pounds a year for the minister's salary.

Lackington obviously fascinated Crabbe, both by the vaccillations of his spiritual temper, and (perhaps) by the success he had despite his worldly period. The poet's treatment of the *Memoirs* is interesting. His "hero", John Dighton, is clearly modelled on Lackington; the copious footnotes to the poem emphasise this. But whereas the bookseller in real life went to a peaceful grave, Crabbe makes his hero suffer bewilderment, alienation, and loneliness at the end of his poem. Beyond "having it in" for the Methodists, the reasons for this alteration—which the poem itself explains and justifies—are characteristic of Crabbe. Dighton is unable to find a settled mean in religion because he never seeks the aid of reason or of a properly qualified pastor. He *is* converted from his debauchery by the sudden, purely instinctual fear of death during an illness, but for Crabbe this is not enough:

> The faith that reason finds, confirms, avows,
> The hopes, the views, the comforts she allows—
> These were not his, who by his feelings found,
> And by them only, that his faith was sound:
> Feelings of terror these, for evil past,
> Feelings of hope, to be received at last;
> Now weak, now lively, changing with the day,
> These were his feelings, and he felt his way.
>
> Sprung from such sources, will this faith remain
> While these supporters can their strength retain?
> As heaviest weights the deepest rivers pass,
> While icy chains bind fast the solid mass:
> So, born of feelings, faith remains secure,
> Long as their firmness and their strength endure;
> But, when the waters in their channel glide,
> A bridge must bear us o'er the threat'ning tide;
> Such bridge is reason, and there faith relies,
> Whether the varying spirits fall or rise.

(*Tales*, XIX, lines 85–102)

92

There is some nicely wrought humour, quiet but not without sarcastic edge, in the section of the poem where Crabbe describes the building up of Dighton's business, and the daily conduct of his life, and even more so in the conversations between Dighton and the brethren, after he has lapsed from the flock. The speech patterns of the brethren, even in secular conversation, and their inflated pulpit manner are wickedly "taken off" by Crabbe, and there is a little scherzo section where the secular books on display in Dighton's window are reprehended by the brethren:

> "What's here? a book of dances!—you advance
> "In goodly knowledge—John, wilt learn to dance?
> "How! 'Go' it says, and 'to the devil go!
> " 'And shake thyself!' I tremble—but 'tis so—
> "Wretch as thou art, what answer canst thou make?
> "Oh! without question, thou wilt go and shake.
> "What's here? 'The School for Scandal'—pretty schools!
> "Well, and art thou proficient in the rules?
> "Art thou a pupil, is it thy design
> "To make our names contemptible as thine?
> . . .
> "We find thee fitted for each evil work—
> "Do print the Koran, and become a Turk!
>
> (*Tales*, XIX, lines 209–28 *passim*)

This is among the richest, most artful and incisive high comedy Crabbe ever penned, yet the tale is not to end in laughter, for though he has been able to see the blemishes in the brethren (it is this, together with a gradually increasing wealth, which has alienated Dighton from them), yet he has no solid base to fall back on:

> . . . when he found his teachers had their stains,
> Resentment and not reason broke his chains.
> Thus on his feelings he again relied,
> And never look'd to reason for his guide.
> Could he have wisely view'd the fraility shown,
> And rightly weigh'd their wanderings and his own,
> He might have known that men may be sincere,
> Though gay and feasting on the savoury cheer;
> That doctrines sound and sober they may teach,
> Who love to eat with all the glee they preach;

Nay, who believe the duck, the grape, the pine,
Were not intended for the dog and swine.
But Dighton's hasty mind on every theme
Ran from the truth, and rested in th'extreme; . . .

(ibid., lines 314–27)

Few more curious defences of latitudinarian living at the parsonage can have been written than this! Yet behind its ingenuous-seeming façade, the passage and the poem as a whole is making a plea for balance, reason, and common sense. The final verse paragraph is even more explicit:

Unhappy Dighton! had he found a friend,
When conscience told him it was time to mend!
A friend discreet, considerate, kind, sincere,
Who would have shown the grounds of hope and fear;
And proved that spirits, whether high or low,
No certain token of man's safety show;
Had reason ruled him in her proper place,
And virtue led him while he lean'd on grace;
Had he while zealous been discreet and pure,
His knowledge humble, and his hope secure—
These guides had placed him on the solid rock,
Where faith had rested . . .

(ibid., lines 448–59)

IX

A reader quickly comes to expect that in Crabbe, the atheists will all go to the dogs. The infidel poacher in *The Parish Register* illustrates this convenient poetic justice at its most simplistic— or would do, were the study not based closely upon reality; "the infidel poacher was drawn from a blacksmith at Leiston, near Aldborough, whom the author visited in his capacity of surgeon in 1779, and whose hardened character made a strong impression on his mind. Losing his hand by amputation, he exclaimed, with a sneer, 'I suppose Doctor Crabbe, I shall get it again at the resurrection!' " (*Life*, p. 140). It is typical of Crabbe's idiosyncratic art that he can turn this sort of character into the material for a poem. It is also characteristic that Crabbe cannot resist the temptation to get Tom Paine—one of his private bogey men— into the picture on the devil's side:

94

> ... he, triumphant spirit! all things dared,
> He poach'd the wood, and on the warren snared;
> 'Twas his, at cards, each novice to trepan,
> And call the wants of rogues the rights of man;
> (*The Parish Register*, "Baptisms", lines 812–15)

Peter Grimes refuses the Holy Word at his father's mouth, while, in a different vein, "The Dumb Orators" (*Tales*, I) shows how the atheistical Hammond gets put down by the conformist Justice Bolt. There is a deftness of touch about this story, which is only apparent to a reader who is aware how closely Crabbe must be involved in the ideas of the poem, and yet how he manages to stand off from it, to be amused by Bolt as well as the discomfited Hammond. Hammond is allowed to put the anti-clerical case:

> Then, voluble and fierce, the wordy man
> Through a long chain of favourite horrors ran: —
> First, of the church, from whose enslaving power
> He was deliver'd, and he bless'd the hour;
> "Bishops and deans, and prebendaries all,"
> He said, "were cattle fatt'ning in the stall;
> "Slothful and pursy, insolent and mean,
> "Were every bishop, prebendary, dean,
> "And wealthy rector; curates, poorly paid,
> "Were only dull;—he would not them upbraid."
> From priests he turn'd to canons, creeds and prayers,
> Rubrics and rules, and all our church affairs;
> Churches themselves, desk, pulpit, altar, all
> The Justice reverenced—and pronounced their fall.
> (*Tales*, I, lines 171–84)

Not surprisingly, this iconoclast turns out to be a rabid republican to boot! The poem is structured so that in due course it is tit-for-tat, and Bolt has the freethinking deist in precisely the position of disadvantage which he was suffering during the tirade I have quoted. Yet, as Crabbe lets the Justice have his say, one senses a quizzical smile on his face at the defences of establishment viewpoints which his hero utters:

> Is it not known, agreed, confirm'd, confess'd,
> That of all people, we are govern'd best?

95

We have the force of monarchies; are free,
As the most proud republicans can be;
And have those prudent counsels that arise
In grave and cautious aristocracies;
. . .

Ours is a church reform'd, and now no more
Is aught for man to mend or to restore;
'Tis pure in doctrines, 'tis correct in creeds,
Has nought redundant, and it nothing needs;
No evil is therein— no wrinkle, spot,
Stain, blame, or blemish: —I affirm there's not.

(*ibid.*, lines 394–409 *passim*)

The verse comes to the bubble as the Justice warms to his work, until the last alliterative tumble is almost apoplectic with indignation. Poor Hammond's rhetoric has, conversely, utterly deserted him. Again, the passage is worth quoting not only because it demonstrates how Crabbe can structure speech rhythms, but because, lo and behold, here is the ghost of Tom Paine yet again!

By desperation urged, he now began:
"I seek no favour—I—the Rights of Man!
"Claim; and I—nay!—but give me leave—and I
"Insist—a man—that is—and, in reply,
"I speak."—Alas! each new attempt was vain:
Confused he stood, he sate, he rose again;
At length he growl'd defiance, sought the door,
Cursed the whole synod, and was seen no more.

(*ibid.*, lines 454–61)

This leaves Justice Bolt in full possession of the field and swollen with his victory, so that Crabbe is clearly suggesting that his own sympathies lie somewhere outside the points of view of both parties. We see him here poking fun at political and religious extremism, which helps to balance the too-prevalent picture of him as a gloomy moralist.

4

The Moral Teacher

> "A moral teacher!" some, contemptuous, cried;
> He smiled, but nothing of the fact denied.
>
> *(Tales of the Hall)*

I

One can see everywhere in Crabbe's work how deeply rooted is
the assumption that political, religious, and moral attitudes follow on from each other. In *Tales of the Hall* the two brothers
whose lives form the background to the frame-narrative, are
sketched for us and from the information given, we can derive
further detail for ourselves. George is a tory, a staid and respectable member of the squirarchy—a static figure, his religious
convictions are predictable:

> He took a solemn and a serious view
> Of his religion, and he found it true;
> Firmly, yet meekly, he his mind applied
> To this great subject, and was satisfied.
>
> He then proceeded, not so much intent,
> But still in earnest, and to church he went.
> Although they found some difference in their creed,
> He and his pastor cordially agreed,
> Convinced that they who would the truth obtain
> By disputation, find their efforts vain;
>
> *(Tales of the Hall, I, lines 128–37)*

Richard, the younger brother, though certainly no republican, has
a more liberal, less formulated creed;

The world he traversed was the book he read;
Hence clashing notions and opinions strange
Lodged in his mind: all liable to change.
　　By nature generous, open, daring, free,
The vice he hated was hypocrisy.
Religious notions, in her latter years,
His mother gave, admonish'd by her fears;
To these he added, as he chanc'd to read
A pious work or learn a christian creed.
He heard the preacher by the highway side,
The church's teacher, and the meeting's guide;
And, mixing all their matters in his brain,
Distill'd a something he could ill explain;
But still it served him for his daily use,
And kept his lively passions from abuse;
For he believed, and held in reverence high,
The truth so dear to man—"not all shall die."
　　　　　　　　　　(*ibid.*, lines 217–33)

The footnotes which cluster around these passages are most instructive, offering clear insights into the kind of liberal tory Crabbe had become in his old age. George and Richard represent aspects of the poet himself. Crabbe's personal tenets are apportioned between the two characters. They show the best side of latitudinarianism—its tolerance, its liberality, and its general eclectic sanity.

The toleration did not, as we have seen, extend to deists, freethinkers, and atheists. The Methodists could strain it pretty far too. The poet bends over backwards to free himself of the criticism that he is being bigoted, partisan, or personal in his famous satire on "Sects and Professions in Religion" (*The Borough*, Letter IV). Crabbe believed passionately that satire should be general, that it should avoid particularities of person or place. Faced with the problem of describing something he strongly disliked, his artistic principles must have been severely strained as he came to write this letter. Yet he could, after all, have left it out. Letter I describes the church in general, and Letter II the principal figures ministering to the church. It is rather disingenuous to offer "strict truth" as the reason for the attack on the Methodists. We cannot clear Crabbe of the suspicion that the old rankling pride-sore, caused by the loss of his congregation to the non-conformists

during his years of absence, is receiving a masochistic scratch-
ing here. In the end, all the fussy exculpation will seem unnecessary to the modern reader, but the length of it telegraphs the
degree to which passions might be raised on the issue in 1810.
For us, it is more important to note that the letter gives us one
of Crabbe's most pungent and well-wrought essays in satire. It
was not, after his early years, a mode he favoured:

> I love not the Satiric Muse:
>
> . . .
>
> What is your angry Satire worth
> But to arouse the sleeping hive,
>   And send the raging Passions forth,
> In bold, vindictive, angry flight,
> To sting wherever they alight?
>   (*Satire, Ward*, Vol. 3, p. 398)

On occasion, forth came the critical bees, indeed, for it is not
only comparatively early in his "second phase" of writing that
Crabbe probed at the more unorthodox kinds of faith, which depended upon instinct more than his own did. Though its tone is
heavy-handed, the *Eclectic Review* had a point when it took him to
task over a couple of passages in "The Maid's Story", *Tales of the
Hall*, XI.

> A man who boldly ridicules that cardinal doctrine of the Reforma-
> tion, Justification by Faith, and who can bring in, for the purpose
> of burlesque, so beautiful a scriptural allusion as the one intro-
> duced may with great consistency, himself being a clergyman, sneer
> at conversion as a substitute for episcopal ordination. After this it
> is perfectly unnecessary to comment on any want of liberality dis-
> covered in his estimate of the dissenters from that Church whose
> priest he is.   (*Eclectic Review*, Feb. 1820, NS. XIII, pp. 114–33)

How deeply his calm, rational, but perhaps tepid faith was
offended by extremes may be easily discerned through the texture
of the verse in Letter IV of *The Borough*:

> . . . none the cool and prudent teacher prize;
> On him they dote who wakes their ecstacies;
> With passions ready primed such guides they meet,
> And warm and kindle with th'imparted heat;

'Tis he who wakes the nameless strong desire,
The melting rapture, and the glowing fire;
'Tis he who pierces deep the tortured breast,
And stirs the terrors, never more to rest.

(lines 20–7)

The fear of these "ecstasies" does more than govern the tone of
the verse: there is a degree of assimilation, which often occurs
when Crabbe is "affecting the Methodists", a degree which almost
suggests a covert sympathy beneath the surface of derision.

The confession at the end of *Sir Eustace Grey* is tonally very
strange. The established clergyman gives an instructive *rationale*
of the nature of this therapy/conversion: "It has been suggested
to me that this change from restlessness to repose, in the mind of
Sir Eustace, is wrought by a methodistic call; and it is admitted
to be such: a sober and rational conversion could not have happened while the disorder of the brain continued" (*Life*, p. 165).
Since the principal criticism in the passage I have quoted from
The Borough is that the terrors stirred in the muddy pool of the
subconscious by Methodism will never more rest, it is bewildering to find in *Sir Eustace*—not far distant from *The Borough*
in date—acceptance of the efficacy of such conversion in at
least one of the three voices around which the poem is structured.

Letter IV of *The Borough* is one of the strongest things Crabbe
ever wrote in generalised satire. Structurally, the most interesting thing about it is its constant desire to become specific:
obviously the controlling voice is that of the narrator—implicitly
Crabbe himself. Yet over half the poem is not uttered by this
omniscient narrator. Six other speakers are allowed to colour
the tone of the poem by damning themselves from their own
mouths. This suggests rather more constructional decorum and
shrewdness than Crabbe is normally credited with, particularly
since he is manipulating the arguments which his speakers use all
the time. The condemnation is not just of their style, but of the
quality of imagination they exhibit. In this passage Crabbe has
taken those creeds which are most abhorrent to him, created a
figurine whose poetic deportment is made ridiculous, and then
let this Frankensteinian monster loose to utter its own condemnation. Yet there is still enough of fact on the speaker's side for us

to retain the interest to hear him out. Attacks on stale sermons, scriptural pedantry, ecclesiastical nepotism, and dull semantic juggling were rife enough to make it likely that the speaker here, a Huntingtonian fanatic, should be using these weapons in his attack on the established church:

> ... now to learning look,
> And see their priesthood piling book on book;
> Yea, books of infidels, we're told, and plays,
> Put out by heathens in the wink'd-on days;
> The very letters are of crooked kind,
> And show the strange perverseness of their mind.
> Have I this learning? When the Lord would speak,
> Think ye he needs the Latin or the Greek?
> And lo! with all their learning, when they rise
> To preach, in view the ready sermon lies;
> Some low-prized stuff they purchased at the stalls,
> And more like Seneca's than mine or Paul's.
> Children of bondage, how should they explain
> The spirit's freedom, while they wear a chain?
> They study words, for meaning grow perplex'd,
> And slowly hunt for truth, from text to text,
> Through Greek and Hebrew—we the meaning seek
> Of that within, who every tongue can speak.
> This all can witness; yet the more I know,
> The more a meek and humble mind I show.
> No; let the Pope, the high and mighty priest,
> Lord to the poor, and servant to the Beast,
> Let bishops, deans, and prebendaries swell
> With pride and fatness till their hearts rebel:
> I'm meek and modest ...   (*ibid*, lines 349–73)

The letter on Sects and Professions offers what, at first sight, appears to be a surprisingly scanty account of the Catholics. The reason is to be found in the entirely subjected and demoralised state of most Catholics during Crabbe's lifetime. In one sense the whole spirit of the eighteenth-century Church—the increasingly political bias of its pre-occupants—had been calculated to achieve this subjection of the Stuart-Catholic-ritualistic party, whilst avoiding the opposite extreme of canting sects like the Huntingtonians. Crabbe seems not to have enjoyed the victory. There is even a touch of nostalgia in the verses which describe the ruins of convents and abbeys:

> . . . the earth where abbeys stood
> Is layman's land, the glebe, the stream, the wood;
> His oxen low where monks retired to eat;
> His cows repose upon the prior's seat;
> And wanton doves within the cloisters bill,
> Where the chaste votary warr'd with wanton will.
>
> *(ibid.,* lines 148–53)

II

There are several of these accounts of religious feelings and of the characters of preachers in Crabbe's work. They serve as a way into the most vital part of any study of him, but they take us no further than a short distance to the heart of his verse. If by "religious poet" one meant no more than "satirist with clerical interests", the topic would not be worth much attention. It is as a student of the human personality, of individuals and individual problems, that one remembers and admires him. But there is no way of separating his humanitarian and his vocational sympathies. By the kind of man he was, and even more, by the kind of church he belonged to, Crabbe was shaped and in turn, shaped his art. There may be inadequacies in the tenets of the Georgian and Regency Church of England—they will be found reflected often in his poetry—but I have attempted to show that there were strengths too, and these likewise inform and sustain it. "His religion furnished him with a rule of moral life—this appears always to have been its chief value to him," as Lilian Haddakin puts it. As we have seen, this religion tended to be sketched in on a broad canvas, where bold strokes and colours are the norm, whatever murky doubts may lurk in the corners. Whether we look at Crabbe through his sermons, his letters, or his poems, we find truisms, generalisations, and abstractions everywhere. From them is wrought a poetry as circumstantial, as detailed, and as personal as any in our language: "Pride" becomes Jachin, the Parish Clerk, "Conscience" becomes Fulham the toyman, "Generosity" and "Meanness" become George and Isaac, the brothers of *Tales,* XX. It is this habit of observing the material of his art through a religious eye which makes it important for the reader never to lose sight of everything lying behind and in the background of Crabbe's mind.

The "moral teacher" tag sticks closely to Crabbe because his religion is so uncomplicated, so obvious, that it may well appear denuded of mystery to the point where it loses all particular character. One misses a vital element in looking at it like this: in giving an account of Crabbe's attitude to other creeds I have tried to suggest a negative virtue which may be present in his own faith. It is not superstitious, it is not hypocritical, it is not bigoted, it does not inflate the pride of the practitioner. Put even thus in the form of negatives, we are moving towards the bases of his art, for it is the vices of cant, self-love, and ingratitude which horrify him in his fellow mortals: horror, with, super-added, a desire to instruct in virtue and to document the processes of temptation and deterioration through which men predictably will pass. Very firm convictions underlie all this. He is unshake-ably certain that punishment will follow sin, and that it will be psychologically appropriate to the error which was committed. In "Edward Shore", (*Tales*, XI) Crabbe speaks of

> ... the time
> (Sure to arrive) when misery waits on crime.
> (lines 374–5)

This sounds, on the surface, as though it will make grim reading, or worse, be a downright bore. It is redeemed by the acuity of the observation. It is difficult to recall two of Crabbe's figures who exemplify quite the *same* "crime" as each other, just as it is rare for Crabbe to punish or blame without justifying his reasons for doing so:

> Man's heart is sufficiently prone to make excuses for man's in-firmity, and needs not the aid of poetry or eloquence to take from vice its native deformity.   (Preface to *Tales of the Hall, Life,* p. 378)

The sermons reiterate the point. Indeed, more than any other attribute of the human mind, Crabbe is appalled by this tend-ency towards self-deception: the struggle to repent, which is diffi-cult anyway, cannot begin until a man has opened his eyes to the need for repentance. The ethos of Crabbe's religion appears harsh or pessimistic to many critics because there is so much emphasis upon the processes of sinning, while he has comparatively little to say about the rewards of not doing so. The critics have always been divided temperamentally into those who share his view that self-deceit and general unhappiness are frequent enough in life to warrant their occupying a major part of a poet's output, and those who believe that such a view exaggerates the general unhappiness of man's position. Hence it is of the same poet that Patmore writes:

> His religion and morality were intolerant, narrow, and scrupulous, and sadly wanting in all the modern graces.
>
> (*Principle in Art*, 1890, p. 137)

and of whom, a more recent writer has said

> His was an enlightened theological liberalism, which sought the best in all the schools . . . Crabbe's theology was, in fact, the doctrinal statement of a type of piety, sincere, devout, and reasonable [his own words], which the eighteenth century often produced, but which also because of its undemonstrativeness is not always recognised at its true worth.
>
> (A. Pollard, *Church Quarterly Review*, No. 157, 1956)

The same bewilderingly divergent views will emerge when we look at the status his art has been accorded over the years.

III

Conscience is perhaps the most important single element in the governing of man's nature, according to Crabbe. The conscience must be trained, and kept in training; to undertake this arduous spiritual exercise one needs Faith, and the tangible end-product is acceptance and stoical courage, together with a genuinely outgoing concern for others. He comes very close to a formal connection between the various attributes in one of the published sermons:

> Holiness is strenuous imitation of Christ in the virtues of humility and meekness, with patience, temperance, and charity; but it is not these virtues, considered in themselves only, which we contemplate, but the practice of them under the most trying circumstances, the hardest temptations. (*Sermons*, p. 127)

The poems tend to divide into those where the agency of mal-aise, the psychic disturbance, comes purely from within, giving us poems about people who tempt themselves; and those where the disruptive agency is external, where man preys upon man. The same firm and influential moral attitude prevails in each group, governed by the authorial attempt to diagnose, to understand, and, in most cases, to sympathise. There are people to whom Crabbe's long suffering charity does not extend: Grimes is one, Blaney another. They have placed themselves beyond the pale of all save the anatomising eye which fixes their fault, and documents it so clearly that no overt condemnation is needed.

One might, looking at the picture of Blaney's downfall (*The Borough*, Letter XIV), argue that Crabbe was loading the dice, that he was cheating in his manipulation of events. But there is a footnote to the poem urging that it is drawn from life. I find it among the coldest and most disturbing of character portraits which Crabbe ever drew. Jeffrey was much struck by its power too, though he found it "offensive from its extreme and impotent depravity". It is the tragic wasteful folly, the utter pointlessness of Blaney's life which is chilling. The character is placed among the inmates of the Borough Alms-house, and is closely linked with Sir Denys Brand, also a study based on personal observation by the poet. It is as an example of Sir Deny's moral taste that Blaney is introduced, for it was Sir Denys, as Governor of the alms-house, who allowed Blaney admission. As an example of structure itself being dominated by the tone Crabbe wishes to adopt—or which his own feelings dictate to him—the poem is of interest. As Jeffrey saw, its manner is Popeian; terse almost to brutality, quite without any flash of warmth or colour, yet holding our attention by its crisp and apophthegmatic power, in describing a man who has killed his own conscience:

> Blaney, a wealthy heir at twenty-one,
> At twenty-five was ruin'd and undone:
> These years with grievous crimes we need not load,
> He found his ruin in the common road: —
> Gamed without skill, without enquiry bought,
> Lent without love, and borrow'd without thought.
> But, gay and handsome, he had soon the dower
> Of a kind wealthy widow in his power;

Then he aspired to loftier flights of vice,
To singing harlots of enormous price;
He took a jockey in his gig to buy
A horse, so valued that a duke was shy;
To gain the plaudits of the knowing few,
Gamblers and grooms, what would not Blaney do?
His dearest friend, at that improving age,
Was Hounslow Dick, who drove the western stage.
(*The Borough*, Letter XIV, lines 13–28)

We meet Blaney at every turn in Regency society: turn the pages
of Pierce Egan and there he is, enter any society drawing-room,
and we shall be introduced to him within minutes. He has cousins
and brothers who go back as far as Ben Jonson, and who mince
and insinuate their way through the pages of Restoration comedy.
But nowhere else is the type touched with so sincere and Christian
a distaste as here in Crabbe. Principally it is moral condemnation
that Crabbe is drawing us to, but the social comment is pungent,
for this useless parasite is to become a place-man, an office-
sponger; thus his world itself is seen to share the corruption of
the individual. The distancing disgust with which his see-saw fortunes are described is the result of deep but controlled feeling on
poet's part:

Yet, thus assisted, ten long winters pass'd
In wasting guineas ere he saw his last;
Then he began to reason, and to feel
He could not dig, nor had he learn'd to steal;
And should he beg as long as he might live,
He justly fear'd that nobody would give.
But he could charge a pistol, and, at will,
All that was mortal by a bullet kill:
And he was taught, by those whom he would call
Man's surest guides—that he was mortal all.
While thus he thought, still waiting for the day
When he should dare to blow his brains away,
A place for him a kind relation found . . .
(lines 33–45)

Blaney makes another fortune in his bought office in the tropics,
and fritters that away too. His moral cowardice is epitomised in
the contemptuous way Crabbe describes his suicide notions, and

the hideous sloth in Blaney's intellectual "efforts" to find *some* justification for his life. It is the old deistic bogey-men who provide the basis of this conduct—or would be if Blaney had the integrity to read them, but no:

> He heard of Blount, of Mandeville, and Chubb,
> How they the doctors of their day would drub;
> How Hume had dwelt on miracles so well,
> That none would now believe a miracle;
> And though he cared not works so grave to read,
> He caught their faith and sign'd the sinner's creed.
>
> (lines 92–7)

He leads a life moved by pride, by habit, and despair, and is finally caught in one of the most tremendous rhetorical crescendos Crabbe ever shaped, no less original for his own insistence in the footnotes that it is an imitation of Pope's manner:

> Lo! now the hero shuffling through the town,
> To hunt a dinner and to beg a crown;
> To tell an idle tale, that boys may smile;
> To bear a strumpet's billet-doux a mile;
> To cull a wanton for a youth of wealth,
> (With [reverent] view to both his taste and health);
> To be a useful, needy thing between
> Fear and desire—the pander and the screen;
> To flatter pictures, houses, horses, dress,
> The wildest fashion or the worst excess;
> To be the grey seducer, and entice
> Unbearded folly into acts of vice;
> And then, to level every fence which law
> And virtue fix to keep the mind in awe,
> He first inveigles youth to walk astray,
> Next prompts and soothes them in their fatal way,
> Then vindicates the deed, and makes the mind his prey.
>
> (lines 142–58)

The culminating irony is that he is admitted to the alms-house at last, yet the whirligig of time brings in his revenges, for he is there, not on the board of governors as he would have hoped and expected, but as a regular inmate, spurned and shunned by all the others.

It is pride which makes Blaney go on sinning when even shame would bid him stop. Here, then, is the very bottom of the pit, as far as Crabbe is concerned. One senses that he has even more regard for Grimes than for Blaney, for at least Grimes finds he *has* a conscience. The poet's feelings may be coupled with frustration that here is a character type which is beyond his aid. Whatever the reasons, this type of sinner who is virtually abandoned by the priest and the poet in Crabbe, is a rare phenomenon in his poetry, for charity (in both its meanings, but principally in its higher one of *caritas*—general all-embracing love) is a vital element in Crabbe's religion. It is straightforward Pauline doctrine, and it makes Crabbe understanding of and pitiful towards sinners. It is also an extension of the poetic doctrine which, following Pope, parson Crabbe avowed:

> Man's vice and crime I combat as I can,
> But to his GOD and conscience leave the man; ...
> Yet, as I can, I point the powers of rhyme,
> And, sparing criminals, attack the crime.
> (*The Borough*, Letter XXIV, lines 450–65 *passim*)

IV

Just beyond this level of *conscious* sinning begin the people Crabbe is really most interested in: those whose crime may initially be venal, or no more than a degree of selfishness, but who allow this to spread like a stain across their whole character until custom has consumed their moral fibre. His sermons return with great regularity to the heinous and insidious effects of habit upon us. One such was obviously a favourite, since he used it at Muston on 19 April 1789, 5 December 1790, 13 November 1791, and at Allington in 1791 and again as late as 1807. It reflects his thoughts on human nature, in other words, during the years which were seminal to *Poems* and *The Borough*. It is worth quoting from the relevant Epistle since it is not only the chosen text itself, but the verses round about, which can help to show the relationship between poet and preacher in Crabbe—and something of the unconscious mind of the man as well, perhaps. The relevant verses of I Peter IV, 1–10, are as follows:

Forasmuch then as Christ hath suffered for us in the flesh, arm yourselves likewise with the same mind: for he that hath suffered in the flesh hath ceased from sin; that he should no longer live the rest of his time in the flesh to the lusts of men, but to the will of God. For the time past of our life may suffice us to have wrought the will of the Gentiles, when we walked in lasciviousness, lusts, excess of wine . . . And above all things have fervent charity among yourselves; for charity shall cover the multitude of sins . . . As every man hath received the gift, even so minister the same one to another, as good stewards of the manifold grace of God.

This is by no means a sombre passage, and indeed is one offering much hope to those who have the will to fulfil its commands, yet Crabbe, lacking conviction in the *will* of his flock, manages a sad and stern moral from his text.

There had, in his early days, been rumours that parson Crabbe's past life had not been all it might. There was supposed to be a rather wild club in Woodbridge of which he was a member, and even suggestions that he lacked popularity at Belvoir through a penchant for liquor which he could not hold—uncharitable rumours, probably without serious foundation in a world where most social drinkers would have seen us under the table, and where the real bottle-artists exhibited a phenomenal capacity: (William Jones' diary records that: "Brothers John and Heighes sat up drinking with Captain Pompier, Mr Goldsboro and a midshipman, all drunk. They drank 3 bottles of wine, and near 20 quarts of cider.") I see no need to believe the stories of Crabbe's inebriety—though the choice of subject for that early poem is interesting—yet I think that, in picking his text, the passages about a debauched past and about charity, will have caught his eye and lent a trenchant personal animus to his sermon.

He begins by stressing that "conscience is the beginning of judgement, the Warning of the World to come and the Terrors of it. The Voice of God and Nature in us." He believes that not only sin, but redemption starts within, that man is responsible for his own moral state. Arthur Pollard has noted this emphasis:

The status . . . Crabbe ascribed to Conscience is similar to that given it by Butler. Both men appear to deify the conscience as the supreme judge of the rightness or otherwise of actions. The criter-

ion of virtue is interior and authoritarian, not as with Paley, who
. . . makes it external and utilitarian.

(Pollard, Church Quarterly Review, loc. cit., p. 316)

No reading of Crabbe's poetry which begins without taking full
cognisance of this fact can possibly be a full and proper reading.
Conscience is the constant element in all his "normative" verse.
The fascination of reading his studies of derangement, or poems
like "Where am I Now?", is that the conscience has been bye-
passed in this dream world.

The sermon on Conscience goes on to look at self-analysis and
self-deceit, the two prime activities of man's intellectual state for
Crabbe. Time and time again we are to see in his poetry, people
falling, not because they are inherently wicked like Grimes or
Blaney, not because they are wretchedly put upon like Jane and
Lucy in "The Sisters" (Tales of the Hall, VIII), but because they
put upon themselves. This is the situation, with shrewd psychological variations, that Crabbe portrays so often.

> There is no deceit so great as that of our Vices and Habits. Vice
> and Habit are both deceitful, but how much more when joined
> . . . We look upon our Temptations, our Youth, our way of Life,
> our Companions or particular inclinations and in one or more of
> these we find a pardon in ourselves for all we have done. We call
> Sin Frailty, Frailty Custom, and Custom Law . . . Our Hearts deceive
> us and our Imaginations dwell upon what we think our goodness.
>
> (Yale mss.)

This sermon takes us yet one step further to understanding the
moral processes as Crabbe presumed them to be, for it concludes
that Salvation will only come from within and that the work required is arduous and continuous. It may well have been this heavy
insistence upon everything coming from within us, with a consequent recognition that helping other people is a near-impossibility
unless they are already in a self-prepared state to want help, that
gives Crabbe so bleak a view of the efficacy of his function as a
clergyman: "I am convinced that instructing Ignorance and correct-
ing Vice are not my Talents, at least they do not suit my turn
of Mind and Temper," he wrote to Miss Charter in November
1815 (Broadley and Jerrold, The Romance of an Elderly Poet,
1907, p. 111).

There is an interesting group of poems in which he shows how even conversion and apparent repentance can be a function of pride, and totally mistaken. Poins, the eponymous hero of one of the *New Poems* demonstrates this false repentance. He is thus reproved by one of the other persons in the poem:

> . . . repenting Sinners fly
> From the sad Pleasures that their Frailties buy,
> They feel their ruined State, lament the Price,
> And spurn the Profit that is made by Vice.
> But thy Repentance is the fruitless Grief,
> That is too light to give the Soul Relief.
> ("Poins", *New Poems*, lines 499–504)

The same poem also discusses the relationship between this rather bleakly isolated humanity, wrestling with its own inward volitions and delusions, and external sources of assistance. If friends and even professional spiritual counsellors are of only partial assistance, where can we turn? At this point the answer given, obvious as it may be, demonstrates Crabbe's Christian, rather than his merely humane orientation.

> . . . he did resolve, indeed,
> But Resolution is a breaking Reed,
> Made by Man's Will alone—He should have known
> Who gives Man Strength superior to his Own;
> Vain his Resolve, who on himself relies,
> 'Tis Grief's Repentence, not Humility's.
> (*ibid.*, lines 297–302)

The process has its less bleak side, though I think it important to stress that Crabbe abhorred that lack of rigour and honesty which palliated the message just for comfort's sake. He made this quite clear to his flock: "we are not so much to consider whether what we preach be pleasant or unpleasant, as whether it be false or true" (*Sermons*, p. 60). There is a curious but very close relationship between this and his literary practice. In the preface to *The Borough*, defending himself against the charge of a morbid over-insistence upon analysis of men's faults, he declares, "It has always been held as a salutary exercise of the mind, to contemplate the evils and miseries of our nature," which, by implication, allows this sermonising literature to be considered as poetry despite its didactic roots. Crabbe has many friends and advocates who want to see him as less grey, sober and conventional than this investigation may have made him appear. I cannot think, from anything he has written, that he would thank us for trying to wring the entertainment out of him at the expense of the instruction:

> Poetry without morality is but the blossom of a fruit tree. Poetry is indeed like that species of plants, which may bear at once both fruit and blossoms and the tree is by no means in perfection without the *former* however it may be embellished by the flowers which surround it. (Shenstone, "Essay on Elegy", *Works*, 1765, Vol. 1, p. 11)

This sums it up very well, though the *practice* of Crabbe, or any moral artist, usually makes its fusion of teaching and entertaining so complete that the conscious mind is never over-aware of being manipulated or preached at.

V

In examining the art by which the Sunday effusion is transmuted into permanently valuable poetry, it will help to look in detail at another of the sermons, since it is perhaps the most analytic statement of the nature and function of conscience which Crabbe has left us. His text is the First Epistle of John, III, 20, a chapter dealing with man's relationship with the community, where he must exercise love and charity; and with God, to whom the deepest motive-springs of his heart will be known. This leads Crabbe into a disquisition on conscience. He likens unassailed conscience to a sundial: it is simple in operation and its clarity is a function of its efficacy. But conscience assailed by indulgence is like a watch, it is mechanistic, and more fallible than the "natural" organ of the sundial. The watch must be constantly set, checked, and tampered with artificially, by man. How then, Crabbe goes on to ask, can we find the spiritual exercises which will enable us to have this clear conscience, and what factors introduce artificial opacity into our view of ourselves? He lists five causes: *neglect*, and *carelessness of self-inquiry*; so that we may not be moved in conscience, but this will not mean that we are sinless:

habit; that is, consistent indulgence in small sins which we deem, simply through customary practice, to be unworthy of our moral attention: (the interesting corollary to this is that there is no such thing as a small sin. We shall see how many of the poems demonstrate this): *imitation*; that is, the belief that we are living as others do, and therefore all must be well. Crabbe adds to this point the observation that in fact nobody really knows how any one else lives, and each of us has a private and interior life. The last of his causes of spiritual obloquy is that *moral sloth* which makes us content to stand still rather than be constantly searching for signs in ourselves of spiritual progress. As he says in another of these published sermons, "We are not born Christians any more than we are born soldiers"—there must be constant training, courage, and constancy.

Clearly, the congregation which is thus exhorted to be constantly vigilant for sunspots upon the face of its conscience, needs to know something of the nature of sin, the more so if the preacher is adamant that there is no gradation into "big" sins which matter, and little ones which don't. The poems demonstrate this: the care and attention which has gone into the artistic documentation of Grimes, murderer, blasphemer and drunkard, is no greater than that with which the pharisaical Dinah (*Tales*, IV) argues herself towards spiritual self-destruction through a slowly growing taste for worldly possessions. The sermon on the text, "The wicked shall be turned into Hell" (Psalm IX, Verse 17) seeks to give some definition. The wicked are the openly abandoned, who have given themselves over to evil, such as blasphemers, sabbath-breakers, the cruel, the unjust, and those who lie, steal, deceive, or are bad parents. This is the category of Blaney and his like. Next come those who, while decent in all other ways, are yet under the sway of one over-riding passion deleterious to their moral nature. Covetousness and drunkenness are cited as examples of such sins. (Both, interestingly, are sins found in Crabbe's own family circle: his father seems to have been a violent alcoholic in his later years, while the covetousness of the Widow Goe in *The Parish Register* is said to be a description of the manners of old Mrs Tovell, an aunt of the poet's wife.) The third category of the wicked embraces those who lack charity. Crabbe returns to this quality very frequently. He clearly construed "charity" in its very widest

sense, to take in everything from specific deeds of alms-giving—
upon which he was very keen—to love of one's fellow men in the
broadest of contexts. Altruistic benevolence was a characteristic
of the poet himself and he valued people who had it. Letter XVIII
of *The Borough* furnishes a good insight into Crabbe's thoughts
on the subject.

In "The Family of Love", the second story in *Posthumous Tales*,
there is a description of a reactionary self-made man's reasons
for not exercising charity. The arguments are those we meet again
and again when we look at Crabbe's relationship to the political
climate of his day. The more he lets his character speak, the more
we can see how Crabbe disapproves of his attitudes:

> "[We're] rich," quoth James; "but if we thus proceed,
> "And give to all, we shall be poor indeed:
> "In war we subsidise the world—in peace
> "We christianise—our bounties never cease;
> "We learn each stranger's tongue, that they with ease
> "May read translated Scriptures, if they please;
> "We buy them presses, print them books, and then
> "Pay and export poor learned, pious men;"
>
> (Posthumous Tales, II, lines 146–53)

In his carping, sneering attitude to "good works" Dyson gives
utterance to things which the poet himself regards as epitomising
uncharitableness. It says much for the temper and independent
mind of a Regency country parson that he can feel and write like
this. It says quite a lot for the technician in Crabbe that he can
make such vigorous and well-rounded rhetorical verse look so easy
to throw off.

The tenets which Crabbe thought worth inculcating into the
minds of his parishioners are, I believe, fundamental to the moral
structure of his verse: the poet and the parson are one. Conscience, Faith, and Repentance are the bases of his fables. They
unite a huge, sprawling output which is broken by a twenty year
time span—into a protean but coherent statement about human
nature. That such a reading can lead to a strong dislike of the
poet must be admitted:

If human nature really is Mr Crabbe's theme, it is the human nature
of Hobbes, in which, for the bond of human love, is substituted

a barrier of universal hatred, and every man is asserted to be the
adversary to his brother. It is the social plan of Mandeville, in
which, what little good we possess is declared to be the produce of
conflicting evils.

(*British Critic*, "On Crabbe, Hobbes and Mandeville", NS XII,
Sept. 1809, pp. 285–301)

Nothing, I think, could be further from the truth, yet the poetry,
if read as purely secular poetry, does lay itself open to such
charges. It is only the over-riding professional, vocational, charity
of the writer which transforms the bleak documentation of frailty,
tawdriness and failure, into a deeply passionate affirmation of the
value of human life, beyond and outside the local prescriptions
of this or that system, but always inside the framework of
Christian love and brotherhood as Crabbe understands them.

Analysis of a couple of poems may help to make the point
clearer. "Procrastination" (*Tales*, IV) is a secular tale about those
"small" sins Crabbe discusses in his sermons. Nobody is murdered
or has his worldly goods purloined; indeed, very little action takes
place at all. The fable is bleakly simple; a young couple, in love
but impoverished, agree to delay their wedding while Rupert tries
to improve his fortunes. He goes abroad to work; Dinah lives with
an elderly widowed aunt. Gradually the aunt seduces the affections
of her niece away from the absent Rupert towards a love of
worldly possessions. No poet can describe furniture, chattels, and
everyday things so pregnantly as Crabbe. It is, I think, one of the
things which made such different authors as Jane Austen and
Dickens admire him, for both, in their very different ways, have
a preoccupation with the relationship between the characters of
people and the physical objects with which they surround themselves.

There is just a hint that jealousy motivates the aunt to seduce
Dinah away from Rupert. The poem is the stronger because this
suggestion is not made overt. It is, ultimately, left as one of
the mysterious but sad truths of our nature that such seductions,
whether consciously or unconsciously effected, take place all the
time. It is no less damaging than physical seduction: indeed, a
mustachioed villain, an Alec D'Urbeville, might have done Dinah
less spiritual damage than her aunt does her. Crabbe gives us a
norm from which the characters all diversify as they interact:

115

The prudent Dinah was the maid beloved,
And the kind Rupert was the swain approved.
A wealthy Aunt her gentle niece sustain'd . . .
(lines 15–17)

"Prudent", "kind", "wealthy": at this point the qualities attributed to the young people are moral ones; the danger comes from the "wealth" of the aunt, and from the atrophy which worldly goods have already effected upon her character.

. . . the poor virgin lived in dread and awe;
Upon her anxious looks the widow smiled,
And bade her wait, "for she was yet a child".
(lines 23–5)

The brief but succinct strokes with which the situation is fixed for us are Crabbe at his best: which of us has not heard some relative or figure in authority employing just the kind of blackmail which Crabbe puts into the aunt's mouth?

The dame was sick, and, when the youth applied
For her consent, she groan'd, and cough'd, and cried;
Talk'd of departing, and again her breath
Drew hard, and cough'd and talked again of death:
"Here may you live, my Dinah! here the boy
"And you together my estate enjoy."
Thus to the lovers was her mind express'd,
Till they forbore to urge the fond request.

(lines 34–41)

The acuteness and accuracy of Crabbe's ear for the dramatic timbre of speech-patterns comes across very clearly here. One can hear again old Mrs Tovell who inspired the Widow Goe, but the transformation now is a for a more serious purpose.

Rupert eventually is given the prospect of making his fortune if he will go abroad. The couple, now approaching middle age, and with no nearer prospect of independence from the aunt if Rupert stays, are forced apart.

Loth were the lovers; but the aunt declared
'Twas fortune's call, and they must be prepared:
"You now are young, and for this brief delay,
"And Dinah's care, what I bequeath will pay;

"All will be yours; nay, love, suppress that sigh;
"The kind must suffer, and the best must die."
Then came the cough, and the strong signs it gave
Of holding long contention with the grave.

(lines 54–61)

The language of the poem is carefully contrived to show the growing moral schism between the lovers. As Dinah is hardened and inured to the worldly materialistic values of her aunt, she becomes "the grave niece"; the gravity set in an ironic context of "hoards" and "comforts" until "love grew languid in the careful maid". "Careful" is a long way from the "prudent" with which the poem opened. When the aunt, after much more play with her voluble cough, does finally die, the poet adopts, on behalf of Dinah, a brusque tone, in which no regret whatsoever is discernable. This ability to control subtle nuances of tone and texture marks most of Crabbe's best work:

Then came a priest—'tis comfort to reflect,
When all is over, there was no neglect;
And all was over—by her husband's bones,
The widow rests beneath the sculptured stones,
That yet reflect their fondness and their fame,
While all they left the virgin's care became:
Stock, bonds, and buildings;—it disturb'd her rest,
To think what load of troubles she possess'd.
Yet, if a trouble, she resolved to take
Th'important duty, for the donor's sake;
She too was heiress to the widow's taste,
Her love of hoarding, and her dread of waste.

(lines 114–25)

Two of Crabbe's principal gifts as a teller of tales in verse are his ability to get straight to the heart of what lies behind the social and public surface in people, and his skill in condensing time, so that a five hundred line poem will credibly span a twenty year time scale while appearing to omit no necessary fact from the analytic account of character which is taking place. "Procrastination" offers an example of these skills. As we read of Dinah's drawing-room—an exquisite picture of the claustrophobic Regency clutter which is so oppressive if not managed with discreet taste—we are aware that this room is a timeless monument to the spiritual atrophy which has overtaken the woman. Up-holstery has superseded sentiment: the exhibitionism of Dinah's dependence upon *things* pads round and masks her total spiritual emptiness. Secular as the poem may seem—and, after all, no "crime" is committed—one is aware by a governing tone behind the narrator's apparently factual voice, that a crushing condemnation is being uttered:

> Within that fair apartment, guests might see
> The comforts cull'd for wealth by vanity.
> Around the room an Indian paper blazed,
> With lively tint and figures boldly raised;
> Silky and soft upon the floor below,
> Th'elastic carpet rose with crimson glow;
> All things around implied both cost and care;
> What met the eye was elegant or rare.
> Some curious trifles round the room were laid,
> By hope presented to the wealthy maid:
> Within a costly case of varnish'd wood,
> In level rows, her polished volumes stood;
> Shown as a favour to a chosen few,
> To prove what beauty for a book could do;
> A silver urn with curious work was fraught;
> A silver lamp from Grecian pattern wrought;
> Above her head, all gorgeous to behold,
> A time-piece stood on feet of burnish'd gold;
> A stag's-head crest adorn'd the pictured case,
> Through the pure crystal shone th'enamell'd face;
> And, while on brilliants moved the hands of steel,
> It click'd from pray'r to pray'r, from meal to meal.
>
> (lines 158–79)

Be it said, our lady was bang up to fashion! The Grecian thing must have been scarcely under way when Crabbe was writing this tale. The room is an amalgam of inward and outward signs, of genuine taste and hideous charlatanism, and the directing voice in the background never needs to intrude. The sensuous, often erotic patterns of the oriental wallpapers and furnishings of the day begin the process of ironic double-entendre which runs through the passage. As early as Pope, the "Indian" motif had rank sexual connotations: the power of Pope's couplet about the bored lady submitting to copulation while she lies stifling a yawn

118

and seeking some object to concentrate her gaze on, comes as an inevitable association with Dinah's wallpaper:

> She, while her lover pants upon her breast
> Surveys the carving on an Indian chest.

That there is no sexual or human contact of any kind in "Procrastination", makes the Crabbe poem with this particular innuendo about Dinah's lack of human normalcy very intense. Were it nothing else, "Procrastination" would be one of the saddest, truest, and most acute studies of the causes and effects of "old maidism". But this woman has killed herself; she positively revels in her living death, and the details of atrophy and emptiness continue to be represented by the physical paraphernalia of sumptuous fullness. The carpet itself rises—is it with a blush of shame at Dinah's insufficiency, or is it as it might be in the work of some surrealistic film-maker? It is worth noting, too, how Dinah's life has been passed. There have been suitors, of a kind. Men have called and have made her presents: their votive offerings are ceremonially laid out around the room. The culminating detail is, of course, the clock—the symbol of time passing and crowned by its unconsciously sexual motif. It ticks with a steely, shiny, empty, mad-house rhythm, clicking Dinah towards a death she has already suffered in the spirit, and against which none of her possessions will shield her when the time comes. The closing line shows how minute and particular Crabbe's artistry can be: he has truncated the longer, more significant word "pray'r" and contrived to extend the emphasis upon "meal" until it becomes something that one's inner sense of rhythm apprehends as a di-syllable.

And then, suddenly, the poem brings us up to date. As Dinah sits listening to the vaguely prurient gossip of "a friendly pair stept in t'admire the view", there is an interruption, superbly managed by the dramatist in Crabbe, which alters the balance of the poem, and shatters its comfortable claustrophobia:

> The friends prepared new subjects to begin,
> When tall Susanah, maiden starch, stalk'd in;
> Not in her ancient mode, sedate and slow,
> As when she came, the mind she knew to know;
> Nor as, when list'ning half an hour before,
> She twice or thrice tapp'd gently at the door;

119

> But all decorum thrust in wrath aside,
> "I think the devil's in the man!" she cried;
> "A huge tall sailor, with his tawny cheek,
> "And pitted face, will with my lady speak;
> "He grinn'd an ugly smile, and said he knew,
> "Please you, my lady, 'twould be joy to you;
> "What must I answer?"   (lines 200–12)

The impetuous Rupert, whose return this servitorial fanfarade is all about, catches the lady off balance, though only briefly. The cold and decimating precision with which she then ousts him from the room and from her life occupies less than a hundred lines, but can never be forgotten. Her speech is mincing, fluttering, coy; his is bluff, brusque, and manly. Yet she has the wealth and position. His naïve attempt to share her wealth by an offer of letting her share his "caritas"—his love of life, of simple virtue, of limpid moral probity and unworldliness—is crushed. He retires to the parish alms-house:

> Behold them now!—see, there a tradesman stands,
> And humbly hearkens to some fresh commands;
> He moves to speak, she interrupts him—"Stay,"
> Her air expresses—"Hark to what I say!"
> Ten paces off, poor Rupert on a seat
> Has taken refuge from the noon-day heat,
> His eyes on her intent, as if to find
> What were the movements of that subtle mind;
> How still!—how earnest is he! ...
>
> But Dinah moves—she had observed before
> The pensive Rupert at an humble door.
> Some thoughts of pity raised by his distress,
> Some feeling touch of ancient tenderness;
> Religion, duty, urged the maid to speak
> In terms of kindness to a man so weak;
> But pride forbad, and to return would prove
> She felt the shame of his neglected love;
> Nor wrapp'd in silence could she pass, afraid
> Each eye should see her, and each heart upbraid.
> One way remain'd—the way the Levite took,
> Who without mercy could on misery look,
> (A way perceived by craft, approved by pride):
> She cross'd and pass'd him on the other side.
>
> (lines 319–49 *passim*)

So the poem, which could, after all, have been the work of any humanitarian author for most of its length, comes back to a specifically Christian point of reference in the end. Apart from its integral excellence it is worth study in the context of an argument that Crabbe's religion was important to him, and still is important to us, reading him today, because it demonstrates the kind of "moral teacher", the kind of Regency parson he was.

VI

It is possible to trace the ideological foundations of this attitude to "sin" through Crabbe's sermons. Dinah belongs in the second circle of his inferno, with all those who corrupt themselves, and in whom charity is absent or suppressed. The authorial voice is not that of a Hannah More or a Mrs Grundy. It has *artistic* authority, and it has a poised, ironic wit. One often feels that it is in the more serious poems that Crabbe shows best his unique humour. "Procrastination" works because the narrative tone can include the external scrutiniser as well as the individual voices of the characters. It sends a sudden chill down the back in *Peter Grimes* that, in the midst of the whippings to which his 'prentices are subjected, the townspeople, hearing the cries of agony, can pass by the shed and say "calmly",

> "Grimes is at his exercise".
> (line 78)

The adverb is devastating in its context.

So long as this controlling tone is exercised, Crabbe sustains his moral verses above the level of the handbooks of "The Goodies and the Noodles", as the incorrigible Sydney Smith designated the pietistic moral manuals which were beginning to proliferate—one of the less happy side effects of evangelical fervour:

> The story generally is that a labourer with six children has nothing to live upon but mouldy bread and dirty water; yet nothing can exceed his cheerfulness and content—no murmurs—no discontent: of mutton he has scarcely heard—of bacon he never dreams: furfurious bread and the water of the pool constitute his food,

121

establish his felicity, and excite his warmest gratitude. The squire or parson of the parish always happens to be walking by and over- hears him praying for the king and for the members for the county . . . and it generally ends with their offering him a shilling, which this excellent man declares he does not want, and will not accept! These are the pamphlets which Goodies and Noodles are dispersing with unwearied diligence. It would be a great blessing if some genius would arise who had a talent of writing for the poor. He would be of more value than many poets living upon the banks of lakes . . .   (Pearson, *op. cit.*, p. 81)

Avoiding the pitfalls of this, of Hannah More's *Practical Piety* or Mary Leadbeater's *Cottage Dialogues* requires in the writer an enormous tact, a rigorous control, as well as a spontaneous sensi- bility. Uniquely among the writers of his day, Crabbe combines these gifts; his wry, sometimes acid humour, is a factor in the control. It is significant that, half way through "The Parish Clerk", another tale of a self-deceiver, the poet pulls himself up short— changes spiritual gear, so to speak, since he has been thoroughly enjoying the commedia of pride taking a fall, yet suddenly recalls that this is a fellow human, a man who will suffer, and who will be destroyed by a "crime" which starts as silliness, and grows beyond control. Ironic, distanced, mocking, the tone of the first half of the poem is almost Jonsonian. Jachin, the overweening Parish Clerk, is here playing the moral advocate, immensely pleased with his own sanctimonious righteousness.

> "Nay, nay, my friends, from inns and taverns fly;
> "You may suppress your thirst, but not supply.
> "A foolish proverb says, 'the devil's at home;'
> "But he is there, and tempts in every room: . . .
> "Think not of beauty; when a maid you meet,
> "Turn from her view, and step across the street; . . .
> "Go not with crowds when they to pleasure run,
> "But public joy in private safety shun . . .
> ". . . heed my council, shut thine ears and eyes;
> "A few will hear me—for the few are wise."
> Not Satan's friends, nor Satan's self could bear
> The cautious man who took of souls such care:
> An interloper—one who, out of place,
> Had volunteer'd upon the side of grace.

There was his master ready once a week
To give advice; what further need he seek?
"Amen, so be it:"—what had he to do
With more than this?—'twas insolent and new; . . .
(The Borough, Letter XIX, lines 54–86 passim)

This is virtually the world of The Devil is an Ass. Yet, at the crisis, when Jachin's pride has taken the inevitable tumble, the poem pauses, as though to adjust its surplice, before changing tone:

Thus far the playful Muse has lent her aid,
But now departs, of graver theme afraid;
Her may we seek in more appropriate time—
There is no jesting with distress and crime.
(ibid., lines 118–21)

For this is a poem about avarice and pride. Jachin dies in the end. It demonstrates not only Crabbe's belief in decorum and propriety within his art, but also his contention that there are no such things as "big" and "small" crimes.

VII

There are, of course, in Crabbe studies of people who do not delude themselves, but who are tested by adversity either beyond their deserving for small errors committed, or, like Ellen Orford (The Borough, Letter XX), upon whom the screw of fate is turned and turned. Ellen makes one mistake: she falls in love with a man richer than herself, allows him to seduce her, and bears his child.

When he comes to tell the tale of Ellen Orford, Crabbe goes about his business in a rather strange, but totally characteristic way. The poet warns us that the tale will be a sad one, but before he gets down to it, he asks us to look at the literary fiction which is the antithesis of the real fact his story is about, and he gives us an extended discussion of types of fiction. What the poet is doing is, first of all, to clear the ground: fiction is so absurd that there is a need for something more credible. This establishes a factual ground for writing about Ellen; it satisfies the sociologist in Crabbe—though that side of him is the least important. The "literary" passage also prepares us stylistically for what Crabbe's poem will be. Obviously it will be the antithesis of the "gush"

123

which characterises the romantic novel. Thus, the poetical side of his nature is placated. But I think the most important justification of a device which, structurally, occupies something like one third of Ellen's tale, is that it gives a moral preparation for the reception of the tale, and for the kind of woman Ellen Orford is. A bare narration of her woes reads like a horror-story. Her mother remarries, and the step-father mistreats her; she is made a general drudge to the second family which arrives. A young man wins her trust, seduces her, and leaves her when she becomes pregant. She is forced to watch his parade of total indifference as he marries a woman of his own class. The illegitimate daughter grows up to be an idiot. When Ellen eventually marries, the partnership turns sour, the husband loses his wealth as their family grows, and eventually takes to a surly form of non-conformity. Back to the poor-house goes Ellen when the husband dies, where she is also separated from her children, except the idiot daughter, and the sickly last son of her marriage. Three of the boys die, and the most promising of them is hanged. Then the idiot-daughter becomes pregnant and, although unwilling to admit it herself, Ellen suspects the sickly son of being the father. She has been earning a sort of subsistence by keeping a dame school. This is now taken from her as she falls blind!

Taken out of all its contexts, the tale is monstrous and absurd. As a *literary* poem it is too much. But if we see it as a moral poem, written by a priest who had frequently before him the book of Job—and also Milton's praise of that book as a kind of tragedy —then its purpose is clear and its detail understandable, even if not still totally acceptable. Ellen Orford supplies a good case in point of Crabbe's organisation and moral methods. In the end these aspects are fused; literature *is* morality. While Crabbe is saying on the one hand, "look at the real life of the poor, not at the absurdities of polite fiction," he is also saying, "here is a secular redaction of the Book of Job, wrought out of everyday and contemporary materials, to inculcate the old scriptural messages of Acceptance and Faith."

These were important virtues to Crabbe.

> Oh sacred sorrow! by whom souls are tried,
> Sent not to punish mortals, but to guide;
> (*Parish Register*, "Burials", lines 629–30)

"Ellen Orford" is littered with texts and epigraphs which are carefully posted to enable us to follow the development of the moral line in the poem. The prefatory discussion on novels is so written as to make us ask for something alternative to and better than the effete fiction Crabbe half jocularly and half seriously describes. Then as Ellen tells her tale—so much in contrast to all this—the texts are placed to sub-divide each section:

We should humbly take what Heav'n bestows . . . (line 125)

Labour and hunger were indeed my part,
And should have strengthen'd an erroneous heart . . . (lines 132–3)

I strove for patience as a sinner must . . . (line 200)

Thus for my age's good, my youth was tried . . . (line 140)

It soothed me . . .
                    to bless the Power who gave
Pains to correct us, and remorse to save . . . (lines 324–6)

And as my mind looks cheerful to my end,
I love mankind and call my GOD my friend.   (lines 336–7)

I cannot regard Ellen Orford as one of Crabbe's more successful poems—though this may be no more than a temperamental inability to *accept*, in the full sense Crabbe and Ellen would have us do—but it is a poem that only Crabbe could have written. Aside from the central moral issues, the fundamentals of Crabbe's broad, simple, and humane creed which it throws into highlight, there are two matters of subsidiary interest worth noting. It is significant that Crabbe does not manipulate his story to show the downfall or repentance of the man who seduced Ellen. He quite simply drops out of the poem—though the poet, with a sympathy rare in his day, notes how unfair it is that the woman bears all the opprobium in such a case, while the man, also without the physical responsibility, may even derive a social kudos from it. It is this honesty which sets Crabbe off from the Goodies and Noodles. The second point thrown to light by a study of the more rigorously moral tales—this one in particular—is that they could not be the work of a humanitarian atheist. All criticisms of latitudinarianism, the half-suggestions of mere deism being Crabbe's secret creed, fall away. This is the work of a man seeking paradigms through which to apprehend the mysteries of faith and trust in a Christian God.

5

A Poet's Politics

"A Changeful World and Woeful Times"
(Sermon at Glenham 4 May 1794)

I

There are plenty of books on The Regency, and it is a period
particularly rich in primary sources for the social historian. Yet it
is essential to trace some of the familiar ground, to place Crabbe
in the context of this world of contrasts, and to gauge his reactions and responses to the struggles of the nation and its individual citizens as they underwent drastic shifts in perspective,
life style and governmental procedure.

Though the technical period of regency lasted only from 1811
to 1820, it is justifiable to extend the term so that it describes
a substantially longer period. It is in the early seventeen-eight-
ies that "Prinny" really began to make his presence felt, not
only politically but socially too. His adherence to and then betrayal of the Whigs helped to shape national attitudes to liberty,
probity and party unity for the years to come, just as his cata-
strophic irresponsibility, his open flouting of moral conventions
and his brash opportunism gave a savour to the spirit of the age.
During the years of his ascendency and rule England became more
and more schismatised: the haves and the have-nots grew further
apart than ever before; the liberals tended to become radicals, and
the cautious to become reactionaries. Town and country became
alienated from each other—partly because for the first time the
town became a major factor in English social life. While some men
volunteer to mount a-horseback to make a sabre charge at their

127

unarmed fellow townsmen assembled for a peaceful meeting, others plot the assassination of the cabinet *in toto*. Few men, certainly few articulate and committed men, could live through a period of such contrast without expressing themselves about the issues raised. In this period many of the literary men became political writers, not in the old eighteenth-century sense of being hired party men, but genuine political philosophers, attempting to articulate the problems of their age, and cures for these problems, whilst retaining the full measure of their artistic independence. Shelley, Byron, Leigh Hunt, Burke, Cobbett, Sheridan were all at the very centre of things in the verbal battles of the day. Crabbe seems, on first reading, not to belong in this epoch, and of course many of his critics have tried to place him in Johnson's world, rather than in Byron's.

"The Regency", in that broad sense in which I wish to use the term, spans exactly the creative life of Crabbe. It begins in about 1783, when the Prince of Wales "finds" Brighthelmstone, and begins to convert it into Brighton. And the ending of the period is marked distinctly, not by the death of King George IV, but by the passing of the Reform Bill, and then by the accession of Victoria. *The Library* appeared in 1781 and *Life and Works*, posthumously, in 1834: there is an almost exact identity between these dates and those of Regency influence. This term serves a more useful purpose than the ones usually pasted over the period; it is possible to comprehend Moore, Campbell, Southey, Bloomfield, Clare, Peacock and Coleridge, not as rivals in antithetic schools at war with each other, but united by period and atmosphere. Crabbe occupies an important position in this world, in his attitudes to its politics.

II

One of the cardinal features of the epoch is its ability to identify and to experience problems, but its almost total failure to bring solutions to those problems. This is not a new thing but the drastic natures of the solutions offered seemed new at the time. The best demonstration of this claim is provided by national attitudes to revolution. Perhaps more than any other single idea, it dominates the period. It may well be that the French, by the convulsive political upheaval they experienced, helped to prevent the same thing happening in England. There were times when it looked like touch and go, when the multifarious factors of poverty, royal ineptitude, parliamentary corruption, and industrial innovation offered a serious threat to the Hanoverian settlement, which Englishmen had tolerated for nearly a hundred years as the price to be paid for a guarantee of stability. The Revolution in France aroused strong feelings. To many Englishmen—Wordsworth and Crabbe were but two—there was a sense of triumph in the early days. The *ancien règime* represented despotic power at its worst, as it had never been in England. It has been noticed by more than one social historian that England had one of the few *working* aristocracies in Europe, in the later eighteenth century. Endeavour, with money and influence, could always raise a man to the highest levels of society. The mildly tory Crabbe was a frequent and honoured guest among the whigs at Holland House where Lady Holland selected her guests more for their merit than their breeding. And the *literary* hierarchy was wider open than it had ever been before. John Clare is by far the best of the "peasant poets" who made their appearance, and commanded a wide audience, in the Regency period, but there were many others like the Bloomfield brothers who came from nowhere to at least a temporary recognition.

The flexibility of the system prevented its rupture along lines as drastic as those in France. Unfortunately, as the period progresses, the flexibility seems—or at the time seemed—to grow less. Having witnessed a political revolution "go wrong" and end in bloodshed and anarchy, Englishmen shuddered and took up arms, rather than have the son of that revolution impose its Jacobin tendencies on them. There was not, in the early days of the war at least, a great animus against the French people, nor, initially, against Napoleon. Fox, who was one of of the most astute and competent statesmen of his day, believed the war against France in 1793 to be inopportune. Crabbe was of this opinion too, unlike his mentor Burke, whose royalist enthusiasm made him an outright opponent of all things revolutionary in France. For nearly twenty years England was at war, ostensibly to save herself from invasion by the Jacobin horrors from across the Channel, who might cut off the King's head, secularise the

state, and establish a military dictatorship. To a few like Cobbett
and Byron these seemed like blessings the land needed to have
thrust upon it, but they are the extreme, and very much the
minority voice. For the main part, a kind of grim union of necessity held the nation together through the decade of adversity when
Napoleon swept across Europe, isolating England, and making
invasion a very real threat. It was the disaster of the Whig party
in this period that it lost Fox, the one statesman who might
have engineered a peace, or held party and nation in a unity of
creative purpose. But from his death in 1806, the Whigs dis-
integrated into factions—the extremists who continued to oppose
the war, and the various cabals of moderate opinion which marched
only half a step out of pace with the Tory governments who, from
the beginning of the war, ruled for nearly forty years with only
one brief coalition. The Prince Regent has often been blamed for
not appointing a Whig government in 1812 when Perceval was
assassinated, and there were selfish considerations in his mind no
doubt, but he would be equally blamed by history if, after all those
years of suffering he had put into power a party which didn't
know its own mind about the war with Napoleon, just at the
moment when the tide was turning. The tragedy of it is that,
though the Tory party did know *its* mind, the mind concerned
was not a very talented or a very long-sighted one.

England emerged victorious from the war by the middle of the
second decade of the new century, to find herself with all those
problems which have since become so familiar. She faced social
disruption consequent upon the unwinding of the war machine,
unfulfilled expectations of a victory-millenium, and a stultified
attitude to social welfare, which had suffered inevitable neglect
during the years of national crisis. Other random factors con-
tributed. The poor-law system took from the indigent what little
human dignity they might have left, the Corn Laws exacerbated
the problems of the agricultural labourer who was already suffering from the new methods of husbandry which the war had
spurred on. Being under siege for so many years England had,
perforce, become self-sufficient as a grain producer. A series of
freak harvests caused by uncertain summers in the post-war years,
simply underlined all these problems.

Though it is possible to exaggerate and over simplify the "industrial revolution", most of which is a Victorian rather than a Regency phenomenon, yet the first and palpable effects of urbanisation, and alienation of population from traditional roots, had begun by the time Crabbe came of age. Industry had turned Trowbridge into a "dirty manufacturing town" by the time he became its incumbent in 1814.

To all the human bewilderment which followed these events, the government had one answer: repress. They suspended habeas corpus, they forbade workmen to form combinations for their advantage in trade, they taxed the cheap opposition press out of existence, made it one of over a hundred capital offences to steal an apple, and when all this failed they set the yeoman cavalry at a peaceful protest meeting at "Peterloo". At least eleven people were killed. Arthur Bryant describes the aftermath:

> The country's immediate response was confused. It did not strictly follow class lines. Before the sabres flashed there appeared to be two Englands, both preparing to resort to force. The effect on the industrial workers was one of stunned shock, followed by intense indignation. The response of the other England was divided. The Tory party, the local magistracy which had precipitated the events, and the advocates of firm action everywhere, regarded the affray as the timely dispersal of a dangerous demonstration by a gallant handful. When Walter Scott heard the news he wrote that the yeomanry had behaved well, upsetting the most immense crowd that was ever seen, and despite the lies in the newspapers, without using needless violence. There had been a blunder, it was true, in using yeomanry instead of regulars. But the meeting had itself been illegal, an organised conspiracy to intimidate for political purposes.
> (Bryant, *The Age of Elegance*, 1958, p. 411)

Scott was both a tory and a snob but he wasn't a fool and he wasn't a brute. That he could see Peterloo in terms like this, shows how real the crisis of conscience was at the period. It is easy to sneer or to denigrate with the wisdom of hindsight, but to men like Scott, Crabbe and Southey, hearth and home were at stake, and an entire way of life, which was not all bad; which was, even by contrast with that in the new France, a life with advantages for nearly every class of society. Reading Cobbett on the diet of the English labourer one sees a starving scarecrow living on an unbalanced and unhealthy fare which would have been spurned by his own grandfather, but if one sets alongside this the observations of travellers from the continent who visited England at this period, with European conditions fresh in their minds, the picture can be a very different one. Suddenly one sees a peasantry better fed and clothed than anywhere else in Europe, with neater cottages, more fruitful gardens, and families with more scope for both leisure and education. It depends upon the spectator's preconceived viewpoint, and upon *where* his observations are taken.

The degree to which England was still regionalised, and consequently compartmentalised must be stressed. The Reading countryside of Mary Mitford is not only an imaginative distance from Crabbe's sun-parched saltings, it is a physical journey of very considerable distance and difficulty, into a world of different avocations, and hence of different politics, different architecture and different social customs. It is not surprising that the poetry of Crabbe's Trowbridge period is so unlike that he wrote in his East Anglian days.

The major issues during Crabbe's active life were reform and revolution. They took a bewildering number of forms and created innumerable problems, each of which, on its own, could have occupied the conscience of a generation: child-labour, slavery, education, prison conditions, parliamentary reform. That an author, as much read and respected in his day as Crabbe was, can steer a middle course between the extremes which all these issues raised, suggests he was a man of some tact.

He confesses in the Preface to *Poems* (1807) that his avoidance of contemporary issues might well seem strange:

> among the poetical attempts of one who has been for many years a priest, it may seem a want of respect for the legitimate objects of his study, that nothing occurs, unless it be incidentally, of the great subjects of religion; so it may appear a kind of ingratitude of a beneficed clergyman, that he has not employed his talent . . . to some patriotic purpose; as in celebrating the unsubdued spirit of his countrymen in their glorious resistance of those enemies who would have no peace throughout the world, except that which

is dictated to the drooping spirit of suffering humanity by the triumphant insolence of military success.

Credit will be given me, I hope, when I affirm that subjects so interesting have the due weight with me, which the sacred nature of the one, and the national importance of the other, must impress upon every mind not seduced into carelessness for religion by the lethargic influence of a perverted philosophy, or into indifference for the cause of our country by hyperbolical or hypocritical professions of universal philanthropy. (*Life*, p. 99)

This mixture of mock modesty and genuine humility is typical of Crabbe. He is both a political and a religious writer, in a broader and better sense than is apparent in the Preface just quoted. The reason why he seems tepid or indifferent to the great events of the day lies in the kind of art he practised:

> ... the poet looks the world around,
> Where form and life and reasoning man are found.
> He loves the mind in all its modes to trace,
> And all the manners of the changing race;
> Silent he walks the road of life along,
> And views the aims of its tumultuous throng;
> He finds what shapes the Proteus-passions take,
> And what strange waste of life and joy they make,
> And loves to show them in their varied ways,
> With honest blame or with unflattering praise.
> 'Tis good to know, 'tis pleasant to impart,
> These turns and movements of the human heart;
> The stronger features of the soul to paint,
> And make distinct the latent and the faint;
> Man as he is, to place in all men's view,
> Yet none with rancour, none with scorn pursue; ...
> (*The Borough*, Letter XXIV, lines 426–41)

There is articulate dignity and restraint about this affirmation which makes Crabbe's withdrawn position on contemporary issues not only explicable, but creditable. On religious issues he did not always live up to his own ideals, as I have shown, but on the great issues of society in his day he can and does speak with wisdom and pity, albeit with an inherently and increasingly conservative voice.

IV

In January 1817, on the way back to Carlton House from the opening of Parliament, the Regent's coach was stoned by the mob. There was some suggestion that one of the holes in the carriage windows had been made by the pellet from an air gun; George himself seemed to be of the opinion that he had been shot at. Parliament in any case responded by passing a series of Acts which rendered free expression of written or spoken liberal opinion virtually impossible. It was in this year that Crabbe was deeply engaged upon his blandest, least outspoken poem: *Tales of the Hall*.

On 11 May 1812, the British Prime Minister, Spencer Perceval, had been assassinated in the lobby of the House of Commons. Later that year appeared *Tales in Verse*. Apart from an anti-game-laws story in the former, and some raillery against the Paine-ites in the latter, one would scarcely know, on the surface, that Crabbe had been living through these alarming manifestations of the threat to established order. He had been an eyewitness at the Gordon Riots in London during the June of 1780, and he lived long enough to see Bristol ablaze in the last months of 1831:

Bristol, I suppose, never, in the most turbulent times of old, witnessed such outrage. Queen's Square is but half standing; half is a smoking ruin. As you may be apprehensive for my safety, it is right to let you know that my friends and I are undisturbed, except by our fears for the progress of this mob-government, which is already somewhat broken into parties, who wander stupidly about, or sleep wherever they fall wearied with their work and their indulgence. The military are now in considerable force, and many men are sworn in as constables: many volunteers are met in Clifton church-yard, with white round one arm to distinguish them; some with guns, and the rest with bludgeons. The Mayor's house has been destroyed—the Bishop's palace plundered, but whether burnt or not I do not know. This morning a party of soldiers attacked the crowd in the Square; some lives were lost, and the mob dispersed, whether to meet again is doubtful. It has been a dreadful time, but we may reasonably hope it is now over. People are frightened certainly—and no wonder, for it is evident these poor wretches would plunder to the extent of their power. Attempts were made to burn the

134

cathedral, but failed. Many lives were lost. To attempt any other
subject now would be fruitless. We can think, speak, and write only
of our fears, hopes or troubles. I would have gone to Bristol today,
but Mrs. Hoare was unwilling that I should. She thought, and perhaps rightly, that clergymen were marked objects ...   (*Life*, p. 88)

These riots were part of the general upsurge of feeling which
boiled to a head as attempts to place a Reform Bill before Parliament were thwarted by the reactionary government. It would have
been surprising if they had ever made a direct appearance in his
work for he was near the end of his life at this time. But the
Gordon Riots don't either, and Crabbe was at an impressionable
enough stage of his development when they occurred in 1780. Nor
does he mention Waterloo, Peterloo, Trafalgar, or Yorktown.

It is unusual that an intelligent and sensitive man should have
had so little overt comment to make upon the loss of a continen-
tal empire, twenty years of island siege, and the profligacy of an
entire generation of Royalty. Yet it is necessary to consider
Crabbe's relationship to the politics and the political figures of his
generation, just as much as it is to see him as a figure within the
Church. He presented himself as a man who remained avowedly
uninterested in politics. The truth is not quite that simple, of
course. Crabbe studies men: not politicians, ploughmen or peers,
as such, but men who happen to have this or that vocation, and
whose total character may be affected by particular beliefs or
professions. Hence the interest he has in politics, peripheral in his
own life, lies below the surface in his analyses of his fellow men,
but one does not have to probe very far to find it.

V

The village which had occupied his thoughts in 1783 was even
then dying. One is never sure whether it is a political attack on the
destruction of a way of life, a sociological attack on that way of
life itself, or a poetic attack upon a superannuated genre, which is
the real motive-spring of the poem which made Crabbe famous,
but which is really utterly untypical of his best work.

. . . the land-owning class, having boldly invested enormous sums
to increase agricultural production, had used its monopoly of

135

political power to secure private acts of Parliament redistributing
the arable fields and commons. With population rising by at least
fifteen per cent in every decade . . . increased corn growing had
become both an urgent national priority and a means of vast private
profits. Between 1796 and 1815 more than eighteen hundred enclosure bills were passed, four hundred more than in the previous
forty years.   (Bryant, *op. cit.*, p. 367)

The most surprising thing about *The Village* is the fact that it
isn't a poem about these conditions. It gives a graphic, if partial,
account of the miseries of living off the land, but every time it gets
close to what we now regard as the central evil of the labourer's
lot at this time, the poem shies away onto other things. Though
Bryant suggests the real tide of enclosure was still to flow in 1782
when Crabbe was planning *The Village*, it *was* on the increase,
and Goldsmith was only the most successful of a number of
authors who had already pointed a finger at the evils which ensued
when common land was purloined from the peasantry. Crabbe's
reticence on the topic is not a calculatedly political one. He was
more radical at this time in his career than at any other, yet the
"argument" of the poem does not even mention the topic of en-
closures. The famous passages attacking false pastoral verse, and
describing the Suffolk fields, take the reader with a curious rapid-
ity into a description of the antisocial rogues who inhabit Aldeburgh and its environs, of their preference for smuggling rather
than agriculture, (or village green games)—and lead to a statement of the poet's urgent desire to quit the wretched place. All
this misery, in the first instance, Crabbe argues, is not the fault of
the squirarchy, the government, overpopulation or poor methods
of tilling; it is Nature who is to blame:

> Nature's niggard hand
> Gave a spare portion to the famish'd land;
> Hers is the fault, if here mankind complain
> Of fruitless toil and labour spent in vain.
> (*The Village*, lines 131–4)

Only then does he go on to consider that there may be human
error behind it too:

> But yet in other scenes, more fair to view,
> Where Plenty smiles—alas! she smiles for few—

And those who taste not, yet behold her store,
Are as the slaves that dig the golden ore,
The wealth around them makes them doubly poor.

(ibid., lines 135–9)

Those five lines take us, a little periphrastically, towards the en-
closures and land tenure problems, but then the poem skips off
again, into detail of the agrarian life and its hardships—hardships
of wind, weather, and season, which would be equally relevant to
a peasant tilling his own fields as to a labourer working for another man. We are then taken through a picture gallery of village
suffering: the ancient shepherd, the parish poor, and the dreadful
doctor and parson who attend them. And there, lo and behold,
Book I of *The Village* comes to an end. Book II is devoted to
a rather half-hearted attempt to see the more cheerful side, and
to an irrelevant panegyric on Lord Robert Manners, the brother
of Crabbe's patron the Duke of Rutland. This is extraordinary if
one thinks about the evils Crabbe *might* have written up in this
poem, even more so if one thinks about the way most critical
histories of English poetry describe Crabbe. Usually it is *The
Village* alone of all his works which receives attention, and that
only for its "social content".

VI

Because it eschews any obvious political stance, *The Village* is,
to this extent a characteristic, if immature, production of Crabbe's
mind. He very seldom strays into social polemics. He hated politicking in his own life, and seems to have made great efforts to
keep it out of his work. Poems like the letter on Elections in *The
Borough* are obvious exceptions, but even there, we shall see, his
object is to ridicule political activity. John Wilson Croker, who
was Tory M.P. for Aldeburgh, a friend of the Regent and a frequent contributor to the influential *Quarterly Review*, wrote, after
Crabbe's death, to the Biographer, as follows:

> I have heard, from those who knew Mr. Crabbe earlier than I had
> the pleasure of doing (and his communications with me led to the
> same conclusion), that he never was a violent or even a zealous
> politician. He was, as a conscientious clergyman might be ex-
> pected to be, a church-and-king man; but he seemed to me to think

and care less about party politics than any man of his condition
in life that I ever met. At one of my elections for Aldeburgh, he
happened to be in the neighbourhood, and he did me the honour
of attending in the Town Hall, and proposing me. This was, I suppose, the last act of his life which had any reference to politics—
at least to local politics; for it was, I believe, his last visit to the
place of his nativity . . .   (*Life*, p. 49)

A-political as Crabbe himself was, he was treading dangerous
ground. To be the favourite of Croker and the *Quarterly*, usually
meant being in bad odour with Jeffrey and the pundits of the
Edinburgh Review. The *Edinburgh* had been started by Sydney
Smith, Jeffrey and Brougham in 1802, to promulgate whiggish
views. *The Quarterly*, starting up in 1809, was designed as a tory
response to the *Edinburgh*'s authority and popularity. Much of the
literary criticism of the Regency period is coloured by the antagon-
ism between these most influential and respected organs of contemporary literary opinion. Yet Crabbe had the plaudits of the
Edinburgh and the *Quarterly*. Whilst this may say something for
the advantages of being outside the battle arena, it is also something to ponder over when we come back to look at his reputation
and standing among his contemporaries.

If he was admired across party boundaries, he repaid the compliment by a most democratic and impartial allocation of the
favour of his franchise. Having a vote, at this time, both in Aldeburgh and in Trowbridge, Crabbe supported the Tory, Croker, in
the former place and the Whig Bennett in the latter:

During the violence of that contested election, while the few friends
of Mr. Bennett were almost in danger of their lives, he was twice
assailed by a mob of his parishioners, with hisses and the most
virulent abuse. He replied to their formidable menaces by "rating
them roundly"; and though he was induced to retire by the advice
of some friends, who hastened to his succour, yet this made no
change in his vote, habits, or conduct. He continued to support
Mr. Bennett; he walked in the streets always alone, and just as
frequently as before; and spoke as fearlessly.   (*Life*, p. 61)

The poet's own letters are peppered with avowals of amazement
and scorn at the fury such elections could cause, though his most
succinct account is the one in *The Borough*, Letter V:

Yes, our Election's past, and we've been free,
Somewhat as madmen without keepers be;
And such desire of freedom has been shown,
That both the parties wish'd her all their own:
All our free smiths and cobblers in the town
Were loth to put such pleasant freedom down— . . .

True! you might then your party's sign produce,
And so escape with only half th'abuse—
With half the danger as you walk'd along,
With rage and threat'ning but from half the throng.
This you might do, and not your fortune mend;
For where you lost a foe, you gain'd a friend;
And, to distress you, vex you, and expose,
Election-friends are worse than any foes;   (lines 1–16 *passim*)

The curious thing about this letter, as about *The Village*, is the alacrity with which Crabbe gets away from his ostensible subject, and begins to frame, in embryo, the sort of character study which represents the best of his art. It is not that he can't do these formal, social set pieces well enough. But most critics have agreed that he gradually comes to find himself in extended narratives, founded upon a human interest rather than in generalised satire. This had been his instinctive bent from the start: what really gives *Inebriety* its vigour—(and let it be said, it's a rattling good, vigorous poem for a first serious "go" at writing)—is the individual portraits; the drunken rector, the ducal chaplain, the pub toper. These, rather than any social or moral comment upon drinking, are what make the poem still worth reading. *The Borough* is the real turning point, for while it undoubtedly demonstrates the emergence of the "mature" manner in the full-length portrait, it brings to perfection the older, and by no means negligible, side of Crabbe—the satirist on abstract set subjects.

At the end of the letter on Elections Crabbe pulls himself up with a self-governing tug, for the poem has begun to reveal him as rather less liberal than he might have wished to appear. Much of it reads like a straightforward attack on the franchise system and upon the probity of those elected by that system. It would not sit well on the shoulders of a disciple of Burke to utter sentiments of this kind. Hence the poem ends with a rather half-

hearted retraction of the attack on the licence and excess which
has been the topic of the Letter.

> But, this admitted, be it still agreed,
> These ill effects from noble cause proceed;
> Though like some vile excresences they be,
> The tree they spring from is a sacred tree,
> And its true produce, strength and liberty.
> Yet if we could th'attendant ills suppress;
> If we could make the sum of mischief less;
> If we could warm and angry men persuade
> No more man's common comforts to invade;
> And that old ease and harmony re-seat
> In all our meetings, so in joy to meet:
> Much would of glory to the Muse ensue,
> And our good vicar would have less to do.
>
> (lines 197–209)

This is by far the weakest part of the poem, both in its technique, and in its ideas. The two are inter-related. All the vigour of
this Letter has gone into the description of the uproar, the anarchy of election time, and into the amused description of the
Mayor, who was so ignorant (despite all his native fisherman's
canniness), that he did not know he could collect interest on his
money were he to lend it out! Crabbe deplores the effects of
election-time, and he writes strongly on its evils. But the coda
of political platitude at the end goes a long way to undoing his
good work. It neatly illustrates one of the difficulties which underlie the satirist's task. Attack is always easier than defence, destructive wit easier to manifest than constructive suggestion, and
it is quite clear that the poet has no ideas whatsoever for preventing the malfeasances he has described. When one has read this
kind of poem in the Crabbe canon, it is both with gratitude and
with applause that one recognises the change in his work, away
from such general exercises, and towards analysis of particular
crises in the individual soul. In this latter type of poem, one is
not looking for a "solution", for the poem propounds an insoluble
problem of human nature. This is a way of stating a fact about
the kind of sensibility Crabbe had: despite his acute eye for
grievances and tragedies, and his intense pity for the objects of
such tragedies, he is not good at offering solutions. Nor, tempera-

mentally, was he equipped for the kind of savage in-fighting to which involvement with major contemporary political or social issues might have led.

VII

The nearest he ever got to this was *The Newspaper*. This, the coldest and least successful thing of any length that Crabbe wrote, seems to have been an attempt at sniping from the under-growth on a very distant part of the battlefield:

> Notwithstanding the philosophical tone . . . it seems highly prob-able that Mr. Crabbe had been moved to take up the subject by the indignation he felt on seeing Mr. Burke daily abused, at "this busy, bustling time," by one set of party writers, while the Duke of Rutland was equally the victim of another." (*Life*, p. 125)

The poem seems to acknowledge its own ineffectuality;

> A TIME like this, a busy, bustling time,
> Suits ill with writers, very ill with rhyme:
> Unheard we sing, when party-rage runs strong,
> And mightier madness checks the flowing song:
> Or, should we force the peaceful Muse to wield
> Her feeble arms amid the furious field,
> Where party-pens a wordy war maintain,
> Poor is her anger, and her friendship vain.
> (lines 1–8)

This is of course quite untrue. Swift, Pope, Fielding had all drawn a good deal of their inner fire from the passion of party spirit. Crabbe is simply making a generalisation about writers, out of his own particular temperamental inability. In its cold and formal way *The Newspaper* has competent patches of writing in it, and probably the ingenuous claim of its author, that it was the only poem written on the topic, is still true today! Its sharpest passage is that where Crabbe individualises his subject:

> Hither, with all a patriot's care, comes he
> Who owns the little hut that makes him free;
> Whose yearly forty shillings buy the smile
> Of mightier men, and never waste the while;

Who feels his freehold's worth, and looks elate,
A little prop and pillar of the state.
    Here he delights the weekly news to con,
And mingle comments as he blunders on;
To swallow all their varying authors teach,
To spell a title, and confound a speech:
Till with a muddled mind he quits the news,
And claims his nation's licence to abuse;
Then joins the cry, "That all the courtly race
"Are venal candidates for power and place";
Yet feels some joy, amid the general vice,
That his own vote will bring its wonted price.

(lines 177–92)

The Newspaper carries the lowest proportion of direct speech of any of Crabbe's major poems. There are none of his racy and beautifully identified speaking-voices which give such vigour to the best of his work to help him out here. Judgements that *The Newspaper* is a "cold" poem, are merely taking cognisance of this lack of an enlivening speaking voice. I shall have cause to come back to this point.

The Newspaper may be ambivalent to the point of being flaccid in its attitudes towards Party spirit, not only because Crabbe simply wasn't interested in politics, but because he is caught between two personal allegiances, at a very difficult time. There is plenty of evidence to show that it was written in the summer of 1784, not long after Crabbe had been appointed chaplain to the Duke of Rutland. The Duke was a Tory, but Burke, who had recommended Crabbe to him, was a Whig. Furthermore, Burke was under considerable pressure at this time both inside and outside his own party. The *Reflections on the French Revolution* looked like turn-coat writing to the Whig Old Guard, whose extreme fringe continued to support the revolutionary cause, even into the Napoleonic wars. But Burke, and the more moderate Whigs, whilst retaining their approval of the ending of absolute despotism in France, came to fear that bad had been replaced by no better. It is this which gives the sonority and the driving force to the rhetoric of Burke's *Reflections*. One sees, I think, how Crabbe's attitudes, both in *The Newspaper* and in *The Borough* Letter V are a pale reflection of Burke:

Of all things, wisdom is the most terrified with epidemical fanaticism, because of all enemies it is that against which she is the least able to furnish any kind of resource. We cannot be ignorant of the spirit of atheistical fanaticism, that is inspired by a multitude of writings, dispersed with incredible assiduity and expense, and by sermons delivered in all the streets and places of public resort in Paris. These writings and sermons have filled the populace with a black and savage atrocity of mind, which supercedes in them the common feelings of nature, as well as all sentiments of morality and religion; insomuch that these wretches are induced to bear with a sullen patience the intolerable distresses brought upon them by the violent convulsions and permutations that have been made in property. The spirit of proselytism attends this spirit of fanaticism . . . England is not left out of the comprehensive scheme of their malignant charity: and in England we find those who stretch out their arms to them . . . applaud them and hold them up as objects for imitation . . .

(*Reflections on the Revolution in France*, ed. H. P. Adams, 1926, pp. 160–2)

This, a fair reflection of how many Englishmen felt, led directly to Paine's spirited rejoinder the following year in *The Rights of Man*, where he attempted to put the revolutionary spirit in a very different context. We have already seen how Crabbe misses no chance to belabour the ghost of Paine in his poetry. He becomes, for the middle-of-the-road parson with a personal debt to Burke, the living manifestation of anarchy.

VIII

The best statement of Crabbe's own political stance is that made by the Biographer.

The truth is, that my father never was a politician—that is to say, he never allowed political affairs to occupy much of his mind at any period of his life, or thought either better or worse of any individual for the bias he had received. But he did not, certainly, approve of the *origin* of the war that was raging . . . nor did he ever conceal his opinion, that this war might have been avoided—and hence, in proportion to the weight of his local character, he gave offence to persons maintaining the diametrically opposite view of public matters at that peculiar crisis. As to the term *Jacobin*, I shall say only one word. None could have been less fitly applied to him at any period of his life. He was one of the innumerable good men who, indeed, hailed the beginning of the French Revolution, but who execrated its close . . . [and] Napoleon had not long pursued his career of ambition, before my father was well convinced that to put *him* down was the first duty of every nation that wished to be happy and free. (*Life*, p. 49)

There is a value in emphasising this political tepidness, since it is remarkable how both sides could agree on Crabbe's merits, perhaps because he claimed allegiance to neither, and had so limpid, almost naïve an integrity that none could doubt him. Thus, Byron, who personally approved of Napoleon (or gestured as though he did), could still hail Crabbe as Nature's best "painter". Wordsworth, whose attitude shifted much as Crabbe's own did from "hailing" to "execrating" the state of affairs in France, could offer uncharacteristically generous praise on occasion, and Croker, one of the true-blue Tories, who governed with such repression through the post-Waterloo years, was equally ready to speak warmly of both Crabbe and his work. Given the openly political bias of the two principal Reviews, given that the Church was often referred to as "the praying part of the Tory party", and given the debt to Tory patronage which Crabbe owed in the Rutland family, his independence is very much to his credit.

This attitude, because it is unusual in an age of extreme partisanship, where Whig and Tory tore each other's verses as well as each other's characters on political principles, is worth stressing. It is the antithesis of the position of a man like Cobbett, no less honest and no less vigorous than Crabbe could be, and yet consumed by a burning conviction that all he saw around him had to be explained in political terms. The author of *Rural Rides* is worth mention here, not only for the obvious contrast of temperament we may see but because Crabbe mentions him as antithetic to his own point of view. Writing to his friend Miss Charter on 11 February 1817—by no means a peaceful or a comfortable year—Crabbe says

I cannot give a satisfactory . . . [opinion of the times] . . . but I dread no Insurrections, no Hunts, no Cobbetts; and I hope cheerfully, and I have comfort in the Benevolence and morality of the country in general. (Broadley & Jerrold, *op. cit.*, pp. 154–5)

Neither the Blanketeers, nor Peterloo, nor the Cato Street con-
spiracy seem to have been able to shake this touching faith in the
"benevolence and morality" of the country. He saw how deep-
rooted the causes of the struggle were:

> ... in these times the causes of our strife
> Are hearth and altar, liberty and life
> (*Tales of the Hall*, XVI, lines 207–8)

but he continued to believe, and to write in the belief that, men
are not corrigible *en masse* or through techniques of general per-
suasion such as a political system can give. Each individual must
remain an individual problem. This it is which gives René Huchon's
deprecatory description of Crabbe's political stance a rather more
apposite and humane application than he may have intended:

> A patriarchal government, with each village taking care of its poor
> under the supervision of its clergyman—this seems to have been
> Crabbe's ideal. (Huchon, p. 463)

It is, of course an impossible system, yet it explains Crabbe's
attitudes not only towards society, but towards the pastoral duties
which were his care as priest and, in later life, as magistrate. Many
members of the Established Church saw social structure in these
terms. The diaries of Jones and Woodforde show men of similar
temper, doing an unselfish and level best to stem the tide of poverty,
ignorance and oppression, from the limited but honest standpoint
which their vocation gave them.

It is not surprising that the parish priest should choose to see
men as individuals rather than as cyphers in a crowd. Nor should
one deride the patriotic sentiments which sometimes intrude upon
the poetry of Crabbe and his contemporaries. They had come
through twenty and more years of siege, for much of the time
quite alone against Europe and latterly America as well. The
imminence of Boney's invasion threats may have receded after
Trafalgar, but it was to be a long, hard and vaccilating struggle
from there to Waterloo. Hence remarks like that Crabbe made to
his neighbour Dr Gordon on hearing of Napoleon's abdication
may seem naïve to us—(so do descriptions of the public rejoicings
on V.E. day if it comes to that): he writes of "this glorious
country . . . which never from the time Caesar first tried its

virtues stood so high as at the present period . . ." There is remarkably little of this in his verse.

IX

It has been observed of Jane Austen that the great events of the
day scarcely enter her novels. Some of her young men are in the
army or navy but we are never aware of the urgency or the brutality of the campaigns they would have fought in. She shares this
reticence with Crabbe, where soldiers and sailors appear in some
of the tales, but few give anything like a first-hand account of the
miseries or the glory of the war. Though Wellington has always
been praised as a general parsimonious in the expenditure of his
men's lives, yet he had five thousand casualties at Badajoz, another
five thousand at Salamanca and two thousand more at the un-
successful siege of Burgos; these encounters represent only one
part of the campaign of one year in the Peninsular war—1812,
when Wellington was on the offensive. The classic battles of the
earlier Peninsular campaigns had been even more costly, and at
Waterloo fifteen thousand of the Allied Army fell. Whilst these are
not the figures for the British casualties, but for the Allies as a
whole, Wellington had grown accustomed to placing his own
troops where the action was most bloody, and losses were often
out of proportion to those of the Spanish, Portuguese and Hanoverian elements of the army. Whilst a few "extremists" like Byron
protested at this butchery, undertaken in a cause they cast doubt
upon, the vast majority of English writers shared Crabbe's simple
sentiments about their "glorious country".

Yet one does see in Crabbe's work the local, human, outcome
of the war. The cottager who had subsistence farmed, depending
on the common land and open woodland which belonged to the
village, was swept away, either into the growing towns, or across
the seas to America and to Canada. It is worth remembering
when reading, say, the *Tales of the Hall*, where a squirarchal
system seems to have been going on since Domesday, and shows no
signs of ever breaking up, that while in 1815 some two thousand
people emigrated from England and Wales, by 1819—(the year
Tales of the Hall appeared)—the figure had risen to thirty-four
thousand. People do go away in Crabbe's poems. "The Parting

146

Hour", and "Procrastination", both depict lovers separated by economic circumstances, but it is not so much the war, as the general hazard of travel at the time, which seems to cause the crisis in these tales. There is some personal experience too:

> Mr. Crabbe's fourth brother, William, taking to a sea-faring life, was made a prisoner by the Spaniards: he was carried to Mexico, where he became a silversmith, married, and prospered, until his increasing riches attracted a charge of Protestantism; the consequence of which was much persecution. He was at last obliged to abandon Mexico, his property, and his family; and was discovered in the year 1803, by an Aldborough sailor, on the coast of Honduras, where again he seems to have found some success in business. This sailor was the only person he had seen for many a year who could tell him of Aldborough and his family . . . This was the first, and it was also the last, tiding that ever reached Mr. Crabbe of his brother William . . . *(Life,* p. 281)

One finds much more of domestic political issues in Crabbe, than of the grandiose ones like the war. The problems only become real to him when they can be related to the vicissitudes of his parishioners, when they become personalised. When he describes the village workhouse, he is aware that it is an evil, yet the alternative was the Speenhamland system, or removal of paupers to a central workhouse away from their own community.

> The parish poor-house was usually a place of horror, some ruinous cottage into which those of all ages, sick or well, were crammed . . . Yet an undoubted claim on such a place was an object of supreme importance to the labourer. The riots in East Anglia in 1765 against the building of large workhouses to serve a number of parishes and supercede the wretched parish poor-houses speak for themselves. The House of Industry, as it was called, on Nacton Heath was threatened by a mob of about four hundred labourers. When the magistrates tried to persuade them to disperse they answered that they came to fight for their liberties. They were resolved the poor should be maintained in their own parishes, they might as well die there as be starved, and they were determined to pull down the house . . . When threatened with troops they said 'If the King was to send 1,000 soldiers it would give them no concern, for they could raise 10,000.
>
> (Dorothy George, *England in Transition,* 1953, pp. 98–9)

Reading Crabbe's description of the parish poorhouse in the light of this account, one sees his humanitarian standpoint the more clearly, but comes to wonder if he has a *political* standpoint at all. Certainly he didn't approve of the Speenhamland system. This required parish relief for the labourer to be paid out of the poor-rates in proportion to the price of corn, and the size of the labourer's family. It was a backlash of sliding scales for grain, which operated very much in favour of the larger landowners, particularly during the war, when no grain could be imported. Whilst "the man on the rates" did gain some immediate benefit, there was a loss of human independence which to many labourers outweighed any material advantage, and the system was another nail in the coffin of the small farmer, who had to find the rates to pay for it. The system encouraged "love on the dole" since, the larger the family, the larger the parish relief. And hence, the old custom of couples waiting until they could afford to marry and maintain a family independent of outside help, was itself encroached upon by the new poor-law. This is the situation which David and Judith experience in "The Parting Hour" (*Tales*, II) as it had been for Crabbe himself and his "Mira":

> The lovers waited till the time should come
> When they together could possess a home:
> In either house were men and maids unwed,
> Hopes to be soothed, and tempers to be led . . .
> . . . . .
>
> Dull was their prospect—when the lovers met,
> They said, we must not—dare not venture yet.
>
> (lines 74–87 *passim*)

These two find their prudence ill-rewarded: David goes abroad to seek his fortune, is captured by the Spaniards (like Crabbe's own brother, whose experiences gave birth to the Tale in question) and at last marries in Mexico. Judith waits ten years for him, and hearing no news, enters into a loveless but prudent marriage. After years of suffering, in which he loses his family, David returns, shattered and enfeebled, to be nursed by Judith who has also lost all her children and been widowed. The story, gloomy as it sounds, is told with so much discretion by Crabbe that it remains, for all its sadness, a defence of the prudence which the lovers exercised.

In *The Parish Register* we see temperance and patience rewarded, as they are not rewarded in "The Parting Hour". It is an
unfortunate fact that the successful couple are by no means as
artistically interesting as the tragic pair. But Crabbe dutifully in-
cludes them in his Register, as examples to the village, and also
one suspects, because for all their dullness, they were *real*; they
exemplify all that Crabbe, as parson, and domestic economist
approved of. Because they existed and were observed by the poet
he felt bound to include them in his work:

> Reuben and Rachel, though as fond as doves,
> Were yet discreet and cautious in their loves;
> Nor would attend to Cupid's wild commands,
> Till cool reflection bade them join their hands.
> When both were poor, they thought it argued ill
> Of hasty love to make them poorer still;
> Year after year, with savings long laid by,
> They bought the future dwelling's full supply . . .
> . . . . .
>
> Thus both, as prudence counsell'd, wisely stay'd
> And cheerful then the calls of Love obey'd:
> What if, when Rachel gave her hand, 'twas one
> Embrown'd by Winter's ice and Summer's sun?
> What if, in Reuben's hair, the female eye
> Usurping grey among the black could spy?
> (*The Parish Register*, "Marriages", lines 435–52 *passim*)

The poet concludes his eulogium of this couple by a simile which
roots them firmly to the earth, and the entire, time honoured
system, of which they are exemplars:

> Yet time, who blow'd the rose of youth away,
> Had left the vigorous stem without decay;
> Like those tall elms, in Farmer Frankford's ground,
> They'll grow no more—but all their growth is sound;
> (lines 455–8)

X

It was Leslie Stephen who, rather acidly, remarked that nobody
portrayed better than Crabbe the process of going to the dogs.
And if *The Parish Register* contains these cameos of contented

149

couples, it is much fuller of the tragic, the foolish and the frus-
trated people who have not been so prudent. No wonder that the
Marriages section of the poem has running through it with a bell-
like insistence, the words "refrain, refrain". Six times, at the end
of key verse-paragraphs, these words, or others which chime with
them, recur in "Marriages". It is an economic, and ultimately
a political warning, as well as a purely human one. *The Parish
Register* shows how even the comparatively early Crabbe prefers
to take his social history and re-shape it into narratives woven
around people and events he really knew. Together with a temperamental disinclination towards politicking, this may explain why
he lived through such troubled times with a muse so apparently
equable and unmoved by current events. Both artistic and social
discretion led him the same way, a way which, as we have already
seen, his moral bent was taking him also.

There is no doubt that anyone who comes to Crabbe after reading Cobbett's *Rural Rides* may, with Cobbett's thunder dinning in
his ears, find Crabbe's verses very milk-and-water in their sociological and political content. If these two totally different men are
allowed to stand as spokesmen for their respective points of view,
the size of the problem and the degree of national alarm and bewilderment are made clear. Cobbett advocated a return to subsistence cottage economy; he wanted to put the clock back to the
years before the War, or perhaps, more accurately, he wanted a
world which he chose to recall as that of his youth but which in
fact had never existed, except in tiny, isolated and a-typical
pockets. He hated with the whole of his magnificently broad and
kindly soul the urbanisation, the stock-broking suburbia, the
racketeering and the political corruption of the English scene after
Waterloo. This of course led him to champion the Americans and
the French against the "THING" as he called it, that is against the
English Establishment of Liverpool, Canning, Wellington, and the
Conservative ministries they perpetuated during the years of repression from 1815 to the Reform Bills of the early 1830s. Cobbett also hated tea, potatoes, Scotch economists, and parsons!
They all become part of the same grand campaign in his mind,
they are all part of a charade of privilege, chicanery, suppression
and jobbery. It is not surprising that not only the tories of his
day, but virtually all shades of whiggery too found his *Political*

Register too strong a diet. He was labelled as "Jacobin", and suffered imprisonment, exile and harassment for his outspoken views. He was no irresponsible revolutionary. His heart was always bigger than his head. Nobody can be more generous to the aristocracy when they are demonstrably managing affairs to the benefit of the community around them. Cobbett is most earnest that he does not want a total upheaval of land ownership. But he does want to see the land properly employed, and something close to a rural subsistence economy. And he wants political reform: the abolition of the system whereby Old Sarum, with something like six inhabitants, returns a Member to Parliament, whereas Manchester is unrepresented, as are virtually all the new industrial centres.

Behind all the rhodomontade and the pig-headedness, Cobbett was the fearless and uncorrupt voice of a part of English life which was suffering abominably. Nor can there be any doubt that much of his laying of the blame at the door of the Government is correct. In this land which protested itself "the envy of Europe" for its freedom, a man could be hanged for a greater number of offences than anywhere on the Continent, any kind of workmen's union or combination was expressly forbidden, and pregnant women would be manhandled across the parish boundaries lest their offspring became a charge in the poor-rates. The official response to the unrest this produced was repression, and more repression:

From the Bourne we proceeded on to *Wrecklesham*, at the end of which, we crossed what is called the *river Wey*. Here we found a parcel of labourers at parish work . . . The account they gave of their situation was very dismal. The harvest was over early. The hop-picking is now over; and now they are employed *by the Parish*; that is to say, not absolutely digging holes one day and filling them up the next; but at the expense of half-ruined farmers and tradesmen and landlords, to break stones into very small pieces to make nice smooth roads lest the jolting, in going along them, should create bile in the stomachs of the over-fed tax-eaters. I call upon mankind to witness this scene; and to say, whether ever the like of this was heard of before. It is a state of things, where all is out of order; where self-preservation, that great law of nature, seems to be set at defiance; for here are farmers unable to pay men for working for them, and yet compelled to pay them for working in doing that which is really of no use to any human being . . . [In Cobbett's rural economy there would be no turnpike roads, travel on horseback across country lanes being his ideal!] . . . There lie the hop-poles unstripped. You see a hundred things in the neighbouring fields that want doing. The fences are not nearly what they ought to be. The very meadows . . . would occupy these men advantageously until the setting in of the frost; and here they are . . . uselessly employed. Is this Mr. Canning's *'Sun of Prosperity'*? Is this the way to increase or preserve a nation's wealth? Is this a sign of wise legislation and of good government? Does this thing *'work well'*, Mr. Canning? Does it prove, that we want no change? True you were born under a Kingly Government; and so was I as well as you; but I was not born under *Six Acts*; nor was I born under a state of things like this. I was not born under it, and I do not wish to live under it; and with God's help, I will change it if I can.   (Cobbett, *Rural Rides*, 1967, pp. 41–2)

The Six Acts to which Cobbett refers epitomise the attitude of government to the problems of England in the post-war years, with wildly fluctuating markets, growing poverty and unrest, and a total social re-orientation under way. Among other things they forbad armed training, made any assembly, other than that of the parish council meeting within its parish bounds, potentially seditious and illegal, made impossible the publication of cheap, (and hence popular), periodicals, and they gave magistrates—who were of course exclusively of the landed interest—far-reaching powers of search, arrest and imprisonment.

Let it be remembered that this is the very year when Crabbe, who had anxiously negotiated a three thousand pounds deal with Murray for the rights of his works, saw *Tales of the Hall* appear. The sum negotiated was three hundred times the average annual income of "labouring people in husbandry, including earnings of the females", to use the terminology of the 1801 census. In *Tales of the Hall* there is only the barest mutter of the uproar Cobbett describes. Crabbe is far less rigorous than Cobbett, far less committed to a programme of any kind which might ameliorate the individual lot, by attacking Institutions in some way. Cobbett's attitude can make Crabbe look like a flaccid, mealy-mouthed adherent to the outworn "THING". Yet, on occasion, Crabbe's accounts of individuals caught within the system can make Cobbett's attacks look like empty-handed rant. Where Cobbett rails against the game laws, and the use of keepers, traps and spring-

152

guns, Crabbe tells the tale which he calls "Smugglers and Poachers" (*Tales of the Hall*, XXI). It is, justly, one of the most highly
regarded of the *Tales of the Hall*, but if one sees it against the
background of Regency England, if one, imaginatively, with Cobbett, passes that estate just outside Canterbury, described in
Rural Rides, with its unconsciously ironic notice

> "PARADISE PLACE. Spring guns and steel traps are set here"

then "Smugglers and Poachers" becomes a very curious poem. It
required a special kind of sensitivity to apprehend the causes of
such a situation, and yet to avoid all suggestion of a sermon or a
diatribe upon the effects of it, especially when those effects are
death and bereavement.

Whilst it would be unlike Crabbe, at this stage of his career, to
write a political poem, yet it is typical that the man who wrote
The Village can still go to the heart of the human situation which
underlies a contemporary political problem. In "Smugglers and
Poachers" we meet two orphan lads. Robert is the bolder and
more extrovert of the two, James a quieter, more cautious soul.
(This dichotomy is typical of poem after poem Crabbe wrote—
the brothers in the frame narrative of *Tales of the Hall* are but
one example. It is possible to see them as aspects of the poet's own
personality, his own forthrightness and diffidence being extended
into two different people, and ultimately his own conservatism at
war with the liberal humanitarian in him.) James becomes keeper
at a local estate, while Robert lives a much wilder, less staid life,
making a living by his wits:

> The brothers met not often—When they met,
> James talk'd of honest gains and scorn of debt,
> Of virtuous labour, of a sober life,
> And what with credit would support a wife.
>   But Robert answer'd—"How can men advise
> "Who to a master let their tongue and eyes?
> "Whose words are not their own? whose foot and hand
> "Run at a nod, or act upon command? . . .
>   (*Tales of the Hall*, Book XXI, lines 74–81)

Though the poet does not label them conservative and anarchist
yet one can see the opposition of ways of life, and how these are
reflected in the chosen avocations of the two brothers for, in-

evitably, Robert's ill-disciplined course draws him towards smuggling. It is interesting that Crabbe has chosen this particular law-breaking as the first step on Robert's downward path. In post Napoleonic England smuggling was big business. So many goods were in short supply, and so many were severely taxed, that the covert importation of lace, spirits, tobacco and other luxuries constituted a profitable, if hazardous business. The attitude of many people was ambivalent. They deplored the ferocious taxes, wanted the goods involved and consequently, by a process of moral gymnastics, persuaded themselves that, even if there wasn't something attractively roguish about smuggling, it represented a variation on the "Englishman's freedom" theme. This background enables Crabbe to put his protagonist in a special moral and social context. Had he written of a young man who went straight into poaching, his own sympathies, and those of most of his readers, would probably be abrogated. Smuggling is a nicely enigmatic half-way house. The moral danger is made quite clear, however. It is James who expresses it as he considers his brother's life:

> He sigh'd to think how near he was akin
> To one [seduced] by godless men to sin;
> Who, being always of the law in dread,
> To other crimes were by the danger led,
> And crimes with like excuse—The smuggler cries,
> "What guilt is his who pays for what he buys?"
> The poacher questions, with perverted mind,
> "Were not the gifts of heaven for all design'd?"
> *This* cries, "I sin not—take not till I pay;"—
> *That*, "My own hand brought down my proper prey."—
> And while to such fond arguments they cling,
> How fear they God? How honour they the king?
>
> (lines 186–7)

One needs to be sensitive to the political nuances under the argument and the speaking voice, to realise exactly what Crabbe is trying to do. He has, in a way, written the two sides of his own nature into a dilemma. As the story progresses we shall see that his sympathies lie mainly with the "lawless" brother, yet he is a magistrate and a clergyman. How can he write as his heart dictates the story should go, and yet not offend the sensibilities

154

of his middle and upper class readers on issues which were fiercely contended at the time he was writing? He achieves his object by making the crime of the attractive brother a matter which he falls into by degrees, through expression of his independence which lacks regular, (servile), employment, into the pen-umbral region of smuggling, and then, almost of necessity, into poaching. For the smugglers fall on hard times:

> Their traffic fail'd—and the adventurous crew
> No more their profitless attempts renew.
> Dig they will not, and beg they might in vain—
> Had they not pride, and what can then remain?
> (lines 257–60)

Poaching, of course is what remains. Crabbe never, anywhere in the poem, shows approval of it. But any reader who has the contemporaneity of the story in mind, can see how close we have been drawn to the borders of where approval would begin. Equally, how close to disapproval of the prudent, law-abiding gamekeeper comes one side of Crabbe's nature. The trite couplet about poachers' chop-logic preventing their respect to King George is a touch of typical Crabbe irony. It shows us inside the mind of James as nothing else could do; there is a pettiness, a conventionality about this man, which is downright uncomfortable.

Crabbe goes on to develop this. Both brothers love the same girl, and she prefers the more flamboyant and attractive poacher to the rather grey and dowdy keeper. Robert is caught by his own brother whilst poaching, and is imprisoned. This would probably be enough to warrant the death penalty, but the crime is compounded: in the struggle one of the keeper's assistants is wounded. By law, even to threaten a keeper in 1819 was a capital offence: Crabbe's readers would know how horribly enmeshed in the vindictive game laws Robert has become. Yet there is one way out: James has the ear of his employer who, as a peer of the realm can —though the poem does not *need* to state this overtly—subvert or stay the course of punishment. And this he will do if Rachel agrees, against the instincts of her heart, to marry James instead of Robert. Whilst Crabbe makes no direct political comment on this part of his story, and indeed goes out of his way to remind us of its kinship with *Measure for Measure*, yet his readers must

155

have recognised the effects of Influence at work in the closed system which English justice had become under Liverpool and Castlereigh. The tendency at once to particularise his story—to create specific people in a specific environment, rather than writing "on the Game Laws"—and to give it a *literary* context through the references to *Measure for Measure*, is typical of Crabbe.

Whether one calls this a pusillanimous refusal to face facts, or whether one sees it as a triumphant ability to write from above the local and transient conditions of 1819 depends largely upon the taste of the reader. Much as I admire Cobbett I do think that Crabbe has a point of view less dishonourable than that which the radical Rural Rider would have us believe is typical of the clergy. That point of view is given humane and genuinely moving expression in "Smugglers and Poachers". If it is more Crabbe's artistry than his politics that one remembers, this may not, in the long run, be a bad thing. It is what he would have wished, certainly:

> With respect to . . . parties . . . I can but think, two dispassionate, sensible men, who have seen, read, and observed, will approximate in their sentiments more and more; and if they confer together, and argue—not to convince each other, but for pure information, and with a simple desire for the truth—the ultimate difference will be small indeed. The Tory, for instance, would allow that, but for the Revolution in this country, and the noble stand against the arbitrary steps of the house of Stuart, the kingdom would have been in danger of becoming what France once was; and the Whig must also grant that there is at least an equal danger in an unsettled, undefined democracy, the ever-changing laws of a popular government. Every state is, at times, on the inclination to change; either the monarchical or the popular interest will predominate; and in the former case, I conceive, the well-meaning Tory will incline to Whiggism—in the latter, the honest Whig will take the part of declining monarchy. (*Life*, p. 380)

That all was not well Crabbe had seen as readily as Cobbett, yet their diagnoses were as different as the subsequent prescriptions they wrote for the sick patient's cure. The pity of it is that, these men would not have been able to "confer together, and argue, not simply to convince each other, but for pure information". The gap is wider than it might appear. For so much of their

ground is, or ought to be common ground. They both admire independence of mind, the sturdy self-reliance which they saw as an
English characteristic. Both pitied the poor by whom they were
surrounded. Both distrusted codified "solutions" which ignored the
rights and the individualities of particular men. Both hated sancti-
moniousness, and the trite moral wisdom of Evangelical tracts.
Yet the times keep them apart.

Physically, they never did meet. Cobbett's furthest flung Ride
took him within five miles of Trowbridge: it would have been
fascinating to have his account of Crabbe's parish, of that "dirty
manufacturing town" to which he ministered for eighteen years
as priest, magistrate and occasionally, as doctor. In 1826 Cobbett
reported the Devizes area to be depressed, mills working at
quarter capacity, many squads out of work, farm labourers mend-
ing the roads to obtain their parish relief money—(always a red
rag to Cobbett and a sign, for him, of total chaos in the economy).
Yet Crabbe reports rather differently to Mrs Leadbeater:

> We are quiet in this part of the land and in fact our tumults depend
> not upon the politics but upon the employments of the inhabitants;
> if they have work they are peaceable if not they are Whigs, Rebels
> and Reformists. 5 November 1819.   (B.L. ms. Eg. 3709. b)

XI

The Whig/Tory division is one to which Crabbe returns time
and again. He uses it virtually as a shorthand method of suggesting character type. Tales like "The Brother Burgesses", or "The
Dumb Orators" show how the pre-occupation followed him
through middle age and increasing prosperity. "The Brother Burgesses" is the twelfth of the posthumous poems, almost certainly
written after 1820. It is only 116 lines long—suffering from that
lack of stamina which vitiates several of the *Posthumous Tales*.
There is a simplicity almost amounting to crudeness about the
"story-line" of the poem. It is couched within the overall framework of the "Farewell and Return" device. The narrator has been
absent from his native village for over twenty years, and now
returns to re-encounter a number of people to whom he bade farewell all that time ago. The subsequent narratives recount the
varied fortunes of these individuals. The sixth of these tales gives

F   157

an account of two step-brothers each belonging to and being a vehement adherent of one of the political parties:

> JAMES is the one who for the people fights,
> The sturdy champion of their dubious rights;
> Merchant and seaman rough, but not the less
> Keen in pursuit of his own happiness;
> . . . . .
>
> JAMES goes to church—because his father went,
> But does not hide his leaning to dissent;
> Reasons for this, whoe'er may frown, he'll speak—
> Yet the old pew receives him once a week.
>   CHARLES is a churchman, and has all the zeal
> That a strong member of his church can feel;
> A loyal subject is the name he seeks;
> He of "his King and Country" proudly speaks:
> He says, his brother and a rebel-crew,
> Minded like him, the nation would undo,
> If they had power, or were esteem'd enough
> Of those who had, to bring their plans to proof.
>   (*Posthumous Tales*, XII, lines 5–22)

The poet sketches in the antipathy, founded on party prejudice, which keeps the pair apart. Then one day, on hearing that his brother has failed in business, Charles's real fraternal nature gets the better of the veneer of party spleen, and he offers assistance to the bankrupt brother. All is forgiven and they afterwards live and die in complete reconcilement. What this seems to amount to is a statement that humane feelings begin when political pre-occupations cease.

The tenth of the *Posthumous Tales*—"The Ancient Mansion" —demonstrates again that Crabbe was by no means unaware of cause and effect of the political and social scene around him. Once more the story is very simple. The narrator takes leave of the local Mansion and of its aristocratic Lady, and returns to find the Lady dead, her woods felled, her house altered to the modern taste. All this is effected by a brash industrialist, without class or background, who has taken over the property: Hardy could well have taken the hint for Alec D'Urbeville from here. The poem ends with a lyric lament couched as a dialogue between the superannuated and blind butler, and his niece. For a subject so controversial on

the one hand—(what would Cobbett have made of the events
Crabbe portrays?)—and so potentially maudlin on the other—
(what kind of moralising monster might Hannah More have made
of the old butler?)—Crabbe steers a nicely judged middle course.
Though this poem is little longer than "The Brother Burgesses",
yet it is filled out with all the detail which marks Crabbe's richest
vein. The downfall of the old system, of the beautiful woods which
surrounded the house, and the decline in the dignity and useful-
ness of the aged butler become fused into one statement of lament.
Crabbe is unequivocal in his praise of the old way of life, as
though for once the mask of impartiality has dropped, and we can
see how far this ex-Whig, once accused of being a Jacobin, has
been driven back by the encroaching tide of vandalising post-war
modernity. It is a common enough phenomenon, perhaps only remarkable in that there are few places in Crabbe where the natural
tendency is so strongly marked. Even so, it is sadness rather than
bitterness which the poem expresses.

The poet begins by describing the Lady's charity; here is a
description which must have fitted hundreds of the miniature
welfare states which village life may have been before the Napoleonic Wars brought to a head the process of agrarian change.
The Lady of the Hall has "the pride of name and character", yet
it is a pride which manifests itself in charity and solicitude for the
welfare of her tenants. Crabbe describes how both parish curate
and doctor are made part of her scheme, and how, just like Sir
Roger de Coverley, the Lady requires attendance at church of all
"her" parishioners. As an ideal type she is difficult to fault:

> Still are her habits of the ancient kind;
> She knows the poor, the sick, the lame, the blind.
> She holds, so she believes, her wealth in trust;
> And being kind, with her, is being just.
> Though soul and body she delights to aid,
> Yet of her skill she's prudently afraid;
> So to her chaplain's care she *this* commends,
> And, when *that* craves, the village doctor sends.
>
> (*Posthumous Tales*, X, lines 18–25)

The surroundings of the Hall are given nobility, and a calculatedly
"old-fashioned" grandeur. The oak trees grow as Nature planted

159

them, and in one of those rare but moving passages when Crabbe
lets himself go on natural description, he catches the cycle of
nature, the old pre-railways, pre-machines, pulse and rhythm upon
which life in the country had been based:

> Unnumber'd violets on these banks appear,
> And all the first born beauties of the year;
> The grey-green blossoms of the willows bring
> The large wild bees upon the labouring wing.
> Then comes the Summer with augmented pride,
> Whose pure small streams along the valleys glide;
> Her richer Flora their brief charms display,
> And, as the fruit advances, fall away.
> Then shall th'autumnal yellow clothe the leaf,
> What time the reaper binds the burden'd sheaf;
> Then silent groves denote the dying year,
> The morning frost, the noontide gossamer;
> And all be silent in the scene around—
> All save the distant sea's uncertain sound,
> . . . . .
>
> And then the wintry winds begin to blow;
> Then fall the flaky stars of gathering snow;
> When on the thorn the ripening sloe, yet blue,
> Takes the bright varnish of the morning dew;
> The aged moss grows brittle on the pale;
> The dry boughs splinter in the windy gale;
> And every changing season of the year
> Stamps on the scene its English character.
>
> (lines 76–99 *passim*)

Neither Cobbett, Borrow, nor Clare, loved the land more than
the poet who wrote this. Yet it is serving a specific purpose in the
narrative. We begin to associate these emotive tokens of the
traditional English seasons, not only with the people of the Hall—
particularly the old butler—but with an entire way of life.
Verbally, pictorially, and emotively the new way is shown to be
ugly as Crabbe describes the alterations at the Mansion:

> What barbarous hand could all this mischief do,
> And spoil a noble house, to make it new? . . .
> Some true admirer of the time's reform,
> Who strips an ancient dwelling like a storm;

Strips it of all its dignity and grace,
To put his own dear fancies in their place . . .
. . . but sighs are vain;
It is the rage of Taste—the rule and compass reign.

                                    (lines 112–39 *passim*)

Then follows a lyric lament in which the blind butler asks about
the neighbouring landscape, to be told by his grand-daughter of
the utter devastation which has been effected. Though it verges
perilously close upon the sentimental, this lyric achieves its purpose
by adopting a deliberately "old-fashioned" metre and language
which suggests nostalgia for a past which is irrecoverably gone,
and also a criticism of the rule and compass school which has
superseded it. Though much of this may be the sentiment of a
septuagenarian of rather conservative bent, it is a deeply felt
lament, the more moving for its total avoidance of fulmination
and "party" writing.

XII

Part of Crabbe's mind never lost its liberal tendency. In the
numerous pairs of men he creates for purposes of contrast, he
always seems to hanker secretly after the manner and life-style
of the freer spirit of the two. His sympathies clearly lie more with
Robert the smuggler than with James the keeper, with Richard, the
younger brother in *Tales of the Hall* rather than with George, the
Tory squire, and with the sailor, George in "The Brother Burgesses", where Isaac, the landsman, is a repellently loveless creature.
This sometimes makes it difficult to discern whether political inclinations are a cause or an effect of character as Crabbe understands it, and certainly it is difficult to discern any party animus in
the poet himself. It was a remarkable feat to have remained so outwardly a-political at a time when the whole state was undergoing a
cataclysmic upheaval. Most of Crabbe's eminent literary contemporaries made political avowals. Shelley, Wordsworth, Byron,
Southey, Scott, Hazlitt, Leigh Hunt all did so. Some like Cobbett
were hounded and persecuted for articulating criticisms of the
society in which they lived, yet Crabbe, for all that he is a social
poet, manages to "remain as neuter", on the surface.

That this is because he can see merits and faults in both parties

161

emerges clearly from the portraits he gives of the brothers in *Tales of the Hall*. Beyond this impartiality, he has a sense of the evanescence of all worldly things, as can be seen in the rejected conclusion to *Silford Hall*, the first and most substantial of the *Posthumous Tales*. In this poem Crabbe reconstructs a visit he had paid, as a lad, to Cheveley, one of the Duke of Rutland's East Anglian estates. Hence, as a village boy with all his life to make, he had wandered, open-eyed, around the settings which were later part of his every-day life as Ducal chaplain. The poem as Crabbe chose to send it to the press, ends on a note of cheerful wonderment, without any conscious *criticism* of the life-style of the aristocracy. The alternative, suppressed, ending however, engages in a discussion of freedom, as experienced by peasant and nobleman— (a theme Crabbe had tried to tackle years earlier in *The Village*)— and of innocence and experience. He splits himself into the now familiar personae, though here they are Youth (innocence) and Age (experience) rather than two brothers. And the narrator addresses the youthful persona, sadly and wisely, in terms which show how far Crabbe had moved outside political wrangling or the urgent immediacy of reform or repression:

> Little didst thou know
> How near approach the lofty and the low!
> In all we dare, in all we dare not name,
> How much the great and little are the same!

> Well, thou hast tried it—thou hast closely seen
> What greatness has without it, and within;
> Where now the joyful expectation?—fled!
> The strong anticipating spirit?—dead!
>
> (*Ward*, Vol. 3, p. 536)

It is easy enough to adopt this tone from the comfort of a parsonage, yet there were plenty of creative spirits who were like Crabbe in this respect, people who were by no means ignorant of, or unsympathetic to the conditions around them, but who mistrusted or were too timid to apply any grand system to the remedy of those ills. Jane Austen, Mary Mitford, Cowper, and the surprising number of noblemen whom even Cobbett allows to be irreplaceable bastions of the old squirarchal way of life, these are not despicable people, nor are they in the broadest sense a-political people. Even a character like James Dyson in "The Family of Love" is not presented in a totally alien light by Crabbe. Though he typifies much of what is least attractive about the upper-middle class Tory, the poet goes out of his way to depict the virtues, such as they are, of the type. He is reliable, frugal, family-oriented, and by no means anti-social. The sociological criticism of this type is, however, the most telling part of the portrait, for Crabbe senses a lack of genuine humanity in the man, and as we have seen in his religious principles, without humanity all else is in vain. Like so much of his best poetry, this tale exists on the frontiers where sociology, religion, politics and pure imagination meet and are fused into a work of art which, whilst recognisably of its time, is also capable of transcending contemporary boundaries.

James is made to express, with great accuracy, a point of view which Crabbe must have heard articulated all around him every day. It is a voice which has not substantially changed in a hundred and fifty years:

> . . . "Vainly we strive a fortune now to get,
> So tax'd by private claims, and public debt."
>
> Still he proceeds—"You make your prisons light,
> "Airy and clean, your robbers to invite;
> "And in such ways your pity show to vice,
> "That you the rogues encourage, and entice."
> For lenient measures James had no regard—
> "Hardship", he said, "must work upon the hard;
> "Labour and chains such desperate men require;
> "To soften iron you must use the fire."
> Active himself, he labour'd to express,
> In his strong words, his scorn of idleness;
> From him in vain the beggar sought relief—
> "Who will not labour is an idle thief,
> "Stealing from those who will;" he knew not how
> For the untaught and ill-taught to allow,
> Children of want and vice, inured to ill,
> Unchain'd the passions, and uncurb'd the will.
> Alas! he look'd but to his own affairs,
> Or to the rivals in his trade, and theirs;
> Knew not the thousands who must all be fed,
> Yet ne'er were taught to earn their daily bread;

163

Whom crimes, misfortunes, errors only teach
To seek their food where'er within their reach;
Who for their parents' sins, or for their own,
Are now as vagrants, wanderers, beggars known,
Hunted and hunting through the world, to share
Alms and contempt, and shame and scorn to bear;
Whom Law condemns, and Justice, with a sigh,
Pursuing, shakes her sword and passes by.—
If to the prison we should these commit,
They for the gallows will be render'd fit.

(Posthumous Tales, II, lines 154–85)

The passage seems to move out of the context of the poem, and to become something from Crabbe's own notebook. It seems to me the strongest statement he ever made about the state of the poor, and their relationship to the affluent in the society of his day. Though the sentiments may appear common-place enough today, they cannot have been so in the parson-magistrate of a depressed industrial town in the eighteen-twenties.

This is one of the very few of his stories which is set in an urban background. Nor is it fanciful to trace a relationship between the murky urban setting and the loveless hearts of the "Family of Love".

The clearest example of Crabbe constructing a character in terms of political opinions and physical environment is in the frame narrative of *Tales of the Hall*. George is a retired merchant who has come back to his native village, and bought the Hall he admired as a boy—(both the "Silford Hall" and the "Farewell and Return" motifs are discernible here: the Hall is also, pretty clearly, an amalgam of Cheveley and Parham Hall, which Crabbe himself had enjoyed as tenant through his wife's family). There is something of the cautious, responsible Crabbe in this man:

George loved the cause of freedom, but reproved
All who with wild and boyish ardour loved:
Those who believed they never could be free,
Except when fighting for their liberty;
Who by their very clamour and complaint
Invite coercion or enforce restraint.
He thought a trust so great, so good a cause,
Was only to be kept by guarding laws;
. . . . .

164

The public good must be a private care;
None all they would may have, but all a share.
So we must freedom with restraint enjoy;
What crowds possess they will, uncheck'd, destroy;
And hence, that freedom may to all be dealt,
Guards must be fix'd, and safety must be felt.
    So thought our squire, nor wish'd the guards t'appear
So strong, that safety might be bought too dear;
The constitution was the ark that he
Join'd to support with zeal and sanctity; . . .

(*Tales of the Hall*, Book I, lines 146–69)

Though this is conservatism, and is presented with a light touch
of whimsy, yet there must have been many and many a worthy
Englishman who read it with relief and a sense of agreement. Few
of Crabbe's contemporaries articulate this kind of reasonable
caution with equal grace or simplicity.

Yet he can move on to set even this in a broader context, by
contrasting the attitudes of the younger brother with those of
squire George—perhaps to give expression to that side of himself which had been a runaway, an adventurer, a gambler.
Richard's religious opinions, veering to non-conformity, have
already been noticed. Crabbe moves straight from them to his
political notions:

He spake of freedom as a nation's cause,
And loved, like George, our liberty and laws;
But had more youthful ardour to be free,
And stronger fears for injured liberty.
With him, on various questions that arose,
The monarch's servants were the people's foes;
And, though he fought with all a Briton's zeal,
He felt for France as Freedom's children feel;
Went far with her in what she thought reform,
And hail'd the revolutionary storm;
Yet would not here, where there was least to win,
And most to lose, the doubtful work begin;
But look'd on change with some religious fear,
And cried, with filial dread, "Ah! come not here."

(*ibid.*, lines 240–53)

There is both a generosity and a shrewdness about this, which may surprise some readers who have read only *The Village*, and "Peter Grimes", those two utterly a-typical poems, by which Crabbe seems to be universally known. There is plenty of genuine radical spunk in Richard—(and one must remember that Crabbe was over sixty when he wrote this)—plenty of ideas which neither Byron nor Cobbett could have faulted. Yet, at the end, there is a sudden drawing-back. This is not Crabbe's loss of nerve. It is a very shrewd reflection by the poet of a loss of nerve which many English liberals did suffer. There were people like Walter Scott and Dorothy Wordsworth, for instance, who became convinced that "Jacobin", "Radical", and "rogue" were inter-changeable terms of denigration, whilst many evangelical extremists failed to throw in their physical lot with the poor they championed, because they believed that it was right for the poor to suffer patiently, and to bear the afflictions of the law as Providential tests of will! The real insight of Crabbe's picture of the liberal Richard comes in those last two lines, where he puts his finger on the precise anomaly in the national character which makes open rebellion so difficult to achieve or even to countenance, for an Englishman.

The brothers of *Tales of the Hall* went straight to the hearts of many contemporary readers, who expressed pleasure at meeting such discernible and clearly defined types of acceptable opinion in the poem.

Virtually all the themes with which this chapter has been concerned have been rural ones, or general issues. Though he spent a third of his ministry in a manufacturing town, there are few references in Crabbe to the specific condition of the urban poor. As early as his Muston days he had seen something of the impending "revolution" in methods of production, for he had struck up a friendship with Edmund Cartwright, the perfector of the power loom, and had indeed paid a visit to Cartwright's factory at Doncaster. Yet neither at that time, nor at any subsequent one, does Crabbe, in his poetry, or in his letters as far as I have been able to trace, make any comment on the situation or his reactions to it. Individual persons, mentioned by name, either for praise or blame in a political sense, are virtually unknown in Crabbe's writings. He seems to have been quite the opposite of the "good hater" which Cobbett was. Like his Irish friend Mary Leadbeater, he is interested only in the individual, not in his political opinion. *The Leadbeater Papers* describes how the Quaker community at Balli-tore, just outside Dublin, suffered first at the hands of one side, then of the other, during the uprising of 1798. Yet the com-munity continued to minister to the needs of the wounded of both parties. Crabbe's christian charity was never tested quite so far, yet it is interesting to read his descriptions of the attempts he made to lead a balanced and a normal life during the disturbances in Trowbridge and district in the 1820s. We find him a little re-luctantly involved with the forces of "law and order";

> I should enjoy the repose of Pucklechurch and particularly after the tumults here; the brief triumph of the rioters, their trial as brief and sending them to prison. Then the dining with officers and listening to stories of distress, all make a medley in the mind which is anything rather than pleasant and there is a member of the Yeo-man Cavalry who has injury from a kick of his horse and lies at the Cross Keys where I visit him, but I hope he will soon be able to return to Chippenham where he keeps an inn I am told . . .
>
> To George Crabbe Junior, Trowbridge 18 May, 1826
> (Earl of Cranbrook's collection)

Ministering to the hated Yeoman Cavalry would scarcely endear the rector to the common people of his parish. The action of these troops at Peterloo had not been forgotten or forgiven. Yet it is "distress" not politics which motivates Crabbe. The man is sick and lies in his parish; he must and shall be visited. That his sympathies lie, not with a party, but with the truth as he sees it, comes out a couple of years later. The atmosphere can have been only slightly less tense than in '26 when he wrote to Mrs Lead-beater, concerning the laws which forbade workmen to combine or form unions. He takes a pre-eminently sane and humane view of this—not at all the standard view of a Tory parson-magistrate as the radicals would have us see him. In 1828 he informed his son George that he had been forced to take note of "A Combination among workmen respecting wages, in which every man is sworn to secrecy, which renders it unlawful". For Crabbe, it is the oath-taking which is illegal, and this alone, for "If the Masters may combine to fix what they will give, servants should be allowed to make agreements concerning what they will take" (Yale mss.). But nothing will justify the secrecy and the oath-taking. These

Crabbe regards as potentially seditious. Unfortunately, one suspects he is very naïve. The movement for reform was so riddled
with informers and *agents-provocateur*, that secrecy became a
necessity. Quite simply he detested and totally failed to understand the need for vicious party in-fighting.

> The man who dwells where party-spirit reigns
> May feel its triumphs, but must wear its chains;
> He must the friends and foes of party take
> For his, and suffer for his honour's sake;
> When once enlisted upon either side,
> He must the rude septennial storm abide—
> A storm that when its utmost rage is gone,
> In cold and angry mutterings murmurs on;
> A slow unbending scorn, a cold disdain—
> Till years bring the full tempest back again.

This is the opening of "The Boat Race", the eighteenth of the
Posthumous Tales. The tone and manner remind one of the much
earlier satire in *The Borough*. But on this occasion Crabbe goes
on to tell a tragic story which provides human substance to the
abstraction of the earlier critique of politics. It is not entirely
successful as a poem, lacking the touches of enlivening psychological detail which are found in his better work. The poet seems
so earnest to make his point, that the natural bizarreté of the story
is exacerbated by his concentration on the didactic element. "No
good can come of party strife" is the burden of the tale. Though
the narrative is moving enough, there does not seem to be a truly
essential relationship between the events which would link politics
with a boating accident. Crabbe tries to write a Romeo and Juliet
story, but fails really to show us that the lovers are star-crossed,
or that they suffer directly for their parents' intransigence. There
is a flaccidness about the plotting of the middle section of the
poem which is unlike Crabbe's usually taut, inexorably logical
story telling.

Two sailors espouse different political parties with particular
vehemence. On his death-bed one of them extracts from his son
a promise to continue supporting the party, come what may. The
son, after making the promise, falls in love with the daughter of
the rival family. The only available compromise seems to be that
the young man should give up his vote. This will save him break-

ing his word to his father and will ensure he is not an active opponent of the family into which he is marrying. Thus far the poem might have been a social comedy, though the poet does not ever treat it as such. But in his endeavours to make it tragic enough to prove his point about party faction, Crabbe strains things. To celebrate the forthcoming wedding a boat race is organised, and against his better judgement the young sailor is induced to take part. A storm gets up, and the boat in which he is sailing with his father-in-law-to-be capsizes, and they are drowned. The trouble with the poem is that there is no cogent reason given why the party politics theme has been welded onto the boating tragedy, since the party rivalry has actually been abandoned before the race happens. Logically then, the moral of this is that if you sink your differences, you will get sunk at sea! Nor can one really read the poem and be carried along by any conviction that the storm is anything other than the most blatant of devices. I do not know whether the poem is based on fact. Even if all the events are true, Crabbe has failed to turn life into art here—a very rare failure, but one worth our attention since it is possibly explained by the earnestness with which he wishes to make the point that party faction is a destructive and futile thing. It is possible to give the poem a highly ingenious meaning in which Crabbe is showing that once party-faction has infected an individual or a community, it may not be possible ever to undo the ill effects it brings—hence the storm which so suddenly and wantonly destroys all the male characters together. But the poem seems neither tight enough nor articulate enough to warrant such a reading.

Crabbe's own political opinions veered to the right as he grew older. He was never a radical either in action or intent and this despite the repressions and the corruption of the system he lived under and was part of. Such is the case against him. But there are enough of the poems, particularly of those written late in his life which show concern and compassion to place him not among the "don't knows" or the "don't cares", but among the majority who, fearing the shadows of the French Revolution, clung to as much of the old order as they could, while the world around them convulsed from an agrarian and static society into an industrial and fluid one. In Crabbe's thought there was a good deal of the viewpoint of his mentor, Burke. Though the system was far from infallible it had advantages as Burke remarked: ". . . it *works*; who can guarantee as much for any other system that has not been tried? Old institutions, like old boots, are more comfortable than new ones." And for Crabbe, within such ramshackle but comprehensible structure, it is always the individual who matters more than the creed, or the party, though he was was far too shrewd and sensitive to the spirit of the times not to see how acutely his fellow man could feel and be affected by political motives. These he records with sensitivity and understanding.

6

The Life Within

> Our Passions on our Virtues prey,
> And when the Conflict is extreme,
> Our Reason in the Strife gives Way,
> And then our Life is but a dream.
> (*New Poems*, p. 79)

I

In a substantial number of his poems Crabbe deals with the theme of madness. The amount of his writing which concentrates upon it grows most noticeably from *The Parish Register* onwards: the miller's daughter, Lucy, in *The Parish Register*, suffers a melancholic derangement after her disappointment in love ("Baptisms", lines 370–402). This is merely a thumb-nail sketch, though done with great insight and sensitivity. Within a very few years *The Borough* provides a number of much fuller studies of derangement —Jachin, Peter Grimes, the condemned felon of Letter XXIII, Ellen Orford, and Abel Keene. The impetus to develop this theme would have come from the enormous success of "Sir Eustace Grey" which was hailed as a masterpiece of its kind when it first appeared in *Poems* in 1807, and which has remained among the most respected of Crabbe's poems ever since. Throughout *The Borough* we can see Crabbe becoming increasingly concerned with what goes on underneath the surface of people's minds.

It is not the least interesting side of his development that he concentrates on this topic even while his mastery of the narrative qualities of the verse tale is progressing in the intensely creative years between 1806 and 1812. As his interest in character study developed, and as he came to evolve the particular form of verse

171

tale which the 1812 volume shows at its best, he must have been aware that his eye for furniture, detail, and accoutrement could be used in a way which illuminates the entire tale to show the condition of a man's mind. As we have seen, Dinah in "Procrastination" falls in love with her aunt's chattels and out of love with poor Rupert, an emotional stultification which the poet demonstrates by loading the poem with descriptions of wealth and furniture. The ability to develop character in this way—one of Crabbe's greatest gifts—had not been shown in much of the work which dates from before his silence of twenty-two years. Catherine Lloyd, from the "Burials" section of *The Parish Register*, shows how acutely the poet's eye is drawn towards this correlation of the outward trappings and the inner woman—an early example of a fusion which is to become characteristic:

> Down by the church-way walk, and where the brook
> Winds round the chancel like a shepherd's crook,
> In that small house, with those green pales before,
> Where jasmine trails on either side the door;
> Where those dark shrubs that now grow wild at will,
> Were clipp'd in form and tantalized with skill;
> Where cockles blanch'd and pebbles neatly spread,
> Form'd shining borders for the larkspurs' bed—
> There lived a Lady, wise, austere, and nice,
> Who show'd her virtue by her scorn of vice.
> In the dear fashions of her youth she dress'd,
> A pea-green Joseph was her favourite vest;
> Erect she stood, she walk'd with stately mien,
> Tight was her length of stays, and she was tall and lean.
> The long she lived in maiden-state immured,
> From looks of love and treacherous man secured;
> Though evil fame (but that was long before)
> Had blown her dubious blast at Catherine's door.
> A Captain thither, rich from India, came,
> And though a cousin call'd, it touch'd her fame:
> Her annual stipend rose from his behest,
> And all the long-prized treasures she possess'd: —
> If aught like joy awhile appear'd to stay
> In that stern face, and chase those frowns away,
> 'Twas when her treasures she disposed for view,
> And heard the praises to their splendour due;

172

Silks beyond price, so rich, they'd stand alone,
And diamonds blazing on the buckled zone;
Rows of rare pearls by curious workmen set,
And bracelets fair in box of glossy jet;
Bright polish'd amber precious from its size,
Or forms the fairest fancy could devise.
Her drawers of cedar, shut with secret springs,
Conceal'd the watch of gold and rubied rings;
Letters, long proofs of love, and verses fine
Round the pink'd rims of crisped Valentine.
Her china-closet, cause of daily care,
For woman's wonder held her pencill'd ware;
That pictured wealth of China and Japan,
Like its cold mistress, shunn'd the eye of man.
      Her neat small room, adorn'd with maiden-taste,
A clipp'd French puppy, first of favourites, grac'd;
A parrot next, but dead and stuff'd with art;
(For Poll, when living, lost the Lady's heart,
And then his life; for he was heard to speak
Such frightful words as tinged his Lady's cheek;)
Unhappy bird! who had no power to prove,
Save by such speech, his gratitude and love.
A grey old cat his whiskers lick'd beside;
A type of sadness in the house of pride.
The polish'd surface of an India chest,
A glassy globe, in frame of ivory, press'd;
Where swam two finny creatures: one of gold,
Of silver one, both beauteous to behold.
All these were form'd the guiding taste to suit;
The beasts well manner'd and the fishes mute.
A widow'd Aunt was there, compell'd by need
The nymph to flatter and her tribe to feed;
Who, veiling well her scorn, endured the clog,
Mute as the fish and fawning as the dog.
                    (*The Parish Register*, "Burials", lines 312–71)

Here Crabbe is able to combine social comedy, moral criticism
and personal observation. He begins by suggesting that nature has
been methodised too far in Catherine's life. The cottage garden is
over-regimented—"tantalised with skill"—and though her death
has released the plants to "grow wild at will", there is a powerful
bringing-together of conflicting ideas which serve to show how

Catherine herself has concealed natural impulse in her life, and so become stultified. It is the same when we move indoors. The room is liberally scattered with the goods of this world; so liberally that they asphyxiate us and destroy each other. The dessication of Catherine's personality is echoed through her pets, and through the aunt, added almost as an afterthought to the jewels, the cat, and the parrot. The writing is crisp, concise, never hurrying over its effects. The poet is aware of the heritage he is drawing on— the world of Gray's *Elegy on a Favourite Cat*, for instance, for the verbal echoes of that exquisite *jeu d'esprit* must be totally conscious on Crabbe's part. Yet because it is Catherine and not the writer who is wallowing in this world of tactile objects, a clear criticism can run behind the gentle mockery of the timbre and language of the verse.

This is a half-way stage in Crabbe's analysis of derangement. Over the years he seems to have become increasingly preoccupied with extending this correlation between people and the things they have around them, so that it will reveal the real inner nature of the character. And thus he is drawn towards a closer study of the mind in all its states of aberration. The poems published by Crabbe's son give a partial picture of this tendency, but the poet had left in manuscript several tales about madness which seem to have been suppressed or rejected, not always because they are inferior to or less finished than poems chosen for publication. The rejected tales can now be read in Arthur Pollard's *New Poems of George Crabbe* where there are at least three full-length studies of various states of derangement. None of these are in the couplet-form which we usually associate with Crabbe. They suggest that his increasing concern with the processes of liberation or dislocation of the psyche may have been reflected in the measure he chose for writing on these occasions, though it is, as always, a moral interest and not simply a clinical one which motivates Crabbe.

> Our Passions on our Virtues prey,
> And when the Conflict is extreme,
> Our Reason in the Strife gives Way,
> And then our Life is but a Dream.
>
> (*New Poems*, p. 79)

II

The poet sees a two-way process at work in mental breakdown. The clergyman—that is, the exterior Crabbe—is still prepared to attribute intellectual distress to moral causes. But another side of him goes on to confess that life is so changed by this stress that it becomes, subjectively, a totally different thing. "Madness" is too simple a term to connote the range of experience which Crabbe embraces in his work on this subject. He covers an area from mild but persistent indulgence of dream fancies to the full flights of unco-ordinated frenzy. The association of derangement with dream is so frequent that the one is best studied as an adjunct to the other, while ghosts and supernatural phenomena also form a part of the same consideration. There need be no surprise in finding this preoccupation with derangement in Crabbe's work: both by background and by temperament he inherits a concern for such matters. His roots are firmly planted in the world of Gothic fancy which had been created by Horace Walpole, Mrs Radcliffe, Beckford, Maturin, Mary Shelley, and other writers in the period from 1760 onwards. Spurious and empty as the "Gothic" craze may now seem to us, it had a considerable influence on the imaginations of poets as diverse as Keats, Coleridge, Byron, and Chatterton. Other related vogues such as the cult of eccentricity in clothing, in architecture, and in personal behaviour, demonstrate the abnormalcy of so many Englishmen in the eighteenth and early nineteenth centuries. This "abnormalcy" is manifested among the poets of the "Age of Reason" by the last mad years of Swift, the periods committed to asylums of Smart and Cowper, the extreme withdrawal from the world by Gray, the melancholia of Johnson and the literary fantasies of Chatterton. Blake, the most personal and unconventional author of the entire period, was drawn more and more to the creation of his own world outside that of everyday, a tendency which both Turner and Blake's disciple, Samuel Palmer, variously exhibit in the graphic arts. Architecturally, the Regency (using the term in the broadest sense of the period 1780–1830) is the great age of the folly and the mock-Gothic extravaganza—Fonthill and Strawberry Hill, not forgetting the oriental exoticism of the Brighton Pavilion.

The English were known throughout the continent for their

175

melancholia. Matthew Green had celebrated it in *The Spleen* earlier in the eighteenth century, and melancholia was known in France as "La Maladie Anglaise". Yet these melancholy islanders were, at one and the same time, great extroverts, capable of going from extreme to extreme in a way they could not explain for themselves.

There is a good example of this in the letters of Gray. Writing to his mother from Rheims in 1739 he is full of complaints about the stuffiness of the English community in the town, the petty social round of cards, cant and class which seemed to make up their social life:

> Very seldom any suppers or dinners are given; and this is the manner they live among one another . . . It is sure they do not hate gaity any more than the rest of their country people, and can enter into diversions, that are once proposed, with a good grace enough: for instance, the other evening, we happened to be got together in a company of eighteen people, men and women of the best fashion here, at a garden in the town to walk; when one of the ladies bethought herself of asking, Why should we not sup here? Immediately the cloth was laid by the side of a fountain under the trees, and a very elegant supper served up; after which another said, Come, let us sing, and directly began herself: From singing we insensibly fell to dancing, and singing in a round . . .
>
> (*Letters of Thomas Gray*, "World's Classics" edition, p. 36)

The party proceed to hire musicians, live it up up until 4 a.m. and then awake the entire town by processing in stage coaches, followed by the band in a cart, and so to bed. Horace Walpole thought it would be a good idea to make this a regular feature of life for the English community in exile at Rhiems, but Gray comments, "I believe it will drop, and they will return to their dull cards, and usual formalities." Perhaps this over-formality of English life helped to stimulate the excesses which characterise the period. Yet there is something pathological in Johnson's or in Cowper's gloom, as in Byron's posturing, which seems to suggest a deep-rooted malaise for which no simple explanation can be offered. In several cases of course, one might offer a drastic shift of social station as a factor: Clare, Bloomfield, and Crabbe all came from backgrounds which were a hindrance to their poetic careers, and they bore the stigma of ill-education. Crabbe's early sensitivity on this subject has already been noted: his distress over the uncouth behaviour of his father, his attempts to manipulate Burke into providing him with the social passport of a university education, and his uneasiness at Belvoir Castle. Each of these can be seen to have an influence on his poetry.

One must also stress the degree to which he was directly influenced by the "penny-dreadfuls", for his taste in light reading seems to have been as bad as that of anyone at the time. His son comments on the lapse of discretion in the *Life*, (p. 44) and adds, significantly:

> . . . I may say that even from the most trite of these fictions, he could sometimes catch a train of ideas that was turned to excellent use; so that he seldom passed a day without reading part of some such work, and was never very select in the choice of them.

What "these fictions" could be, Jane Austen, in *Northanger Abbey*, and Peacock in *Nightmare Abbey* have given us some inkling, as has Wordsworth more soberly in the Preface to the second edition of *Lyrical Ballads*. The titles of their works provide further testimony to the taste for the macabre, the horrific and the sensational for which people like Maturin and "Monk" Lewis catered.

We need also to take note of Crabbe's rather uncritical interest in folk and ballad literature, which he appreciated not through that scholarly concern which led Gray back to Anglo-Saxon, but rather from a living, if uninformed, current running through the eighteenth century at a lowly social level, where the broadsheet and the fairy tale had never been quite submerged. The description of the cottage bookshelf in *The Parish Register* recaptures this world for us:

> Unbound and heap'd, these valued works beside,
> Lay humbler works the pedler's pack supplied;
> Yet these, long since, have all acquired a name:
> The Wandering Jew has found his way to fame;
> And fame, denied to many a labour'd song,
> Crowns Thumb the great, and Hickerthrift the strong.
> There too is he, by wizard-power upheld,
> Jack, by whose arm the giant brood were quell'd; . . .
> These are the peasant's joy, when, placed at ease,
> Half his delighted offspring mount his knees.
> (*The Parish Register*, "Baptisms", lines 111–28)

177

John Clare's autobiographical sketch of his early years lists almost identical material among the scanty literature he could come by.

III

Crabbe's personal circumstances in early manhood seem also to have left an indelible stamp on his imagination. The years of struggle to establish himself, the dread of debt, hunger and humiliation are often present even when he is apparently at his most assured, or when dealing with topics in no way concerned with his personal life. His London Journal for 21 July 1817 records the way in which these memories could attack him when least expected. It should be borne in mind that this Journal belongs to that period of apparent tranquillity and prosperity in which he wrote *Tales of the Hall*—long after the struggle for recognition was over.

> I returned late last night, and my reflections were as cheerful as such company could make them, and not, I am afraid, of the most humiliating kind; yet, for the first time these many nights, I was incommoded by dreams such as would cure vanity . . . None, indeed, that actually did happen in the very worst of times, but still with a formidable resemblance . . . Awake, I had been with the high, the apparently happy: we were very pleasantly engaged, and my last thoughts were cheerful. Asleep, all was misery and degradation, not my own only, but of those who had been.—That horrible image of servility and baseness—that mercenary and commercial manner! It is the work of imagination, I suppose; but it is very strange. I must leave it. *(Life,* pp. 70–1)

The company, as his journal for the previous day informs us, included Murray the publisher, and Sir Harry Englefield in "the pleasantest of all parties".

Crabbe's moods of depression were very strong, and any study of his pre-occupation with madness and lack of control over fancy and thought must pay full heed to them. To all these factors must also be added his trying experience with a wife subject in her latter years to fits of gloom alternating with hysterical high spirits. Normally a sociable and gregarious man, Crabbe had been forced by his wife's illness to eschew company, and the experiences of this period of his life seem to have increased that concern with the balance and working of the mind which he took as priest and

178

as poet. The resultant picture of the human scene is often a spare and chastened one. Furthermore, the insight into his own mind is remarkable. He wrote to Alethea Lewis, only a few weeks after his wife's death, and in response to her letter of condolence, a reply which is sufficiently revealing to be worth quoting in full. It offers all sorts of insights into the struggle between overt and covert motivation in Crabbe's mind (a major theme in his poetry), between the "gallant" and the "sober" sides of his nature.

Muston Grantham 25 Oct 1813.

My dear Mrs Lewis

I give you thanks for remembering me & for showing that you did remember me at the present time. My sister informed Mrs Say that I was left, & Mrs Say wrote to you: this was not the mode of correspondence many years since, but now we have nothing to do with many years: you are very right: we are all about the time of our departure: a little sooner: a little later: nor does life appear short: it seems a long time since I met for the first interview you & the inmates and inhabitants of the little old woman's little old house.

She has been dying these ten year: more I believe & I hope I am very thankful that I am the survivor, though with such young men, it took much from the sadness of that prospect, nor would both have wearied I think in her life, but it is otherwise & it is best: she is gone. I cannot weigh sorrows in a balance or make comparisons between different kinds of affliction, nor do I judge whether I should have suffered most to have parted with my poor Sally as I did part (if indeed such was parting) or to have seen her pass away with all her faculties, feelings, senses acute & awake as my own. When I doubt of our parting (a conscious feeling on both sides that we were separating) you will judge of the propriety of such expression, for with respect to intellect & the more enquiring and reassuring of the faculties, she, dear creature, had lost those even years since: the will sometimes made an effort, but Nature forbad: the mind was veiled, clouded & by degrees lost. Then too were the affections wrecked: no I was no more than another! not so much as the woman who administered to the hourly calls for small comforts. The senses remained & even too acute but I hope, I believe there was not pain with the restlessness which preceded the evening of the 20th of Septr & for her there was no morning here! *after* that.

Appetite & thought had been decaying for 2 or 3 years, but very gradually. We had often talked of London & our sons were strongly invited to Beccles: so it was agreed they should go and return by way of Town where we would meet them. It seemed to please & I hoped something from novelty & even from hurry. The journey was pleasant & the first week: on the third I perceived encreased symptoms of debility & hurried down. It was indeed a trying and anxious time. On our arrival all things indicated a speedy change. Medical men could do nothing: my poor Mrs Crabbe only lived to the present: we could not speak of the past. We could not hope together for the future: all was centered in the moment's feeling & when I stood over her & carried my thoughts backward to the mind that was, the intelligence that might have been gained, the improvement, the communication that we should have made if— but it is not in men to foresee nor to repine but to submit. God Almighty grant to me a spirit of absolute & total resignation.

I must yet dwell a little more on self & then you will know as much of me as I dare say you can wish. The night before we meant to do our last offices for the wife and mother when I had taken leave of my sons & indeed of all things, for I was profoundly sleeping, & then pain and other symptoms, which gave no preceding tokens of their presence awakened me & with that violence as seemed to indicate that sleep would not quickly come again. I just recollect the coffin against my chamber door & my selfish feeling for it made no other impression than another noise would have done which affected the head. Indeed I have often remarked the engrossing selfishness of pain at least in my own case. From that time to this I have been better & worse but never well & eat more or less but nothing with appetite. I never was a stout fellow, but Oh! my poor shrunken limbs & hollow features; you would smile, for I will not allow you to laugh, I looked in the glass this morning & do say, it is a very respectable looking old sick face, Chop-fallen to be sure, but as handsome as ever it was—but it is time to leave this & thank you once again for your letter—I am truly and heartily glad that you live in so much comfort, for surely that your letter indicates & indeed I heard in Suffolk no little that I was pleased with; not maliciously pleased as I sometimes have been on your A^{cct} because it was vexatious I conceived here or there, but now I was pleased after a Christian temper & I pray for your continued peace and comfort here so far as is consistent & I trust a great degree of them is perfectly so, with what is of infinitely greater importance than this world's pe[ace] [o]r Comforts. Mr Lewis is kind & I am well pleased with his ideas of the probable friendship between us had situations etc admitted: I should be anyway with myself if I were to seek declarations, but Stella! had we been a year together Mr L would have sought your ear: "I am mistaken in this George who you talk of, in his opinions he seems modestly to comply & to recede, & so on but notwithstanding his manner he is as obstinate as a mule, & so with regard to his will & inclination, one would think him for a while the most complying and complacent of beings but he is a self-willed wearying-out spirit & so much the worse for seeming so much the better. He is comfoundedly vain too, tho that is a little slacked I believe"—Shall I go on? I could, I assure you.

Yes! my boys are with me, & comforts they are: rational comforts: rational Christians as I trust: kind: attentive, I say not, dutiful, I doubt if *that* motive has had a moments influence: that comfort we have: there is I think affection on their side: I would not be too sure, but I think it. It certainly is not often so, when children reach 20–25 then very seldom indeed & now I am at the end of my paper, the subject returns in all its force: my dear Sally! when did I last see you, hear you converse with you? alas I know not. You have left me: long, long left me! God give me, again I pray, intire submission. I wish you both all the world can give, all it cannot. God bless you, George Crabbe.

[Outer cover:]   Mrs Lewis
                Preston Hall
                 Pinkridge,
                 Stafford^{shr}

I did not mean to write slightingly, much less unkindly respecting Mrs Say: I know her to mean the best & to wish it could be effected. There were subjects in the manner of treating which, we varied much in opinion, but no explanation ever took place. Perhaps I judged her more severe than she really is & she me less affected by guilt than I ought to be: I know not, I only know that looking forward to my last day (& I supposed it near & near it may be) I felt nothing in my mind respecting my friends, but what I wished to feel—   (Bod. ms. Autog. c.9)

The comparatively early poem "Reflections upon the Subject: Quid juvat errores" (*Life*, pp. 160–2) epitomises the struggle between the extremes at war. The preface to *Poems* suggests that this poem is about the irreconcilable tension betwen the creative and the repressive sides of nature—between free art and discip-

181

line—and that the stamp of guilt on the human mind may well be indelible. When we are young we have the power to create, but are prevented by "passion". As discretion comes to us, we turn back to creativity again, but now the vital spark has been extinguished. The struggle is between Reason and Passion and man is nullified by the exhausting tug-of-war. Couched in a lyric metre remote from his customary couplets, the poem is an early attempt to understand the source of that deep inner consciousness of alienation, bewilderment, and remorse, to which Crabbe, like so many of his contemporaries, was a prey.

IV

The difference between Crabbe and many of his contemporaries lies not in the quantity of verse he allots to the theme of derangement (although this is considerable), but much more in the quality of insight, the near-clinical and yet highly imaginative treatment which he affords the topic. His years of experience as doctor as well as priest brought him understanding of the problem from the outside just as his own temperamental constitution illuminates his work on madness from within.

As in much late eighteenth- and early nineteenth-century poetry on derangement, Crabbe frequently associates the phenomenon with sleep, and with ghosts. While he naturally acknowledges a debt to Shakespeare in this, a strong element of personal experience seems to underlie his attitude. Sleep frees the fancy from the control of reason, and thus projects it into a dangerously undisciplined world: we have already seen Crabbe's dreams at work in this way. This in itself is true of much of the less individual poetry of the period which touches on the subjects of melancholia and madness—Young's *Night Thoughts* is an example. But in Young there is none of that self-revelatory imaginative force which distinguishes Crabbe's contribution to this genre. The importance of Young in helping to shape the imagination of many of the poets of the generation which followed him cannot be over-stressed, however. Everybody read him; even Cobbett had dabbled, though his pragmatic mind was repelled by the bombastic parsonising of Young's self-conscious gloom. Young seldom correlates the states of derangement and guilt with Crabbe's psychological insight, nor

182

apportions types of insanity to clearly defined types of crime with
Crabbe's nice discrimination. Few pre-Freudian writers have out-
lined the liberation of the ego as succinctly or as imaginatively
as Crabbe. "In sleep what forms will ductile fancy take?" he asks
in *Tales of the Hall*, XVI—a question he has already taken up in
the same poem with the observation:

> . . . in sleep those horrid forms arise
> That the soul sees . . .
>
> (lines 39–40)

This appears very close to the experiences recorded in his London
Journal.

Dreams are, to Crabbe, a release of the mind's moral sensibility. Many of his tales work by showing how a man's innate core
of integrity is worn away by consciously evil action, while many
more illustrate the further process in which the Unconscious rebels
and substitutes an image either of what should have been, or of
the punishment covertly anticipated for the conscious sin. It is at
this juncture that dreams or delusions begin to trouble the protagonist. The hallucinations of Peter Grimes are the most obvious
example of this. "The Insanity of Ambitious Love" (*New Poems*,
pp. 33–45), illustrates the process even more comprehensively.
However robust the outward resistance to conscience, moral probity is asserted at last. Where the experiencing mind is less re-
silient the process will take place more rapidly.

> . . . forms delicately made
> These dreams and fancies easily invade;
> The mind and body feel the slow disease,
> And dreams are what the troubled fancy sees.
> (*Tales of the Hall*, XVI, lines 801–4)

As already suggested, ghosts and supernatural phenomena are
closely linked with the motifs of dreams and derangement. In
Tales of the Hall, XVI, "Lady Barbara, or the Ghost", from which
the above quotation comes, Crabbe gives us a lengthy discussion
on whether ghosts appear to the outward eye or only to the inner
vision of conscience. It is worth noting that in this, his most explicit poem on the subject, the ghost *is* a dream. The cold voice
of reason speaks thus on the subject of dreams:

". . . some as we awake
"Fly off at once, and no impression make;
"Others are felt, and ere they quit the brain
"Make such impression that they come again,
"As half familiar thoughts, and half unknown,
"And scarcely recollected as our own.
"For half a day abide some vulgar dreams,
"And give our grandams and our nurses themes;
"Others, more strong, abiding figures draw
"Upon the brain, and we assert 'I saw';
"And then [will] fancy on the organs place
"A powerful likeness of a form and face.

(ibid., lines 818–29)

This is commonplace enough, and might have come straight from Hartley's *Observations*. One feels that it is what Crabbe the conservative parson would have liked to believe, but that Crabbe the artist and Crabbe the psychologist is less certain of a conclusion so pat and straightforward. The poem ends with a characteristic touch:

If our discretion tells us how to live,
We need no ghost a helping hand to give;
But, if discretion cannot us restrain,
It then appears a ghost would come in vain.

(ibid., lines 965–8)

But both these observations come from biassed sources. The first is the argument of a young lover trying to talk Lady Barbara out of her premonitions, the second from the moralising narrator tying up the strands at the end of an old Wiltshire story. Even those voices of reason, however, imply that ghosts are not sent from an outside agency to warn us of our fate; they are the pricks and stings of acute conscience at work in our own breasts, and they therefore belong to the moral assumptions behind Crabbe's delusion and hallucination poetry. It is in this that the poet goes beyond the commonplaces of *Night Thoughts* and the *Observations*, and even more in the delineation of individual case-histories.

v

The vehicles of a Crabbe poem on derangement, therefore, are often dreams or ghosts. Waking hallucination is more rare—

184

(Grimes suffers this kind)—but conscious indulgence of wish-fulfilment can also lead to a delusive and dangerous state of mind. "The Lover's Journey" (*Tales*, X), light though it is in tone, illustrates the process by which self-deception warps judgement through indulgence of idle fancy. "The Lover's Journey" is one of Crabbe's most popular poems. He intends it as a *jeu d'esprit*, partly as a joke against himself, for it seems to have been based upon his own experience, but if it shows his wry humour at its best, it is, at the same time, a poem akin to the early "Reflections", in its insistence that there is a life within which is not at the control of the senses and the phenomena of everyday existence:

> It is the soul that sees; the outward eyes
> Present the object, but the mind descries;
> And thence delight, disgust, or cool indiff'rence rise.
> . . .
> Our feelings still upon our views attend,
> And their own natures to the objects lend.
> (*Tales*, X, lines 1–11 *passim*)

Such a belief, taken to its extreme, makes for an anarchic and subjective world. In the case of Orlando, in "The Lover's Journey", it doesn't matter. There are other poems where it becomes extremely important. Once he has started to indulge this inner world, a man is open to attack from all sorts of directions. Jachin, the Parish Clerk, allows a subjective voice to blinker his vision of the "proper" world outside himself. He becomes sealed in his cocoon of deception, and when it is publicly shattered, he cannot go on living. John, in "The Patron", indulges wishful expectation to a point where disappointment of his hopes leads directly to insanity.

Beside his imaginative bias and his factual knowledge there can be no doubt that Crabbe's normal attitude adds force and cogency to his poems on derangement. Wordsworth's encounter with his leech-gatherer takes him only a few paces down that alley of introspection which Crabbe walks resolutely, and the madman observed by Shelley's Julian and Maddalo fails to bring the reader the prick of shared remorse which Eustace Grey and Edward Shore can inspire. Crabbe rarely uses madness or hallucination merely for purposes of sensationalism or theatrical effect. Here, as in other respects, his work is primarily *utile*, and *dulce* as a secondary consideration. People go mad because of things they have done, or that have been done to them, and Crabbe analyses their madness because of the salutary effect it may have on us.

VI

The degree of madness is varied subtly in Crabbe's subjects. Only Shakespeare seems to have attempted as much in the field of demarcating and differentiating types and purposes of madness. Crabbe seems to have been aware of this. In the preface to *Poems* (1807) he remarks:

> It is said of our Shakespeare, respecting madness,—"In that circle none dare walk but he":—yet be it granted to one, who dares not pass the boundary fixed for common minds, at least to step near to the tremendous verge, and form some idea of the terrors that are stalking in the inderdicted space. (*Life*, p. 100)

Mrs Leadbeater saw this ability in him:

> On the melancholy variety of insanity, on the descriptions of it, I mean, thou cannot but be conscious how much thou excells—how distinct is every shade from another.
>
> (*Leadbeater Papers*, Vol. 2, p. 378)

Crabbe can do equally well "the solemn wanderings of a wounded mind" in Lucy, the miller's daughter (*The Parish Register*, "Baptisms"), the poignant illusion of a condemned felon (*The Borough*, Letter XXIII), and the derangement of insane pride in a maniac (*New Poems*, pp. 34–44). Within this range of madness types, however, certain unifying tendencies can be seen at work. The poet presupposes a clear dichotomy between the derangement of guilt and that of disappointment or misfortune. The former comes as a punishment, the latter as a barrier between the sufferer and his grief. Differing causes yield predictably and consistently diffentiated effects. The consequences of insanity in Edward Shore (*Tales*, XI) are quite distinct from those in Jane (*Tales of the Hall*, VIII) because their causes originate in very different moral and social problems. Shore falls through his own intellectual pride, and ends a simpleton, intellectually below the children of the village; Jane is the victim of circumstance and thus has the buffer of illusion interposed between herself and reality. If Crabbe's

near-clinical knowledge of diseases of the mind helps to explain
this striking exactitude his moral bias helps yet more. Pride and
guilt may be further distinguished. Guilt-madness usually arises
out of some consciously fostered and ingrained ruling passion; the
insanity of pride is even more dangerous because it comes from
*un*conscious habit of mind.

In some cases, moreover, even where true repentance follows sin
and derangement, an abnormal state is preserved by nature as a
safeguard against further relapse into complete lunacy. Religious
conversion is sometimes a part of this process. Crabbe delineates
Sir Eustace Grey's state of mind as follows:

> . . . the wanderings of a mind first irritated by the consequences
> of error and misfortune, and afterwards soothed by a species of
> enthusiastic conversion, still keeping him insane.
>
> *(Life, p. 100)*

Since, to Crabbe, enthusiastic religion is itself of dubious intellectual validity, a moral judgement on Sir Eustace and on his pride
is clearly suggested. This is quite distinct from the

> . . . Madness, chiefly of the Kind
> Where Passions agitate a vicious Mind,
> Where some absurd Desire affords the Cause
> Of Frenzy's Triumph over Reason's Laws.
> *(New Poems,* "The Insanity of Ambitious
> Love", lines 1–4)

and the resultant behaviour patterns are equally distinct, as the
word "frenzy" denotes.

Whereas Lucy, in *The Parish Register*, sinks into apathy which
epitomises her hopeless worldly lot, Peter Grimes runs violently
wild and needs forcible restraint from that self-violence which
would be so consistent with the brute's conduct to others. The
imagery used in these contrasted portraits plays a major part in
evoking response from the reader. Lucy is described in language
which is all plangency, whispering, halflight, and hopeless ennui:

> Throughout the lanes she glides, at evening's close,
> And softly lulls her infant to repose;
> Then sits and gazes, but with viewless look,
> As gilds the moon the rippling of the brook;

And sings her vespers, but in voice so low,
She hears their murmurs as the waters flow:
And she too murmurs, and begins to find
The solemn wanderings of a wounded mind.
                (*The Parish Register*, "Baptisms", lines 391–8)

Lucy's introspection echoing the wound within, when the surface presents an ostensibly happy picture, is caught in the inverted word order in the fourth and sixth lines, giving a contortion behind simplicity which is most appropriate to the girl's plight. It is slightly surprising to find this technical awareness in a poem as early as *The Parish Register*; and what a powerful impression is made by that phrase "She . . . begins to find . . ." where the verb is everything to the matter.

The imagery and the verse-organisation for Grimes is very different. Here the imagery is full of noise, blood, hellfire, and Horror. It is, however, full of far more than this, for most bad "Gothic" poetry and prose contains the rant and the sensationalism while lacking the trenchant eye with which Crabbe observes, and the moral judgement with which he selects. The airlessness and desolation of the marshland in "Peter Grimes" are finely evoked, and so is the inner landscape of moral distress which echoes and underlines it. The shadeless oppression of the outward scene underlines Grimes' self-imposed isolation and un-naturalness. The use of compound terms linked by a hyphen is worth noting; they are rare in Crabbe but here the emotional tension reaches such a pitch that no other technique could convey an equally cogent and accurate impression of the fisherman's affronts to man and nature, especially "hot-red" for the more normal "red-hot". Again one feels that emotional and imaginative power is being generated by faith in a moral order.

In one fierce summer-day, when my poor brain
Was burning hot and cruel was my pain,
Then came this father-foe; and there he stood
With his two boys again upon the flood; . . .
And when they saw me fainting and oppress'd
He with his hand, the old man, scoop'd the flood,
And there came flame about him, mix'd with blood;
He bade me stoop and look upon the place,
Then flung the hot-red liquor in my face;

Burning it blazed, and then I roar'd for pain,
I thought the demons would have turn'd my brain.
(*The Borough*, Letter XXII, lines 347–61 *passim*)

VII

Justice is always strictly done at the end of a Crabbe poem. Whilst some of his madmen die, others are not allowed this termination to their delusions. Grimes dies, and dies unregenerate, horror-filled and crazy. No worse punishment can be meted out by the poet: but when Jachin, the melancholy-mad Parish Clerk turns to the wall and silently expires, a quite different aspect of Crabbe's code is revealed to us. By comparison with the excesses of Grimes the sins of Jachin are venal. Indeed, he has offended his self-esteem more than he has hurt the parish. Death comes, therefore, as a termination to his sad isolation. Lucy, in *Tales of the Hall*, VIII, as already suggested, has committed no real sin: the cause of her derangement is in no way of her own contriving, and Crabbe arranges his tale to show how the girl's subconscious has employed a gentle, almost fey withdrawal from brutal reality, not as a punishment, but as a defence mechanism. This tendency to rationalise types of delusion into a moral and ethical code becomes more pronounced as Crabbe grows older. The poems of his early and middle periods (up to *Tales in Verse* 1812) reveal it less consistently than those of his later period.

Certain image patterns and symbols recur in Crabbe's studies of delusion and derangement. These are important to an understanding of the poet's intentions. Loneliness is the attribute of all his madmen. They are people who, by heightened or introverted sensibility, are given a vision of things beyond the normal and the tangible. They have, consequently, lost the key to contact with their fellow men, and the ego suffers atrophy and perishes in the vacuum of their own inner conscience. Crabbe's personal instinct for company and his gregarious sociability may in part underlie this view of what madness is. Both "The World of Dreams" (*Life*, pp. 268–71) and "Where am I Now?" (*New Poems*, pp. 52–9) record aspects of the poet's personal ventures into this inner convoluted world of self-and-nothing, and both are discussed more fully below.

189

The symbols of loneliness are constant. Water is one of the most frequently repeated of these. The passages from "Peter Grimes" and *The Parish Register* cited above both employ water as a symbolic token of derangement. In the one case it underlines the attrition of grief, and the narrow passing moment of awareness and sensitivity for Lucy in her isolation: in the other it represents the force of retribution inherent in nature which rises to scald and overwhelm the repressed guilt in Grimes. Because of his unnatural crimes he comes to live in a world where the elements seem to change attributes—water burns and fire drowns. There is nothing remarkable in the fact that Crabbe, brought up within a few yards of the sea and the river at Aldeburgh, should employ imagery of water. The sea destroys or vitiates human relationships; it imposes barriers between lovers; and its implacable winter fury gives testimony to man's insignificance and ephemerality. But the poet's individual usage of these seaboard commonplaces is remarkable. It anticipates that of the mature Dickens fifty years later.

Ruined buildings play an important part in Crabbe's symbolic landscape. I do not know if he had seen the work of Sebastian Pether. This artist enjoyed great popularity around 1820 and his "Romantic Landscape" is in complete harmony with Crabbe's evocations of a mysterious moon-filled atmosphere of decayed castle, shattered trees, and withdrawn mystery. These are customary accoutrements to the Gothic fancy. Both Crabbe and Pether manage to give them a dignity and integrity.

> Upon that boundless plain, below,
>   The setting sun's last rays were shed,
> And gave a mild and sober glow,
>   Where all were still, asleep, or dead;
> Vast ruins in the midst were spread,
>   Pillars and pediments sublime,
> Where the grey moss had form'd a bed,
>   And clothed the crumbling spoils of time.
>   ("Sir Eustace Grey", stanza xxv)

> I know not how, but I am brought
>   Into a large and Gothic hall,
> Seated with those I never sought—

Kings, Caliphs, Kaisers—silent all;
Pale as the dead; . . .
> ("The World of Dreams", stanza xxviii)

Greece was the land he chose; a mind decay'd
And ruin'd there through glorious ruin stray'd . . .
Till, with the dead conversing, he began
To lose the habits of a living man,
> (*Tales of the Hall*, XVIII, lines 286–92 *passim*)

Abel Keene's melancholy ruin-world is a graveyard (*The Borough*, Letter XXI). Jachin, too, seeks "the blind courts" and "the church-way walk". Singular appropriateness is inherent in both these descriptions. Jachin fell through being one who followed the Church's way without following its spirit, and his inner blindness is emphasized heavily by the poet. These factors are much more important than any echo of Crabbe's reading of Blair or Young which may underline the extracts. There are similar scene-settings and motifs in "Where am I Now?" and in "The Insanity of Ambitious Love" (*New Poems*, pp. 33–44). The Gothic novel, and the eighteenth-century delight in landscape gardening are likewise recognisable as elements in the formation of Crabbe's imaginative landscape in these poems, but the manner of their employment is unlike that of any other of the "Graveyard" or "Splenetic" writers. Crabbe often evinces a near metaphysical concern with time and duration, and his descriptions of ruins in the context of the madness poems evoke with a concise power the transience of all things mortal. Equally they give to otherwise vague and general pictures a discernable and individualising touch. His work is also set apart from that of the usual "Gothic" writers by its moral emphasis. He shares with Lewis or Maturin an ability to convey gloomy, decayed grandeur, but his purpose is other than theirs, and arguably, a higher one.

The relationship between the symbols of ruin and those of loneliness is obvious. Both darkness and unnatural light are employed as manifestations of mental instability. Sir Eustace Grey is first plunged into derangement by "two fiends of darkness" (stanza xxii) and he is later mocked by atmospheric changes of light and shadow which seem to suggest a gigantic pulse throbbing and ebbing in his mind, something very close to the physical

191

sensation of migraine. Gifford's criticism of the poem is interesting here. He remarks:

> In the struggle of the passions, we delight to trace the workings of the soul; we love to mark the swell of every vein, and the throb of every pulse; . . .　　　　　　　　　　　　　　　(*Life*, p. 164)

Crabbe had, since 1800, been taking opium for his neuralgia. M. H. Abram's book *The Milk of Paradise; The Effect of Opium Visions on the Works of De Quincey, Crabbe, Francis Thompson and Coleridge* shows how unusual awareness of bright light or vivid colour seems to be a characteristic of opium dreams, and Althea Hayter, in *Opium and the Romantic Imagination*, pursues the topic further and more rigorously. The fact that "Sir Eustace" was written "during a great snowstorm" (*Life*, p. 162) may also play a part in explaining Crabbe's daring and evocative use of light and darkness in this poem.

> They placed me where those streamers play,
> 　　Those nimble beams of brilliant light;
> It would the stoutest heart dismay,
> 　　To see, to feel, that dreadful sight:
> So swift, so pure, so cold, so bright,
> 　　They pierced my frame with icy wound,
> And, all that half-year's polar night,
> 　　Those dancing streamers wrapp'd me round.
> 　　　　　　("Sir Eustace Grey", stanza xxviii)

Here there is a full range of sense experience—sight, feeling, movement—yet none of them correlate with the experiences of normal waking life: "to *feel* that dreadful sight"—"dancing streamers *wrapp'd* me round". There is a most unusual sensibility at work here, heightened beyond the boundaries of everyday experience. This extract also embodies another of the reiterated motifs of Crabbe's derangement poetry—the alternation of rapid motion with the suspension of all life. This device augments the effect of a pulsating rhythm which has been noted already. While the usage of darkness is standard, that of light is far from being so. Moreover, the alternation of light and darkness suggests the changes of remorse and self-will in the hero's mind. Just as the outward eye is confused by a rapid change from light to dark so is the mind's eye blinded by these shifts of temper and conscience.

In practice, of course, it is the fusion and the inter-action of the individual techniques so far enumerated which creates the characteristic flavour of Crabbe's derangement and dream poetry. His own dreams and his own mental state furnish the material for some of the most powerful poetry he wrote on these subjects. "The World of Dreams", for example, is usually passed over as a superficial and conventional exercise in a time-honoured genre. But the movement and the suggestiveness of the verbal activity beneath the surface of the poem is often under-estimated. It provides a revealing slant on "Pope in worsted stockings". Crabbe is writing here with immediacy and personal conviction: the poem is vital to a study of his attitudes towards derangement and dreams, and towards the material he thought appropriate for poetry.

His sleep-world is an unpredictable fusion of nightmare and joy, and "Spirits of Ill" haunt his unconscious mind. He attributes his dreams to "Quick Fancy", and the rational and sober tenor of his daily life is laid on one side.

> . . . all is gloom, or all is gay,
> Soon as th'ideal World I gain.
> ("The World of Dreams", stanza ii)

Apart from the inherent struggle between the instinctive and the rational, one senses the conscious effort Crabbe made to restrain a naturally excitable temperament which may well have prompted this release in sleep. His excitability is well illustrated by his reaction to the sudden appearance of a meteor during a ride near Beccles in 1783:

> He had raised himself from his horse, lifted his arm, and spread his hand toward the object of admiration and terror, and appeared transfixed with astonishment.　　　　　　　　　(*Life*, p. 35)

This note is by George Crabbe junior. His evocation of contrasts between light and shade in the narration of this episode is curiously similar to his father's practice in his poetry. The words may be a recollection of the poet's own description. Such spontaneous reactions are rare with Crabbe. There is usually a moral undertow to his response to nature. Say what we will of release from tension, and indulgence of notions inconsistent with the parish priest's waking round, the impression we are left with is that these disturbing emotions, of which dreams are one kind, come from an uneasy conscience. In "The World of Dreams", "My sin" (stanza iv) leads Crabbe into this interior world. The first-mentioned of his ill-spirited visions embodies the alienation and rejection themes so applicable to his early years of struggle. All turns sour, just as it did in the dream recorded in prose in the London Journal. Even the brother he lost in his youth

> ... meets me with hard-glazèd eyes!
> He quits me—spurns me—with disdain.
> ("The World of Dreams", stanza x)

The brother mentioned here is possibly William Crabbe, who also inspired "The Parting Hour" (*Tales*, II), and whose adventures seem to have suggested to Crabbe the themes of journeying and parting which occur so often in his poetry. Memories of an early incident in which Crabbe was nearly drowned may help to account for the constant brooding pre-occupation with water as an overwhelming force in his dream poetry. In stanza xiv the poet describes his dream-sensation of drowning in language curiously similar to that with which his son describes the real-life accident. There is yet another of these drowning episodes in *Tales of the Hall*, IV. Richard, the "liberated" brother, was washed overboard during his first trip to sea. Though I can find no direct reference to Crabbe reading Cowper's *The Castaway*, there are marked similarities in the descriptions the two poets give of the experience, and both see it as a trauma, equivalent to a living death. Alternations of light and dark, varied animation and suspension, characterise the Crabbe description, and make it akin to the opium world, the world of the "other" self, (*Tales of the Hall*, IV, 209–33). It may also be worth noting the narrow escape Crabbe had from being asphyxiated while still at school, as helping to explain the same re-iterative dream-notion. Yet autobiography takes on a new significance within the context of the poems. The struggle against nature, the fear of instability, and the sense of oppressive forces around the personality suggested by the drowning imagery are revealing insights into Crabbe's temperament and his creative impulses.

Irrational motion and suspension, water, darkness, rejection: all
these elements are present in "The World of Dreams", together
with "gothic" trappings, but their fusion into a self-revelatory experience is new and startling, qualitatively akin to *Christabel* or
The Ancient Mariner. "Where am I Now?" is another personal
testimony to the potency of the poet's own dreams. He describes
how he dozes in his chaise on the way to a social encounter (em-
bodying the theme of warmth and acceptance), and undergoes a
series of chastening hallucinatory experiences (arising, apparently,
out of a fear of rejection, scorn, and coldness). The verse suggests
the haste and flickering light, already noted as a characteristic of
his derangement poetry, and fuses the real ride with its dream-
substitute.

> ... whither ...
> In this deep Road, with Oaks on either Side,
> And these tall stately Trees, on w^h the Rays
> Of the Moon fall? they have their foliage dyed
> With that sweet Light! That now the Branches hide
> And there admit! & as we swiftly move,
> The shifting Scenes approach & past us glide,
> And the Mind wanders in her Worlds above.
>
> ("Where am I Now?", lines 10–17)

Even Thomas, the poet's coachman, becomes confused with

> Thomas true of Ercledom,
> When He beheld his Elfin Love
> Rode fast to her delicious Home,
> Where Satan once a Year w^d come
> To fetch some Guest to his Abode,
> From fairy light to fatal Gloom.
>
> (lines 28–33)

Delight and the devil, (how suggestive the unexpected adjective
"delicious" is in this context), light and gloom, safety and danger
—here again are all the elements of Crabbe's dream world.

At last the poet arrives at a mansion (as he expects to in his
waking state), but the dream palace is significantly altered:

> ... numerous Lights are bursting on ye View
> From Every Window of a mighty Dome,
> And Every Light is a lovely Hue.
>
> (lines 44–6)

195

This palace of pleasure, so reminiscent of Xanadu, is surrounded by a garden of fear, a garden which contains the now familiar "Water, wide and clear" and where the deer (images of true nature) cower mysteriously "Behind the Statues dimly seen" (images of the artificial world). No sooner does the poet enter this mansion than the inhabitants flee, and their seductive music and dance melt into the vision of a gloomy corridor down which resounds the iron tongue of a bell "as tolling for the newly dead". At last the dreamer is led into the ominous presence of a monk who tempts him:

> . . . let me help you while I may,
> The golden Minutes giv'n Embrace,
> (lines 152–3)

The Tempter knows of the "strong Desire! That lives in thy unquiet Breast" and a struggle between the poet's spiritual and sensual appetites ensues. Even when he has rejected the temptation he is left in doubt and fear: there is no final relief and purgation.

> Above a Bridge my Carriage flies,
> Above a River broad & slow,
> Or is it not the Night fogs rise
> Above the Fen that spreds below?
> Hark, do not sullen Waters flow
> With Murmur indistinct? . . .
> (lines 229–34)

The poem breaks off soon after this but even in its fragmentary state its value cannot be over-emphasised. It is the clearest and most immediate testimony we have of Crabbe's hyper-sensitive involvement in his dream world, its workings, and its implications. Nor is it possible to read this deeply personal and private poetry without believing that he knows perfectly well what he is doing, and that he is aware of the symbols which come to his subconscious mind.

IX

Many of the poems so far used in illustration for this chapter are not in Crabbe's normal couplets. This in itself is significant.

It is not merely that he wants a more "romantic" medium; he seems to write these poems from immediate and personally urgent impulses other than those which control the verse tales, and the poetry ebbs and flows spontaneously with the emotional tempo of the feelings expressed. The dreams are concerned with the throwing-off of restraint, and the verse itself echoes this. "Where am I Now?" goes to the limit of this metrical freedom; it has no regular stanzaic pattern at all.

Perhaps the most extraordinary of all the poems in this group is "The Insanity of Ambitious Love". It tells the story of the derangement caused by unnatural pride working in a weak nature. The subject of the tale dwells completely in a world of his own creation, and through indulgence of his wish-fulfilment he loses control of both himself and his imagination. In many ways he is the direct precursor of Peer Gynt in demonstrating the poetic force which fantasy can breed. Even more disturbing than the graphic skill with which Crabbe delineates this strange aberration is his ability to project the reader into the madman's world: an ability to move beyond clinical observation towards empathetic re-enactment of the scene. We lose ourselves with the madman in his curious tissue of related sense and nonsense. Indeed, it is not until the concluding stanzas that we are led to doubt his claim to be the son of a wealthy industrialist, though even this claim proves false at last. The poem is an extension of Crabbe's personal dreams—never very far from the truth, never mere extravaganza, and "still with a formidable resemblance" to the waking world. The motive-spring of "The Insanity of Ambitious Love" is the moral struggle between pride and reason, and for all its lurid trappings, it is a most earnest and serious exercise. It describes

> . . . a Being . . . so vain
> That hungry, naked, in reproach, in pain,
> His Load of Anguish was at times forgot,
> And he could, glorying, bless his happy Lot.
> While Reason thus was driven from her Seat
> He would his favourites to his House intreat;
> To his Hall's Splendor . . .
> His Flights were all ye true poetic breed;
> The Dream of Madness is a Dream indeed.
>
> (lines 5–11 and 28–9)

This terrible self-willed delusion caused by discontentment in an ambitious and selfish mind has come to comprise the protagonist's entire world. He claims that it is scorn for the humdrum routine of his father's mill which leads him to aspire to Byronic adventures. Through pride he loses humanity, and engages upon a course of callous seductions—or at least, subsequently claims that he has done so. Such reduction of heartless people through the inner workings of conscience is a frequent theme in Crabbe's poetry. It is only at the conclusion that we learn that all these circumstantial details are part of the delusion. The maniac is in fact the son of a poor ploughman, whose unrewarded honesty has offended the grasping son.

Despite his amorous success (real or imaginary) the madman's pride urges him to seek supernatural power and knowledge to further his advancement. He consults a gypsy fortune-teller. As the narrator now becomes heated by his own fancy, reality and vision become fused. The Gypsy-Queen becomes a dual persona, both real and metaphorical. The same figure appears in "Where am I Now?" as the tempter monk who, again, can see the future but offers only a world of sybaritic self-indulgence. It is hard to resist the conclusion that the figure is a projection of Crabbe's own worldly self, a self which the priest in him would wish to repress. To reach the lair of this daemon the aspirant passes through an ambiguous landscape—one by now familiar to the student of Crabbe's dream and delusion poetry.

> I past By [?Tentry's] Spire and Street,
>   I past her River soft & slow,
> And woods wherein the wild-Deer's feet
>   Bruize the broom Moss that spreads below,
> And I had past the Abbey's Walls,
>   Where all confess the Fairies be,
> Till I could hear the distant Calls
>   Of Sailors rowing in the Sea.
>
>   (lines 102–9)

He passes, in fact, from the solid and peopled world of religion and social intercourse into the egocentric world of his own pride and delusion. As in "Where am I Now?" there is a journey through a mysterious passage filled with the ominous echoes and with

198

"Strange Fire that shone with coloured Blaze" and again, as in the other poem, a dance of revellers disappears to leave the visionary alone with his mentor.

He is shown an almost mediaeval panorama of the world at work—a vision called forth from his own proud rejection of law, order, and oeconomy. Through the pride of his warped judgement mankind's lot appears as a brutal and degrading drudgery.

> Poor jaundic'd Men at sick'ning Trades,
>   I saw, in Palsies, half Alive,
> Soon to depart, & now but Shades,
>   And those yet fated to survive,
>   Intent with idle Hopes to thrive,
> All servile in their Thrift, & mean—
>   "Enough! dear Guide," said I "contrive
> To shift this Soul-appalling Scene."
>   (lines 264–71)

The Temptress, in answer to this exhortation shows him, instead, a "bower of bliss"—which is obviously a delusory extension of his own appetites and desires.

> There came not Hymen to this Seat,
>   Jealous & vex'd at Lover's Joy,
> There came not Avarice to intreat
>   Reluctant Youth to mean Employ,
>   (lines 312–15)

The maniac, it must be remembered, is in his delusion-world awaiting the arrival of his mistress, another man's wife. He accepts the world offered by the sibyl and she ominously declares

> "Thou hast of no Instruction need;
>   The Dictates of the Heart obey."
>   (lines 350–1)

This marks the culmination of the delusion. The maniac boasts to the onlookers that the mistress he awaits is a countess who regards him alone as worthy of her person. But here the impatience of the two witnesses breaks his dream, and they reveal to us the true state of affairs:

> Be still; then madly vile & proud,
>   Wilt thou thy Father disallow?

199

A parish Clerk that sang aloud,
  An honest Man that drove a plough!
  And a vain, worthless Servant thou,
Who dar'd to gaze with sinful View
  On One *whose pity feeds thee now,*
Thy Lady pious, pitious, true.
                    (lines 384–91)

The horror evoked is a moral and valid one, not a mere morbid sensationalism. The strong contrasts help to bring this about—honesty set against wilful delusion, chastity against lust, pity against self-interest. Furthermore the Christian values here stressed have been so signally absent during the nightmare course of the story that they now strike us with redoubled force. Crabbe's sense of dramatic timing, a feature of the conduct of most of his best tales, is well illustrated. The horror too, is enhanced through the sudden realisation that the phantasmagoric vision which the reader has been led to share with the maniac has been woven entirely by blind pride out of a madman's cell, and out of an effigy he has made from "straw . . . chips and Sticks . . ." The impression that we are all close to this state, that sanity is a tenuous rope to which we cling through the blinding fog of our passions and desires, guided only by faith, gives the poem a disturbing slant. Indeed, this little known poem is the most powerful of all Crabbe's studies of delusion. Its blending of the real and the delusory is consummate. It also avoids Jeffrey's criticism of "Sir Eustace Grey" that

> there is something too elaborate and too much worked-up in the picture

if, as I believe, Jeffrey means by this that the technique of "Sir Eustace" is too obviously controlled and regular to be entirely appropriate to its theme. "The Insanity of Ambitious Love" creates an atmosphere of spontaneity which the earlier "Sir Eustace" lacks, and its moral implications are more searching.

x

Not all Crabbe's works on delusion and hallucination are as stark as those so far discussed, which seem to derive their atmosphere directly from the poet's own experiences. Many of the evil-doers in his tales approach the borders of derangement without ever crossing over. "The Struggles of Conscience" (*Tales*, XIV) exemplifies this type. Fulham, its subject of scrutiny, is a trader who, by luck and fraud combined, contrives to build up a fortune. The poem hinges upon the constant war between Fulham the worldly-wise, and the voice of probity which is his conscience. There is a good deal of sardonic humour in the processes by which poor Conscience is duped, drugged, and double-crossed. But the effect of the constant war—of continual guilt-repression—is ultimately a serious one. From ironic and remote mockery the tone changes to one of reproof as Fulham reduces himself to near-insanity.

> Such was his life—no other changes came,
> The hurrying day, the conscious night the same;
> The night of horror—when he, starting, cried
> To the poor startled sinner at his side:
> "Is it in law? am I condemn'd to die?
> "Let me escape!—I'll give—oh! let me fly—
> "How! but a dream—no judges! dungeon! chain!
> "Or these grim men!—I will not sleep again.—
> "Wilt thou, dread being! thus thy promise keep?
> "Day is thy time—and wilt thou murder sleep?
> "Sorrow and want repose, and wilt thou come,
> "Nor give one hour of pure untroubled gloom?
>   (*Tales*, XIV, lines 480–91)

Editors have often taken too little heed of Crabbe's punctuation. Mercifully, the son seems to have left this passage well alone, and the impact of the constant stops and starts gives a dramatic sense of the disturbance of Fulham's rest.

The passage is full of Shakespearian echoes. The movement of the verse is much akin to that used by the dying Cardinal in *2 Henry VI*, III, 3, and the suggestion of remorse vainly at work is furthered by the echo of Macbeth in line ten. "Conscious night" suggests both the inability of Fulham to sleep, and the participation of Nature in the punishment of his villainy. Fulham's vision is one in which no judges appear to see justice done. This is singularly appropriate to one whose crimes have all been self-generated. Thus by imaginative redeployment of standard material Crabbe is able to create a fresh and startling impact; an impact with clear and rigorous moral implications.

The outburst quoted above follows Fulham's deliberate prostitution of his wife in order to contrive a divorce from the feeble and unfortunate wretch whom he married only for her fortune. "The restless enmity within" of Conscience thus destroys everything for which Fulham had ignored and betrayed her. His state of torment is much akin to that of Crabbe's madmen and dreamers and is best understood in this context even though the derangement is not here extended to its limits. Fulham is punished more by being kept under the threat of insanity than he would be by a release into that state.

While Fulham exemplifies the near-deranged guilt of remorse, "The Mother" (*Tales*, VIII) provides example of a different course of mental disturbance. Humiliation and disappointment lead Lucy, the heroine, close to the boundaries of insanity. The poem's psychological force and validity lies in the insight with which its characters are exposed and judged, and especially in the aptness with which Lucy falls prey to melancholia. In normal circumstances her pliant temper would not have been disturbed; but thwarted love makes her dangerously strong in that it provides a centre of tension and dogmatism in a mind unfitted for passionate struggle. When the lover abandons Lucy because of the interference of her mother, the girl has nothing to fall back on but a rejection of the world which takes the appropriate form of religious delusion. The poem is a perfect example of the claustrophobic and introverted world into which Crabbe's subjects of scrutiny are often forced, while the enforcement itself leads towards derangement and extra-normal sensibility. It also shows the range of Crabbe's understanding, and one of the more important sides of his much discussed "realism". It is true of real life that the innocent suffer as often as the guilty, and Crabbe is not afraid to point this out. Here again moral conviction underlies poetic craftsmanship.

Natures such as Lucy's are frequently examined in his work; natures unable to face the brutal pressures to which ironic circumstances subjects them; natures retreating defensively into a world of their own creation. Disappointment destroyed both John, the patronised boy in *Tales*, V, and Robin Dingley (*The Parish*

Register, "Burials"), through its operation on a particular weakness of character. Edward Shore (*Tales*, XI) portrays the tragedy of a "vascillating (sic) mind" led to the sin of inflated self-esteem, calling from Jeffrey the following comment:

> The ultimate downfall of this lofty mind, with its agonising gleams of transitory recollection, form a picture, than which we do not know if the whole range of our poetry, . . . furnishes anything more touching, or delineated with more truth and delicacy.
>
> (*Life*, p. 325)

Again in this poem the trappings and mechanics of derangement have a mordant, almost brutal aptness. Shore sins through pride inspired by over-estimation of his own talents and he is reduced in the end to mere childishness:

> Simple and weak, he acts the boy once more,
> And heedless children call him *Silly Shore*.
> (*Tales*, XI, lines 466–7)

XI

It must be observed that in all these studies there has been no mention of congenital idiocy. Crabbe never writes of the village simpleton, although as parish doctor and parish priest he must have encountered the phenomenon frequently. There are no Johnny Foys in his work because he sees no occasion for moral instruction arising out of this particular misfortune. "Rachel" (*Posthumous Tales*, IV) is closest to this kind of insanity, and the poem is unsatisfactory precisely because of its lack of moral direction. It is what no other of Crabbe's derangement studies descends to be —a mere macabre fantasy.

For the main part, then, Crabbe's work of delusion, derangement and hallucination reveals the author as a shrewd and sympathetic student of his fellow men, firmly if anxiously clinging to a belief in Reason, but evincing a personal strain of melancholia and doubt which illuminates his poetry with profound insight.

> Man upon man depends, and break the chain,
> He soon returns to savage life again;
> (*Posthumous Tales*, II, lines 76–7)

The causes of the breaking of the chain are manifold, as are its effects; both in the range and in the depth of his understanding of delusion and derangement Crabbe occupies an important place among the English poets. The studies of insanity add a new, and hitherto neglected dimension to any appreciation of his work.

7

'To Make Us Better or Wiser'

"Well turned periods in eloquence, or harmony in numbers . . .
however highly we may esteem them, can never be considered
as of equal importance with the art of unfolding truths that are
useful to mankind, and which make us better or wiser."

(Reynolds, *Discourse VII*)

I

For an author who was so prolific, the amount of space Crabbe
devoted to describing and analysing his own art is small. For the
main part his Prefaces are uninformative. He likes his sense of
structure to be elicited from his material, and in a theorising
exercise like a preface, he cannot write in that way. Hence we
shall look in vain for the rigorous kind of defence which Wordsworth attempted of his misunderstood art in the Preface to
Lyrical Ballads. Nor, for better or worse, is Crabbe so consumed
by an overriding concern for poesy that it spills over into his
letters, making them the source of information which those of
Keats or of Clare can be.

The poems and the prefaces do sometimes give us clues to his
thoughts about his work though. In the little poem called "Satire"
Crabbe deplores that kind of poetry which seeks to be specific
in condemnation of particular persons. Though the *Rejected
Addresses* extract a moment of splendid fun from this lothness to
name names, one feels that Crabbe is right, or that he has judged
his own temperament aright:

> Attack a book—attack a song—
> You will not do essential wrong;

205

You may their blemishes expose,
And yet not be the writer's foes.
But, when the man you thus attack
  And him expose with critic art,
You put a creature to the rack—
  You wring, you agonise, his heart.
No farther honest Satire can
  In all her enmity proceed,
Than, passing by the wicked Man,
  To execrate the wicked Deed.
              ("Satire", stanza ii, *Ward*, p. 398)

This is helpful, as far as it goes, and when one sets it against later
prefaces, where there is not any mention of satire at all, but rather
an earnest consideration of "atmosphere" in character drawing,
one sees a recognition by the poet that his methods and his objectives have shifted. We have already seen—at the beginning of
"Ellen Orford", for instance—that there are plenty of illustrations
of Crabbe's literary taste scattered through his poetry. They have
a direct relationship to the purely self-criticising remarks. The
love/scorn feelings which popular ballads and folk-tales arouse
in Crabbe's mind are the more important because the poems remind us of them so frequently, though the prefaces never do! In
the letters too, though there are few serious discussions of poetic
techniques or ideas, there are occasional glimpses of his methods,
and strong suggestions that Crabbe had a regular stream of corres-
pondents who sent him stories, which he versified. These were
often lurid episodes, as can be seen in "Lady Barbara" (*Tales of
the Hall*, XVI), which had been sent to Crabbe from a correspondent in Wiltshire.

Mary Leadbeater asked Crabbe outright what proportion of his
tales were "invented", and how many of his characters were based
on people he really knew. The poet answers:

Yes! I will tell you readily about my Creatures, whom I endeavoured
to paint as nearly as I could, and *dare*—for in some cases I dared
not. This you will readily admit; besides Charity bade me be
cautious: thus far you are correct. There is not one of whom I had
not in my mind the Original, but I was obliged in most cases to
take them from their real situations and in one or two instances
even to change the sex and in many the circumstances; the nearest

to real life was the proud ostentatious man in The Borough, who disguised a little mind by doing great things; yet others were approaching to reality at greater or less distances: indeed I do not know that I could paint merely from my own Fancy and there is no cause why we should. Is there not diversity sufficient in Society? And who can go, even but a little, into the assemblies of our fellow Wanderers from the way of perfect rectitude and not find characters so varied and so pointed that he need not call upon his imagination.

dated 1 December, 1816.

(B.L. ms. Eg. 3709.b)

More of this would be helpful, but we do not get very much more.

II

Among the poems, we have a very early attempt by Crabbe to identify and describe his objectives and methods. He wrote *The Candidate* in 1779–80, and below all its jejeune and stilted mannerisms one can discern an element of genuine self-scrutiny. Crabbe wrote many a better poem, but he certainly wrote few which are more consciously personal than this one, and it is capable of telling us quite a lot about his art at this early stage in his career.

What an extraordinary poem *The Candidate* is! Nothing could be more gauche, more crass than the conception of this piece. In effect, the poem says to the reviewers, "Please do you think I could write poetry if I set my mind and my talents to the task?"; but instead of the poetic epistle giving a proper sample of that poetry by demonstrating it in practice, the letter itself has to serve as appeal and evidence. Yet there is no doubt that the poem epitomises an element in Crabbe's make-up which we have to understand if we are to encounter the full range of his art. He remained, for the whole of his creative life, very close to his readers. It is not actually a pulpit manner which he has, but it is the manner of a man who is used to talking directly to people. His prefaces, as a whole, are characterised by this note: as late as *Tales of the Hall* he can write that Prefaces are never read, they are a bore, and established authors have no need or excuse for them at all . . . yet here is a preface! This is the same huffingly factual mind which must break off its narrative to reassure us that, whatever the appeerence of things, he means no personal animus to be drawn from his attack on Sects in *The Borough*, or that material is appearing in a certain place because otherwise it might never have appeared at all:

> For the Alms-House itself, its Governors, and Inhabitants, I have not much to offer in favour of the subject or of the character. One of these, Sir Denys Brand, may be considered as too highly placed for an author, who seldom ventures above middle life, to delineate; and, indeed, I had some idea of reserving him for another occasion, where he might have appeared with those in his own rank: but then it is most uncertain whether he would ever appear, and he has been so many years prepared for the public, whenever opportunity might offer, that I have at length given him place . . .   (*Life*, p. 223)

There is a quaint factuality about this mind, which may at first sight suit ill with the "first moral poet of the age". Only a reading which can reconcile the sophistication with the simplicity in Crabbe has any chance of getting to the basis of his art, either in message itself, or in the execution.

Both sides are there in embryo in *The Candidate*. It is worth a closer look, both because the poem is so early—one of the first extended uses of Crabbe's couplets that we have—and because it has, in patches, more merit than either the contemporary critics allowed it, or later commentators have seen fit to accord it. Perhaps the first point to make is that Crabbe patently failed to follow the promise he made in the poem. He offers this odd first-born child to the scrutiny of the world, declaring that, should the judgement go against him, he will retire, discomfited but duly chastened, and write no more. I do not think, in fact, that the most optimistic author could have drawn much comfort from the review notices *The Candidate* achieved: the *Monthly Review*, to whom it was addressed, found little to praise though its half-hearted encouragement came, interestingly, from Cartwright, who was to become a close friend of Crabbe ten years later, through the fortuitous circumstance of having a neighbouring parish.

The Candidate opens with a brief introduction in which the author prepares to send off one of his poems to act as ambassador for all the rest, and to make his plea for recognition. The language is, on the surface, that dreary verbiage which, in the mouths of the poetasters of the previous forty years, had been

wearing thinner and thinner. The grand generalisations are par-
aded—"Genius", "Fancy"—and the stereotyped concepts are
trotted out in their neatly pre-packaged forms. His secular love
poetry has been

> Taught but to sing, and that in simple style,
> Of Lycia's lip, and Musidora's smile.
> > (*The Candidate*, Introductory Address,
> > lines 7–8)

The personae chosen to illustrate poetic vices are, very significantly, not those of 1775 but of 1725—Cibber and Blackmore—
whilst the geography of the poem is that of Pope's London, not of
Crabbe's Aldeburgh: "mad Moorfields, or sober Chancery Lane".
The very manner itself might seem to be a generation behind the
times. The verse strives for polished epigram, and achieves only a
flailing antithesis:

> Praise without meanness, without flattery stoop,
> Soothe without fear, and without trembling hope.
> > (lines 45–6)

And yet, if the passage contains all too blatantly the faults which
remained in Crabbe's work for the rest of his life, it also, at whatever obscure distance, suggests some of his merits as well. Its very
oddness suggests that behind the stereotypes of language there is
an original mind at work. There are flashes of self-awareness, as
when Crabbe calls his poems an "eccentric race", traces of the
insight with which he can surprise us, of the beautifully exact eye
with which he can observe the scene around him, as here, where
he is describing a neglected bookshelf:

> . . . where spiders silent bards enrobe,
> Squeezed betwixt Cibber's Odes and Blackmore's Job;
> Where froth and mud, that varnish and deform,
> Feed the lean critic and the fattening worm;
> > (*ibid.*, lines 17–20)

That, in its way, is worthy of a better context, of a more sustained background to carry it along. No blame, I think, attaches
to the *Monthly Review* for not seeing the merit of such writing
at the time. It is only in retrospect that one apprehends how

Crabbe-like those four lines are, with their ability to make metaphor take on an almost uncomfortably tactile reality.

The main part of the poem is a similar mixture of tumid and
hackneyed platitudes, occasionally interspersed with uncut jewels.
There is not much remarkable in the execution, perhaps, but the
intention and the message which strive to come through, are very
interesting. Behind all the absurd disavowal and the circumlocutory machinery, Crabbe seems to know, even in 1775, the sort
of poet he wants and intends to be:

> ... a bard, who, neither mad nor mean,
> Despises each extreme, and sails between;
> (*The Candidate*, lines 21–2)

Furthermore, through the clumsy allegorical trappings which
stultify the real vigour which the piece has in places, one can
discern a shrewd assessment of where his own strengths will lie.
After confessing that his early failures may have had a salutary
effect on his style and manner, the poet attempts to define the
areas of experience with which he wishes to deal. Turning away
from the allegorical creature with whom he has been conversing,
Crabbe adopts a much more serious tone:

> For O! thou, Hope's—thou, Thought's eternal King,
> Who gav'st them power to charm, and me to sing,
> Chief to thy praise my willing numbers soar,
> And in my happier transports I adore;
> Mercy thy softest attribute proclaim,
> Thyself in abstract, thy more lovely name;
> That flings o'er all my grief a cheering ray,
> As the full moon-beam gilds the watery way.
> And then too, Love, my soul's resistless lord,
> Shall many a gentle, generous strain afford ...
> (*ibid.*, lines 174–83)

Love and Mercy are indeed to be cornerstones of Crabbe's
writing throughout the long years ahead. The love will take very
different forms from those he adumbrates in *The Candidate*, but
as late as 1826 we can still see him following this programme in
the posthumously published "Poins" (*New Poems*, pp. 97–125),
and if lack of love as expressed through betrayal and indifference

is to become the burden of his tragedies, it is of great interest to trace his awareness of the importance of it back to this very early stage in *The Candidate*. The disclaimers of his later prefaces about his inability to write on patriotic or epic themes go back to *The Candidate* too, whilst in its periphrastic way it gives a shrewd account of the process of self-preparation and dedication that the poet must undergo before he may be a serious exponent of his testing craft. The melange of outdated embroidery and the clumsy allegorising should not blind us to what the poem can tell us about Crabbe and his poetry. There is a good deal of debate between the two sides of his own nature foreshadowed here. He hankers after the comfortable old world which existed in the ideal landscape created by Salvator Rossa, James Thomson, and Mrs Radcliffe, in unholy alliance, though he clearly sees the dangers inherent in this fanciful world where control, discipline, and all the qualities he sums up as "Virtue" are wilfully held in abeyance. This takes us right to the heart of his mind and art as they are presented in his mature work, for the "stern moralist" in Crabbe is always at war with a sybaritic appetite in his rebellious other self. Poems like "Poins" or "The Struggles of Conscience" represent the enactment of this debate.

The remarks he makes on technique in *The Candidate* are also of some interest. By and large Crabbe was regrettably less informative on this area of the poet's craft than on any other, and it is left for the anecdotes and judgements of Rogers and Fitzgerald to temper our assessment of the craftsman in Crabbe. Rogers of course reported him thus:

> Crabbe's early poetry is by far the best as to *finish* . . . I asked him why he did not compose his later verses with equal care. He answered, "Because my reputation is already made".
>
> (J. P. Clayden, *Samuel Rogers and his Circle*, 1910, pp. 136–7)

It would be quite wrong to see this as the whole truth of Crabbe's attitude to composition:

> Oft would he strive for words, and often begin
> To frame in verse the views he had within;
> But ever fail'd: for how can words explain
> The unform'd ideas of a teeming brain?
> ("Silford Hall", *Posthumous Poems*, I,
> lines 170–3)

211

He continued striving to polish and to shape his work until the very end, and he took pride in getting it right. Even when on holiday in London as late as 1817, he takes himself to task if he falls short of his allotted number of lines: "My thirty lines done; but not well I fear; thirty daily is the self-engagement" (*Life*, p. 69). A few days later he reproves himself again: "Thirty lines today but not yesterday: must work up," and two days later again: "Make up my thirty lines for yesterday and today." These are entries from the London Journal of July 1817, when Crabbe was at work upon *Tales of the Hall*, but under no particular pressure except that which his own creative urge put upon him. That urge seems to have been stronger in old age than it had been in his youth. Typically, when he has to go to an oratorio, he manages an extra stint: "23rd (July). A vile engagement to an oratorio at church, by I know not how many noisy people; women as well as men. Luckily I sat where I could write unobserved, and wrote forty lines" (*Life*, p. 71). On holiday in Scotland in 1823, he insisted to Sir Walter Scott's wife that he must have a night-light lest he should miss the chance of getting on paper the thoughts which might come during the hours of darkness.

III

The notebooks and fascicles which contain much of his verse in manuscript are the most eloquent testimony of Crabbe's diligence and of his discrimination. When a subject engaged his imagination he worked and worked at it, until he was satisfied that it bore the stamp he wished it to carry. This is far less uniformly the stamp of the heroic couplet than is sometimes imagined. He often began with a prose outline of the fable, then tried as many as half-a-dozen metres before finding the one appropriate to the story as it was evolving. And in several cases, he has deliberately mixed patterns, where the effect of ballad or lyric rhythms are contrasted with the timbre of the heroic line. The established canon of poems—the ones selected by the poet in his lifetime and added to by his son in the 1834 *Collected Works*—is a little misleading as an impression of what Crabbe actually wrote; of the proportion of his work which is in measures other than that couplet we associate him with. The *New Poems* are helpful in reminding us that Crabbe can use metrical variety most effectively. "Where am I Now?", which I have discussed in Chapter 6 principally for the content of the poem, furnishes a good illustration of the rhythmic ingenuity he can employ. The poem begins, as it were, in the world of Trollope, with the elderly narrator—presumably Parson Crabbe himself—dozing on the way to a party:

> Where am I now? I slept to wake again
> And to forget. O now I recollect.
> I'm in a Chaise that takes me o'er a Plain,
> Of Eaton Bassett, where my Friends expect
> That I shall sleep, & where they now collect,
> Three & our Host. Ah! joyful shall we meet,
> And there discarding Thoughts of Party, Sect,
> We shall at once be merry & discreet,
> Our moments all will tell, & every one be Sweet.
> ("Where am I Now?", lines 1–9)

This is so low-keyed, and so matter of fact, that the quasi-Spenserian form in which it is couched seems most odd. The second stanza, in which a nervousness and a change of atmosphere sweeps the poem, is itself "nervous", being one line shorter than the first one, and much more atmospheric. Then, as the familiar countryside of Eaton Bassett and Canon Bowles' comfortable rectory recedes, the patterning of the poem becomes more and more fey. Even the "romantic" Spenserian form melts and transforms into pure ballad measure, associated in Crabbe's mind with the tales of his childhood, and with folk-lore, magic, and imaginative release. Both poet and the mysterious interlocutor to whom he is introduced, continue to use this metre until Crabbe, struggling through the mists of his dream-world, recognises his adversary.

> "It is the Tempter!", so I thought!
> (*ibid.*, line 179)

Once recognised, the figure changes its speech rhythm back to that with which the poem opened, as though the act of exorcism allows Crabbe back to the safety of his stanza pattern. After Crabbe banishes this spectre there is a brief return to the hurried octosyllables as his coach dashes onward:

213

And now we hurry thro' ye Park,
   Like Lenora in dark Midnight,
Who, boldly mounted in her Sark
   On fiery Steed with fleshless Knight,
   Intent on Love! & wild with fright,
Trampt, Trampt. The Hills behind them flee,
   They leave ye Land, & in their flight
   Splash, Splash, Acros ye restless Sea.

                        (*ibid.*, lines 211–9)

It is more than the trappings of fear and ghostly ride which reminds one of Schubert's "The Erl King". The music achieves atmospheric and rhythmic effects similar to those which Crabbe seems to be after in his poem. We have journeyed from the world of Barchester to that of Xanadu, through these extraordinary metrical aberrations.

Were this poem unique in Crabbe's work we might argue that it is still in a raw state, and would have eventually been moulded back into couplet form, but there is quite enough verse like "Where am I Now?", using the same techniques of metrical break, juxtaposition, and dislocation, for us to be sure that we are watching Crabbe consciously and deliberately striving for special effect when he writes in this manner. "The Hall of Justice", which had been written as early as 1798, has a similar, if less extreme sense of changing pulse-beat behind it. Couched in dialogue form, the Magistrate has a simple four-line stanza as his norm for nearly the entire length of the poem, whilst the Vagrant, appropriately, has a more wandering, freer medium of expression. At the very end of the poem when the Magistrate is most moved and most eloquent, there is a final shift into yet another stanza pattern, where the two voices are assimilated within the textural design. "Sir Eustace Grey" has a similar dramatic structure, and again, when the patient approaches his spiritual crisis, the rhythm of the verse changes, for Sir Eustace has experienced "a methodistic call". Crabbe has, with great skill, caught the timbre as well as the language of "enthusiasm":

            "Pilgrim, burthen'd with thy sin,
            "Come the way to Zion's gate,
            "There, till Mercy let thee in,
            "Knock and weep, and watch and wait.

"Knock!—He knows the sinner's cry;
"Weep!—He loves the mourner's tears;
"Watch!—for saving grace is nigh;
"Wait!—till heavenly light appears.
("Sir Eustace Grey", stanza xliv)

As Crabbe grew older he seems to have become more free in the readiness with which he introduced measures other than the couplet into his poems. "The Sisters" (*Tales of the Hall,* VIII) ends with a gently irregular lyric put into the mouth of Jane, disappointed, melancholic, and indulging a "romantic" disposition. The process by which composition as therapy and as doctrine becomes confused in her mind is well worth illustration, since covertly it may well tell us something about Crabbe's own attitudes.

"Jane, as these melancholy fits invade
"The busy fancy, seeks the deepest shade;
"She walks in ceaseless hurry, till her mind
"Will short repose in verse and music find;
"Then her own songs to some soft tune she sings,
"And laughs, and calls them melancholy things;
"Not frenzy all; in some her erring Muse
"Will sad, afflicting, tender strains infuse;
"Sometimes on death she will her lines compose,
"Or give her serious page of solemn prose;
"And still those favourite plants her fancy please,
"And give to care and anguish rest and ease.

" 'Let me not have this gloomy view,
" 'About my room, around my bed;
" 'But morning roses, wet with dew,
" 'To cool my burning brows instead.
" 'As flow'rs that once in Eden grew,
" 'Let them their fragrant spirits shed.
" 'And every day the sweets renew,
" 'Till I, a fading flower, am dead.
(*Tales of the Hall,* VIII, lines 793–844 *passim*)

There may be flaws in the execution of such a passage, but about the *concept* behind this piece of writing, there can be no doubt. Crabbe is trying to pull off something extremely ambitious and difficult—the fusion of rhythm, ideas, language and sound into the meaning of the poetry. Behind it lies a strong sense of the dramatic. That Crabbe had tried (and failed) to write novels is well enough known. But there are several manuscript fragments of dramas in the Murray collection, and Crabbe the would-be playwright is not a familiar figure. Surprisingly, perhaps, the play fragments are utterly dead. They have none of the vigour of observation or the finely judged speech timbre which makes the best of the narrative poetry so dramatic in its own right. "Why not insist on the unwelcome reality in plain prose?" asked Hazlitt (*The Spirit of the Age*, 1886, p. 312), and an equally apposite question would, at first sight, appear to be, "why not in dialogue for the stage?" If one gift more than any other lifts Crabbe into a special place where he has his own excellence, it is his ability to construct and interweave patterns for the speaking voice. At every occasion he will twist and manipulate the pattern of his narrative so that the characters speak for themselves. Sometimes he adds his own voice on top of the created ones, so that a complex pattern develops. The technique is already well-developed by the time of *The Parish Register* and in that poem one sees it coming to final maturity. The poem opens with the poet himself talking to us, and studiously disclaiming any voice or mode other than his own "natural" one:

> No Muse I ask, before my view to bring
> The humble actions of the swains I sing—
> (*The Parish Register*, "Baptisms", lines 7–8)

Both "Muse" and "sing"—the terminology of "poesy"—are used very suggestively by Crabbe here, with a quizzical look over his shoulder at the traditional manner in which rural subjects have hitherto been "sung" by poeticising bards. His is the voice of truth, not of poesy: "Full well I know—these records give the rest": hence the poem's normative tone is to lie between the personal voice of the parson–reporter and the factuality of the parish records he is conning. This insistence on defining the speaking tone of the poem leads Crabbe into a digression which is essentially a repetition of the burden he took up in *The Village*, for if a poet is to speak normatively about village life, then he must have a clear idea of what the village and its "reality" comprises. Hence he turns our face to the village street: "Behold the cot", and dives inside to investigate the ruling taste of the inhabitants. Crabbe describes the bookshelves, the furniture, and the ornaments he remembers from his own home—the passage is the more interesting for that. The point is that this virtual duplication of material in *The Village* is not an excrescence, it is a vital exordium, which controls the rather novel manner and matter of *The Parish Register* itself. Within the cottage there are royalist pictures—illustrating the kings of France as well as of England, and hence demonstrating the unshakeable conservatism of the peasant; Louis is used as a pictorial reminder to the cottage children of what will happen if they stray from the old-fashioned respect they should have for Authority! King Charles serves as a nearer reminder of the same sad lesson. Then we turn to the books of the cottage library:

> The tale for wonder, and the joke for whim,
> The half-sung sermon and the half-groaned hymn.
> ("Baptisms", lines 75–6)

There is an illustrated Bible, the inevitable copy of Bunyan, and, alongside these, works for interpreting dreams, moral fables, and the dross of "romanticism" in the form of broadsheets on The Wandering Jew, Tom Thumb, and Jack the Giant Killer. On such a curiously mixed diet is Crabbe's villager brought up. It is an accurate reflection of his own literary inheritance, and no assessment of him can afford to ignore his early diet of fairy tales and folk stories mixed with quaintly pictorial or emblematic works of popular instruction and dogma. He can speak with and view with the voice and eyes that belong to all these various genres.

The Parish Register is, then, most carefully designed to allow for various attitudes and tones, from which we are to draw inferences about the moral tenor of the episodes and characters discussed, and about the narrator. "Baptisms" proper—the part of the poem which begins with the description of Lucy, the miller's daughter—takes us straight into the mixed-voice structure on which the entire work is based. The intransigent miller, the carefree sailor, and the love-lorn maid each have their differentiated voices:

"For ah! my father has a haughty soul;
"Whom best he loves, he loves but to control . . ." (lines 309–10)

217

"Cheer up, my lass! I'll to thy father go—
"The Miller cannot be the Sailor's foe . . ." (lines 321–2)

"Ha!" quoth the Miller, moved at speech so rash
"Art thou like me? then, where thy notes and cash?" (lines 329–30)

The intense, brief, and economically detailed tragedy is largely
played out by these three voices, with that of the controlling narrator interspersed. Crabbe, at the climax of the episode, is stirred
enough to adopt yet another speaking voice, that of the poet who
is moved beyond mere reportage:

> Throughout the lanes she glides, at evening's close,
> And softly lulls her infant to repose;
> Then sits and gazes, but with viewless look,
> As gilds the moon the rippling of the brook;
> And sings her vespers, but in voice so low,
> She hears their murmurs as the waters flow:
>
> (lines 391–6)

This is a quite different voice from that of bustling Parson Crabbe,
thumbing over the year's doings in his vestry accounts.

He continues to intersperse his own persona with those of the
original voices of the parishioners he recorded. He has an alter-
cation with the village harlot, who has burdened the poor-rate
with yet another mouth to feed. The tone of musing sympathy
in the description of Lucy gives way to that of the parish priest
at his most irate:

> "Again, thou harlot! could not all thy pain,
> All my reproof, thy wanton thoughts restrain?"
> "Alas! Your reverence, wanton thoughts, I grant,
> Were once my motive, now the thoughts of want".
>
> (lines 451–4)

This is well-managed, for without ever losing the seriousness
with which he views such behaviour both socially and morally,
Crabbe is able to allow the village drab to come parlously near
having the best of the exchange. The semantic quibble with which
she answers his stern admonitory tone is exactly right for her.
Insolence, integrity, and self-assertion go into the framing of this
quibbling response. It is worthy of Shakespeare, from whom it
undoubtedly comes, at however many removes. No poet in the
Regency period (when, after all, Shakespeare studies received a

218

strong uplift from Hazlitt, Coleridge, Lamb and Keats), admired or understood him better than Crabbe did. It is significant that the *Tales* of 1812 were each individually prefaced by one or more epigraphs from the plays of Shakespeare—often from very obscure and *outré* places. Crabbe owes a great debt to Shakespeare, principally in this matter of the dramatic organisation of his speaking voices. He has the same ability to create from outside his own pre-determined viewpoint, and to give an authentic tone to people he hates as well as those he approves of.

The Parish Register's simple, list-like structure might have become tedious, but is kept alive and on the move by the range and variety of these voices. The controlling voice, that of the narrator himself, is able to assume degrees of involvement or distance, by the extent to which it follows or opposes the voice given to the character under scrutiny. Thus the pretentious gardener who gives his children names like Lonicera and Hyacinthus, can be set in exactly the right satiric context by the attention Crabbe gives to organising the voices which describe him. The parson and the gardener's wife have a brief exchange, then the parson comments in his own voice, and gradually allows this to melt into a tone where the manner of Erasmus Darwin is parodied in the voice of the gardener himself, as he talks of the arts of cross-pollination— an artificial voice for an artificial topic.

> Would you advance the nuptial hour, and bring
> The fruit of Autumn with the flowers of Spring;
> View that light frame where Cucumis lies spread,
> And trace the husbands in their golden bed,
> Three powder'd Anthers;—then no more delay,
> But to the Stigma's tip their dust convey;
> Then by thyself, from prying glance secure,
> Twirl the full tip and make your purpose sure;
> A long-abiding race the deed shall pay,
> Nor one unblest abortion pine away
>
> ("Baptisms", lines 645–54)

Crabbe lets him have his say, and the reality is even more deliciously absurd than the Darwinian original; the cross-currents of *poetic* pretence and *real-life* pretence become very complex, assuming a response from a well-read audience.

Conversely, the deliberate withholding of the speaking voice when we expect it, can be used for telling effect. The story of Richard Monday illustrates this. He is a foundling, foisted on an unwilling parish vestry, and, like Oliver Twist, he is made to experience the uncomfortable charity of "the Board". Though bare sustenance cannot be denied him, he is deprived of love, human intercourse and humane teaching. Despite this, he eventually thrives, and on his death is found, to the dismay of the parish officers, to have left all his wealth to charities outside the village, whilst the parsimonious and unlovesome Board are left enough to supply forty loaves to their poor each quarter day, and no more:

> A stinted gift, that to the parish shows
> He kept in mind their bounty and their blows!
> (lines 765–6)

Crabbe wishes to present this episode from a point of view where he can criticise the Vestry for their inhumanity, yet where he can suggest that Sir Richard may not be guiltless. His method of doing this is to allow direct speech to creep grudgingly and sparingly into the texture of the verse, and very obliquely at that. The parish officers are anonymous, cold, and officious. They are curiously distanced in the writing, though they are accorded the device of quotation marks around their speeches:

> First, of the fact they question'd—"Was it true"?
> The child was brought—"What then remained to do?"
> "Was't dead or living?" This was fairly proved:
> 'Twas pinch'd, it roar'd, and every doubt removed.
> (lines 694–7)

It is as though a ghost narrator takes over when Crabbe does not wish to be involved, for here we sense a tone which is more condemnatory than that of the poet himself. The manipulation of oblique voices continues throughout the episode, and indeed, through to the end of the section, for Richard Monday is followed in the Register by Barnaby, the poor farmer who is the butt of the cruel wit of all his fellows in the village. Here the poet dissociates himself from this cruelty by devising a speech pattern in which he is not directly and personally committed:

> A humble man is he, and when they meet,
> Our farmers find him on a distant seat;

There for their wit he serves a constant theme—
They praise his dairy, they extol his team,
They ask the price of each unrivall'd steed,
And whence his sheep, that admirable breed?
His thriving arts they beg he would explain,
And where he puts the money he must gain.
They have their daughters, but they fear their friend
Would think his sons too much would condescend;
They have their sons who would their fortunes try,
But fear his daughters will their suit deny.
So runs the joke . . .
His cares, his sighs, provoke the insult more,
And point the jest—for Barnaby is poor.

(lines 771–86)

In Crabbe's original manuscript the voices of the village wags are here represented by giving direct speech marks to what is in fact only indirect speech. It is a device Crabbe uses very frequently. On the page it often looks clumsy and indeed, many modern editors have abandoned the device including Ward, whose text I am following. One tampers with the text at considerable loss to the overall impact which nuances of tone can have on a Crabbe poem.

IV

The proportion of a poem which is likely to be given in direct speech grows as Crabbe's sense of form and his confidence increase. *The Newspaper* is almost without it: I have already commented on the dullness and deadness of that poem. At the other end of Crabbe's career "The Farewell and Return" takes the form of conversations between a man coming back to his native village, and a friend who has resided there all his life, so that the entire poem is in dialogue between two sharply contrasted persons, one having, and one seeking, knowledge. But inside this framework of dialogue, other incidental conversations take place between the people of the inset narratives. Hence voices, time scales, and points of view are all mixed. Many of the "Farewell and Return" series show a sketchy development of the returning visitor as a melancholic and contemplative man, whilst his friend seems younger and more vigorous. This dramatic division is not fully evolved, for the scheme was still in its embryonic stage at Crabbe's death. He may, by his seventy-eighth year, have begun to lose something of the sharpness with which he had formerly differentiated tones and types of speaking voice, but he was still willing to experiment, certainly as late as *Tales of the Hall*. The fourteenth of the poems in this collection, "The Natural Death of Love" takes us to the limits of the "tale-within-a-tale-within-a-tale" idea, for it opens with the narrator (Crabbe) setting the scene, moves rapidly to the voices of the villagers criticising their parson —that is, Jacques, *not* Crabbe himself—passes to the point of view of Richard, one of the principal characters in the frame-narrative, and then to dialogue between the two brothers.

The conversation turns to domestic felicity, and George promises to tell his younger brother a story about a couple who are less happy than Richard and his wife. He tells his story in the form of a dialogue written out as though it were being presented in a play-text. Jeffrey was struck by the life and vigour of it, on a first reading. His review of *Tales of the Hall* for *The Edinburgh Review* singled the poem out:

> This tale is perhaps the best written of all the pieces before us. It consists of a very spirited dialogue between a married pair, upon the causes of the difference between the days of marriage and those of courtship; in which the errors and faults of both parties, and the petulance, impatience, and provoking acuteness of the lady, with the more reasonable and reflecting, but somewhat insulting manner of the gentleman, are all exhibited to the life.
>
> (*Edinburgh Review*, Vol. xxxii, July 1819)

Nearly always, when we are made aware of how much "to the life" Crabbe has managed to exhibit his characters, the success is ultimately attributable to his gift for creating and mixing speaking voices. He achieved an unusual facility for doing this in heroic couplets, where one might have thought it would be a difficult task. Not many of the Restoration dramatists, for instance, ever managed to combine the exigencies of this verse form with the presentation of an individualised personality.

Curiously, when one looks at Crabbe's very rare efforts in blank verse, the result is disappointing. "In a Neat Cottage" (*New Poems*, pp. 59–66) has nothing of the tense, character-revealing power of the rhyming poems. The proportion of the poem which is couched in dialogue is remarkably low, if one accepts its likely date as around 1820. It is only at the very end of the fragment that we get anything like Crabbe's most creative deployment of dialogue. Elizabeth, the heroine, is watching the struggles of a ship at sea to avoid being wrecked. Full of commitment and humanity, she questions a passing sailor, to whom it is all a matter of unconcern, both factually and imaginatively:

> To Sailors, as they walked the Window by,
> She said!: "When will it be that they are [?sav'd]?"
> One answer'd: "What o'clock?", & she replied:
> "Eleven!" "Good! & yesternight the Moon
> Was in her 2d quarter! Wind at East!"
> "But is there Safty"—"If they ride it out".
> "But will they ride it out?" "Perhaps they may,"
>
> (*New Poems*, p. 66, lines 256–62)

There is drama here—the drama of the sailor's refusal to make an emotional commitment to the moving object of the distressed ship, but the passage lacks the terse, tense vibrancy which comes through Crabbe's best couplet verse, and leaves one without much regret that he wrote so little in blank verse, though the very early poem "Midnight" is so promising in the same metre.

v

The answer to Hazlitt's question," Why not insist upon the unwelcome reality in prose?" is, as this look at Crabbe's blank verse helps to demonstrate, because he had a unique gift for making the form of his work of inherent assistance to its meaning, and in neither "In a Neat Cottage" nor in prose, according to his own estimate of the three novels he wrote, was he able to achieve the same compression, accuracy, and cutting power that he could bring through couplets. The fragments of prose narrative still extant in the Cambridge University notebooks confirm this. Far from being a "careless old fellow", as Fitzgerald would have us believe, Crabbe was a diligent and intelligent worker at his own manuscript first thoughts. There is every evidence that the daily thirty lines were subjected at various subsequent times to rigorous scrutiny and re-working. Passages scored through, reworked, changed from form to form, are covered with pen and pencil marks from clearly different dates. In his early days he tended to keep good things by him, and to bring them out whenever a semi-appropriate occasion occurred. He confessed that the governors of the poor-house in *The Borough* had been tacked onto the poem from an earlier piece of writing. On the whole the added-in passages don't show. Without Crabbe's confessions, I doubt if many readers would ever tell stylistically that these episodes are not contemporary with the main body of the work. For what it is worth, it *is* possible, almost infallibly, to distinguish the very early Crabbe from the mature writer, by checking the number of feminine rhymes, the number of triplets, and the proportion of direct speech in a poem. We do not need to rely on this laborious research method, because the canon is well-established, and the dating not in dispute, yet the change in style and method is worth noting.

His method of constructing his verse changed over the years, and the statistics may be of some passing interest. Up to and including *The Parish Register* his lines tend to be end-stopped. He uses enjambement for less than ten per cent of the lines in these early poems. There is still a hankering after the crisp, close effect of the Popeian manner, which the ear begins to sense is on the wane in *The Borough*, scarcely present in most of *Tales*, and quite dead by the last two volumes of his work. There is a direct relationship between matter and manner: it is when he perfects the particular form which much of his best work uses—the verse tale —that epigrams and chiasmus appear less frequently. He begins to think his ideas out through blocks of verse, rather than in couplet groups, and even his triplet rhymes (for which the proportion increases in his later verse) become less emphatically points at which the entire flow of the narrative is brought to a halt. This will be caused, partly at least, by the changing nature of the subject-matter. Writing on "Sects" or "Elections" the need to epigramise will be greater than it is in a narrative poem. On occasions the greater flexibility of the later verse—that is, its tendency to run to a natural pausing point rather than be restrained by the pauses dictated by the end-stopped line, becomes an effect of declining power; in later years Crabbe did not always have the nervous energy left, and did not feel his poems deeply enough, to infuse them with the dynamic driving force of his very best work. But such instances are rare, and on the whole it is fair to say that his manner becomes less epigramatic because he had chosen to adapt or modify his earlier style to his later purpose. Any discussion of such technical matters is also bedeviled by the punctuation employed in the normally established texts. Crabbe's own punctuation is eccentric. Entire letters are composed without a single full-stop, leaving him with a heavy reliance on the colon and semi-colon. Where he may have had a say in the appearence of the printed page he seems to have carried over the methods of his private correspondence. The difficulty of reconstructing Crabbe's punctuation is exacerbated by the unstandardised house-practice of the printers concerned—Brettell, during Crabbe's years with the publishing firm of Hatchard, and Davison, who printed for John Murray, and who hence dealt with all the Crabbe work after 1818. The point is worth making because the excessive semi-colons tend to make the eye read Crabbe in fits and starts, with exaggerated pauses, whereas an intelligent "live" reading shows him to be an altogether more coherent poet, and a conscious organiser of verse units. He also learns the value of breaking up the individual line during his poems on derangement, to create an effect of a wandering mind, or of thought trains so rapid that the speaker himself cannot keep pace with his own ideas.

"The Preceptor Husband"—a typical piece of Crabbe jocose-ness—will illustrate how flexible his unassuming but skilful manner can be. The story is of a young man who falls in love with learning whilst lacking all the discretion and worldly sense of proportion which should accompany it. He chooses for his wife a lady who leads him to believe that she will be responsive to his schemes for her educational improvement. She is too cunning for the unworldly Finch, who marries her out of his wilful and unshakeable delusion, and has to learn of her triviality of mind by the hard process of trying and failing to teach her. The full range of the comedy emerges only from a fairly extended quotation:

> " 'Augusta, love', said Finch, 'while you engage
> " 'In that embroidery, let me read a page.
> " 'Suppose it Hume's; indeed he takes a side,
> " 'But, still an author need not be our guide;

" 'And, as he writes with elegance and ease,
" 'Do now attend—he will be sure to please.
" 'Here at the Revolution we commence—
" 'We date, you know, our liberties from hence'.

" 'Yes, sure', Augusta answer'd with a smile;
" 'Our teacher always talk'd about his style,
" 'When we about the Revolution read,
" 'And how the martyrs to the flames were led:
" 'The good old bishops, I forget their names,
" 'But they were all committed to the flames;
" 'Maidens and widows, bachelors and wives—
" 'The very babes and sucklings lost their lives.
" 'I read it all in Guthrie at the school—
" 'What now!—I know you took me for a fool;
" 'There were five bishops taken from the stall,
" 'And twenty widows, I remember all;
" 'And by this token, that our teacher tried
" 'To cry for pity, till she howl'd and cried'.

" 'True, true, my love, but you mistake the thing—
" 'The Revolution that made William king
" 'Is what I mean; the Reformation you,
" 'In Edward and Elizabeth.'—'Tis true;
" 'But the nice reading is the love between
" 'The brave Lord Essex and the cruel queen;
" 'And how he sent the ring to save his head,
" 'Which the false lady kept till he was dead'.

"That is all true; now read, and I'll attend;
" 'But was not she a most deceitful friend?
" 'It was a monstrous, vile, and treacherous thing
" 'To show no pity, and to keep the ring;
" 'But the queen shook her in her dying bed,
" 'And 'God forgive you' was the word she said;
" 'Not I for certain'—come, I will attend;
" 'So read the Revolutions to an end'.

"Finch with a timid, strange, enquiring look,
"Softly and slowly laid aside the book
"With sigh inaudible—'Come, never heed,'
"Said he, recovering 'now I cannot read'.

(lines 204–45)

All Finch's naïveté comes out in his first speech. His circumstantiality, his finicky doubts about Hume's suitability are, of course, absurd, given what we know of the monumental ignorance and lack of interest which the lady really has. How beautifully the scene is pictured, with the earnest young man with his nose so far into the book that he cannot see the grimaces of the lady as she sits and sews! The couplet in which Finch tries to convey "useful crumbs of culture for young female persons" is exquisitely wrought —"Here at the Revolution we commence . . ." We relish the triteness, the dip and rise in the second line as he painfully makes his point. Augusta's muddling of Revolution and Reformation is richly funny, not just verbally, but structurally, from within the texture of the verse itself, for she babbles and tattles in a manner which clearly reveals the emptiness within. Her ability to turn a serious history lesson into the plot of a penny dreadful is very neatly done, and for all its unobtrusiveness, the verse itself is doing a great deal of the work for us. The dashes are clearly Augusta's breathing spaces as she rushes on with her disconcerting version of Tudor history, which she manages to reduce to "nice reading". She is every bit as good as the tattle-mongers of Jane Austen or Trollope, both of whom are kindred spirits with Crabbe in this mood.

Thrown out of humour and purpose by his failure so far, poor Finch takes his wife for a peripatetic botany lesson. The style ranges from the beautifully casual and informal tone of the dialogue exchange between the husband and wife, to the botanical terminology a little later:

> "They walk'd at leisure through their woods and groves,
> "In fields and lanes, and talk'd of plants and loves,
> "And loves of plants.—Said Finch, 'Augusta, dear,
> " 'You said you loved to learn,—were you sincere?
> " 'Do you remember that you told me once
> " 'How much you grieved, and said you were a dunce?
> " 'That is, you wanted information. Say,
> " 'What would you learn? I will direct your way.'
>
> " 'Goodness', said she, 'What meanings you discern
> " 'In a few words! I said I wish'd to learn,
> " 'And so I think I did; and you replied,
> " 'The wish was good: what would you now beside?

227

" 'Did you not say it show'd an ardent mind;
" 'And pray, what more do you expect to find?'

  " 'My dear Augusta, could you wish indeed
" 'For any knowledge, and then not proceed?
" 'That is not wishing'—
      " 'Mercy, how you tease!
" 'You knew I said it with a view to please;
" 'A compliment to you, and quite enough—
" 'You would not kill me with that puzzling stuff!
" 'Sure I might say I wished; but that is still
" 'Far from a promise: it is not,—'I will'.

  "Now o'er the grounds they rambled many a mile;
"He show'd the flowers, the stamina, the style,
"Calix and corol, pericarp and fruit,
"And all the plant produces, branch and root;
"Of these he treated, every varying shape,
"Till poor Augusta panted to escape.
"He show'd the various foliage plants produce,
"Lunate and lyrate, runcinate, retuse;
"Long were the learned words, and urged with force,
"Panduriform, pinnatifid, premorse,
"Latent and patent, papulous, and plane—
" 'Oh!' said the pupil, 'it will turn my brain'.
" 'Fear not,' he answer'd, and again, intent
"To fill that mind, o'er class and order went;
"And stopping, 'Now', he said, 'My love, attend.'
" 'I do', she said, 'but when will be an end?'—
" 'When we have made some progress—now, begin,
" 'Which is the stigma? show me with a pin;
" 'Come, I have told you, dearest, let me see,
" 'Times very many; tell it now to me.'
" 'Stigma! I know,—the things with yellow heads,
" 'That shed the dust, and grow upon the threads;
" 'You call them wives and husbands, but you know
" 'That is a joke—here, look and I will show
" 'All I remember.'—Doleful was the look
"Of the preceptor when he shut his book—
"The system brought to aid them in their view,
"And now with sighs return'd—'It will not do.'

         (lines 246–305)

Beyond the social observation, the command of the human voice, and the comic vision which can shape these scenes, the very texture and structure of the lines themselves add immeasurably to the total impact. I doubt if any critic of Crabbe has given sufficiently forceful articulation to the distance which exists between this and, say, *The Village*—a distance created quite consciously by Crabbe as he recognises the shift in his own interests, purposes and abilities.

VI

It must be confessed that there are lapses, frequent lapses, in Crabbe's prosody, though I suspect more of them to be due to his curious and idiosyncratic taste than to rank carelessness. If the pun was Shakespeare's fatal Cleopatra, then Crabbe cannot resist the syren song of a chiasmus lurking somewhere over the horizon. He will go out of his way to coin such gawky and often unilluminating things as

> A QUIET simple man was Abel Keene;
> He meant no harm, nor did he often mean.
> (*The Borough*, Letter XXI, lines 1–2)

or, describing a diligent and sober young farmer,

> No fair, nor fair one, kept him from the farm.
> ("Poins", *New Poems*, line 196)

though this latter example is not strictly chiasmus, but rather an irksome quibble. He also engages in what Lilian Haddakin calls "prosaisms". She observes:

There may be different opinions on whether they are *excessively* prosaic. The classic example here is the couplet:

> And I was asked and authorised to go
> And seek the firm of Clutterbuck and Co.

Isolated from its context, this couplet is, indeed, ludicrously flat . . . But if it is taken in its context the jar given by "Clutterbuck and Co." can be seen as intentional—and also (dramatically) ironical, since the speaker is aware both of the cacophany and of the mercantile association. It is through the visit to Clutterbuck and Co that he discovers the woman he has romantically and extravagantly loved since youth. He finds her, (to quote Jeffrey) "in a very unexpected way, and in a way that no one but Mr Crabbe would have either thought of, or thought of describing in verse. In short, he finds her established as the *chère amie* of another respectable banker". This, of course, we do not know when we read the couplet in question. But an observant reader will be aware that Crabbe does not as a rule name minor characters; the fact that this firm of bankers is named, and the choice of name, will strike him as significant. Crabbe's insistence here on his own lack of elevation should indicate that this part of the room is one of those "flats" from which something is soon to emerge.

(L. Haddakin, *The Poetry of Crabbe*, 1955, p. 162)

Clutterbuck and Co. have been discussed by nearly every commentator who writes on Crabbe, or to be more accurate, every *recent* one. It is interesting that few of his contemporary arbiters seem to have been bothered by it.

Dr Haddakin's suggestion that poetry of the kind Crabbe was writing will inevitably have flat patches is worth stressing. C. S. Lewis makes the same point with regard to Milton, though the sense is entirely relevant to Crabbe as well.

. . . the kind of poem Milton meant to write is unfamiliar to many readers. He is writing . . . a species of narrative poetry, and neither the species nor the genus is very well understood at present. The misunderstanding of the genus (narrative poetry) I have learned from looking into used copies of our great narrative poems. In them you find often enough a number of not very remarkable lines underscored with pencil in the first two pages, and all the rest of the book virgin. It is easy to see what has happened. The unfortunate reader has set out expecting "good lines"—little ebullient patches of delight—such as he is accustomed to find in lyrics . . . [but] . . . finding that the poem cannot really be read in this way, he has given up. (C. S. Lewis, *A Preface to Paradise Lost*, 1956, p. 1)

One would add that ill-informed reading is exacerbated by sheer lack of stamina; we have grown accustomed to expecting our poems to run no more than a couple of dozen lines. Crabbe's average, in the narrative poems, is about six hundred. In point of fact this is by no means excessive for the task he sets himself, and one is rather struck by his compression, denseness, and urgency, than by

any sense of a tale spun out or of excrescent *longueurs*. Certainly
no reader in his own day would have complained of Crabbe's
length when compared with Byron or with Southey, for instance,
or with Wordsworth in *The Prelude*.

Crabbe has an admirably business-like way of opening a poem
which sets the tone and gives all the requisite background for
what is to follow, within the space of ten or twenty lines. Sometimes this is done by physical description, sometimes by the succinct expression of a general thesis that the poem is to illustrate.
The first twenty-three lines of "The Patron" are full of suggestions
which the tale will pursue:

> A BOROUGH-BAILIFF, who to law was train'd,
> A wife and sons in decent state maintain'd;
> He had his way in life's rough ocean steered,
> And many a rock and coast of danger clear'd;
> He saw where others fail'd, and care had he
> Others in him should not such failings see;
> His sons in various busy states were placed,
> And all began the sweets of gain to taste,
> Save John, the younger; who, of sprightly parts,
> Felt not a love for money-making arts.
> In childhood feeble, he, for country air,
> Had long resided with a rustic pair;
> All round whose room were doleful ballads, songs,
> Of lovers' sufferings and of ladies' wrongs;
> Of peevish ghosts who came at dark midnight,
> For breach of promise guilty men to fright;
> Love, marriage, murder, were the themes, with these,
> All that on idle, ardent spirits sieze;
> Robbers at land and pirates on the main,
> Enchanters foil'd, spells broken, giants slain;
> Legends of love with tales of halls and bowers,
> Choice of rare songs, and garlands of choice flowers,
> And all the hungry mind without a choice devours.

Crabbe has shaped his exposition to achieve a number of purposes. He establishes a strong sense of contrast between the
dreamy and effete John, and his more sturdy but less sensitive
kindred. The image of the good pilot steering clear of the rocks
will become tragically appropriate to the fate of John. The father
has a shrewd ability to distinguish kinds and characters among

men: his son is to lack this altogether. Yet Crabbe does manage to suggest that this admirable pragmatism is uncomfortably close to charlatanism; it is not surprising that John rebels against the mercantile and spiritless world of his family. Physically he is different from the rest, being naturally cursed with a classically "poetic" physique. At an impressionable age he is thrust into a world quite different from that of his home, a world where Romance runs riot—and, though the poet does not actually say so, a world where John may well be over-indulged and under-reproved: a world where the life will be all imagination and little discipline. Crabbe even manages to pre-figure poor John's tragedy in the choice of themes for the romances he reads. He is to suffer (in his own mind) "lovers' sufferings", to endure "breach of promise" from his patron, and in the end to be virtually murdered by Lord Frederick's cruelty. The world will take all the themes of his fanciful reading, and turn them against him. There is an element of condemnation in all this: Crabbe's own upbringing as the "poetic" son in a mercantile household had taught him the value of keeping one's feet on the ground. But the condemnation is tempered by understanding; it wasn't John's fault he was born with a dreamer's temperament, that he was cursed with ill health, and sent to a household where the reading matter was of the wrong kind for his inclinations.

All this is managed in those twenty-three lines. To expect poetic bravura at the same time would clearly be folly. Fine writing would only draw the attention away from the very things Crabbe is seeking to achieve. The verse is fairly to be described as "flat" in the strictly lyrical sense, but of course it *isn't* lyrical verse. It has a tough, manly air of practical self-sufficiency about it—no chiasmus, no epigrams, no rib-nudging puns, but a simple, direct ability to move us forward to the desired objective. But in order to do this, Crabbe has written much more skilfully than might appear at first sight. The unobtrusive holding back of the verb "maintained" in line two gives a slightly old-fashioned and stilted ring to the line which is entirely in character with the atmosphere Crabbe wishes to build up around the bailiff, for purposes of contrast with his poet-son. The trite metaphor of life's journey as a sea-voyage helps to characterise the bailiff, as one feels it is a metaphor he has coined about himself. It draws upon the world of mercantile, worldly, tough affairs, which is precisely the world John does not know, and which is to wreck him. The language chosen to outline John's romantic reading is appropriate, and the last line has a provocative *double entendre* which carries us across the paragraph-break of the alexandrine and into the next section. It suggests first of all that "hungry" minds like John's are naturally undiscriminating, but it can also be read to suggest that poor John, lacking all other intellectual employment, naturally fell into the way of reading this dangerous material.

The poet is thus able both to sympathise and to judge; a tendency which is usually present in Crabbe at his best. Even in his most jocose poems there is an undertow of earnestness: "The Frank Courtship" (*Tales*, VI) and "The Lover's Journey" (*Tales*, X) are both high comedy, yet they suggest a serious purpose behind the fun. They offer illustration of Crabbe's own contention about the balance between entertainment and instruction which all literature must seek to achieve. The discussion of course has a venerable history, and Crabbe adds little new to it, but the primacy which he gives to entertainment in literature is worth underlining in a man we have too often labelled as "stern moralist" and whose serious-minded and doctrinal intentions I have been at such pains to outline in my earlier chapters. In the Preface to *Tales of the Hall* Crabbe writes:

> The first intention of the poet must be to please; for, if he means to instruct, he must render the instruction which he hopes to convey palatable and pleasant . . . I will not assume the tone of a moralist, nor promise that my relations shall be beneficial to mankind. (*Life*, pp. 377–8)

This is not how we customarily choose to see him, but if we will allow him to entertain us, by paying proper and detailed heed to his manner as well as his matter, then there is a rich benefit to be gained, even though he will occasionally trip us by the heels with gauche, irksome, or banal tricks.

VII

It is a pity that Crabbe is so ungenerous in the amount of comment on his own work and methods. The snippet from the Preface to *Tales of the Hall* which I have quoted, is the only portion of that preface which is of any real help to the reader. The Preface to *Poems* (1807) suggests rather nervously that a poet so amateur and occasional as Crabbe may not develop as much as the reader would expect, which seems a strange piece of self-unawareness, in that most of us, looking back over Crabbe's career, date the "progress" or change in him from precisely this point. The manner in which he designates and explains his chosen area of poetic activity is interesting:

> . . . an endeavour once more to describe village manners, not by adopting the notion of pastoral simplicity, or assuming ideas of rustic barbarity, but by more natural views of the peasantry, considered as a mixed body of persons, sober or profligate, and hence, in a great measure, contented or miserable.
>
> (*Life*, p. 100)

What a telling sentence this is, drawing a logical bond between what people choose to be and what their destinies then become. It may be rather more informative than the poet was aware. In any case, it does provide a real flash of insight into the ideological assumptions upon which Crabbe's narrative art is based.

The Preface to *The Borough* is likewise illuminating only in flashes. The poet's insistence upon the dramatic independence of the narrator gives us another example of the quaint factuality that Crabbe often exhibits. "You must not think it is me, George Crabbe, who writes these letters", he says. "It couldn't be me after all, for I live in Leicestershire and the correspondence concerns the inhabitants of a borough on the East Coast." This is an odd way of looking at dramatic propriety, but quite a lot of the savour of Crabbe's manner comes from his adherence to this kind of factuality. Some of his most famous pieces owe their existence to it. One feels that he doesn't particularly *like* describing hovels and harridans, but they are there, and hence it becomes his duty to include them and to draw no sentimentalising veil over their real nature and appearance. It is a manifestation of that moral toughness and courage with which Crabbe had taught himself to face life, and furnishes the answer to the attack on him by Hazlitt as a "Malthus turned metrical romancer" (*op. cit.*, p. 313).

Crabbe also discusses the area of life he is writing about in this preface. He has chosen the "middling classes" he explains, because they form "that order of society where the least display of vanity is to be found". On first sight this too seems a strange claim. One of his principal themes is the vanity of ordinary man. Poem after poem turns upon the exposure of vanity. I think Crabbe has been a little imprecise or skimpy in his explanation here. He is saying—or wanting to say—that human nature is least overlaid with coverings of social pretension in the middle classes, and that less artificial conventions hedge life around in the world the borough-dwellers inhabit. This seems true enough and suggests an artistic discretion which Crabbe is not always credited with. It is well enough known that his world changed from the time of his move to Trowbridge and that he moved in a higher rank of society there, becoming a magistrate, and having a good deal of contact with Bath and London. Crabbe always writes about the people immediately round him; the change in the poetry comes less from conscious choice than is sometimes assumed.

This certainly places *Tales* at the heart of his work, both by the time of composition—the years between 1808 and 1812—and by nature of the social range he embraces—magistrates, tradespeople, gentlemen farmers, clergymen's daughters, a lady's maid, and a general handyman. The great strength of the volume comes from the breadth of the world it touches, so that Crabbe's own nervous gestures at structural coherence, which the Preface to *Tales* bring forward, are in fact quite unnecessary. Jeffrey had suggested in *The Edinburgh Review* that "an extended chain of adventures" might enhance the attractions of Crabbe's character-drawing skill. The poet took this to mean that he was being asked to write something in epic style. His confusion was quite justifiable, for Jeffrey *did* seem to be hinting at an epic or a verse novel or something of the kind. After reading Crabbe's disclaimer, he seemed to change his mind.

> We did not wish Mr Crabbe to write an Epic . . . we are perfectly satisfied with the length of the pieces he has given us . . . But we should have liked a little more of the deep and tragical passions . . .
> (*Life*, p. 272)

In answer to the point Jeffrey thought he had made, Crabbe quite rightly and shrewdly argued that his characters were not of the kind which would be susceptible to epic treatment, either by rank or by the nature of the way he presents them. Epic, after all, is not a character genre—it deals with archetypes: Crabbe deals with eccentric individuals. His whole art is in distinguishing and documenting the unique individual qualities of a man's nature, not the ideal or the typical. The Preface to *Tales* is by far the richest of his critical writings. One regrets that it is not even more extended, but here one can see a craftsman who knows his own strengths and weaknesses: this is not an aspect of Crabbe on which his critics bestow enough attention:

> . . . these characters which were at my disposal were not such as would coalesce into one body . . .   (*Life*, p. 272)

He makes the analogy of Epic structure with an army where all the troops have to be going in one way for one purpose. Nothing could be more destructive to the very heart and essence of what Crabbe's own gifts yield. Jeffrey claimed to want more poems like "Sir Eustace Grey", "with less jocularity than prevails in the rest of his writings". Poor Crabbe, who is so often castigated for his unremitting gloom, is thus reproved by one of the first judges of his day for not being serious enough!

He has the wit to reject Jeffrey's kind of grand design. His troops are guerillas and irregulars, not the regular infantry. Crabbe recognises that it would be possible to create a loose amalgam, like that of *The Canterbury Tales*, though where, he asks, in Regency society, would one find a similar assemblage which covered the social spectrum? Any loss in unity of design which he suffers is offset by "more minute display of character", together with diversity of scene and change of mood. The last of these seems to me very important. We do not give him nearly enough credit for it. It is not present in *The Village*, and begins to make itself felt only tentatively in *Poems*; but *The Borough* and *Tales* work extremely hard to create variety of tone and mood. *Tales of the Hall* shows what happened when Crabbe went half-way to meeting Jeffrey's criticisms. He created a frame-narrative which meant that the evolution of character in the two brothers had to be spread over twenty-two letters, while at the same time individual and local character sketches were built up but not sustained. Crabbe was, in fact, trying to combine two quite different types of narrative. In addition, the shift in social emphasis had rather flattened out the peaks and hollows in his work. In *Tales* Crabbe defended the isolated narrative as the only means he possessed of engaging the reader's attention. That, at the age of sixty, he was prepared to try to extend that range on Jeffrey's advice, suggests both courage and humility.

> . . . describing as faithfully as I could men, manners, and things.
> (*Life*, p. 273)

Thus the poet designates his own art.

It was an art for which he cared rather more than we sometimes allow, for there have been suggestions that such descriptions do not warrant the name of poetry. His mind slips back into the time-honoured analogy between poetry and painting. Nobody questions the artist "who takes an accurate likeness of individuals", whereas a perversity in public taste punishes the poet for doing exactly the same thing. Perhaps it depends on one's definition of poetry. By the definition given to Theseus in *A Midsummer Night's Dream*, Crabbe admits he may fail to qualify. Such an author, by his use of pure imagination

> taking captive the imaginations of his readers, . . . elevates them above the grossness of actual being into the soothing and pleasant atmosphere of supramundane existence. (*Life*, 274)

Whilst he accepts the great pleasure such writing can give, he points out that it is not a pleasure arising from the characters. It is allowed to be the only kind of poetry that can claim to be "inspired". Yet there is another kind, that which is addressed to the "plain sense and sober judgement" of the reader. Dryden and Chaucer are named as belonging to the latter kind. It is sad that he does not anywhere mention by name any of the poets of imagination.

This account of Dryden as a poet whose accuracy of description needed no assistance from authorial fancy, leads Crabbe to formulate his own idea of "poetry without an atmosphere". If one has been following his argument through the Preface to *Tales*, the phrase is clear enough. He believes, quite simply, that if one describes a character, there is neither need nor reason to superadd qualities or effects. One does not have to imagine situations or

attributes extraneous to the moment and the crisis at which the
character exists properly for the poet, the moment which in itself
motivates his attention. This allows him to describe the death of
Buckingham in Pope's third *Moral Essay* as being without "atmosphere". There lies behind this insistence on not tampering
with the particulars of a situation that same desire for "Truth"
which we have seen elsewhere in Crabbe's thinking.

He also voices the claim that his principal interest is to "engage
the attention of his readers". It has always been a puzzle to those
who, temperamentally, do not find Crabbe easy to like, that he
can try to entertain his readers by depressing or shocking them.
His defence is that however oppressive an episode may be, it can
help to take us from "the painful realities of actual existence".
Provided that these episodes do not exactly coincide with the
reader's problems, they will "soothe his mind, and keep his curiosity pleasantly awake". Here is the explanation of that sometimes
quaint evasiveness Crabbe can adopt about the realities on which
his characters were based, and his earnestness not to give offence,
which caused such amusement to the authors of the *Rejected
Addresses*.

Crabbe's last point is that pleasure comes, in the end, not from
the events related, nor from the characters, but from the manner
in which the poem is conducted; a judicious management of manner will place fictitious and factual material on the same plane.

VIII

The letters take us very little further forward to meeting
Crabbe the artist talking to his fellow practitioners. He scarcely
talks to anyone on a serious level about his craft, not even to
Scott. He knew most of the poets of the Regency world, and
there was a scheme for Crabbe, Moore, Rogers, and Campbell to
start a poet's club at one time. The objects of it seem a bit vague,
and not surprisingly it was still-born. One cannot believe than any
one of these men would have learned much from his fellow members. Crabbe's difficulty in learning from others was, by this time,
partly age and partly temperament. Perhaps, in the end, it was
diffidence too, despite the accolades which Regency Bath and
London heaped on him. That struggle between the world within

and the social surface, which he attributes to his youthful self in
"Silford Hall" (*Posthumous Poems*, I) may explain the paucity of
theoretical comment he has left for us:

> Oft would he strive for words, and oft begin
> To frame in verse the views he had within;
> But ever fail'd; for how can words explain
> Th'unform'd ideas of a teeming brain.
>
> (lines 170–3)

What he omitted to tell us in precept can be grasped from his
practice, however. Certainly he is over-copious: he reveals his own
flaws and weaknesses as well as his strengths through his enormous output. His indiscretions and excesses are easy enough to
isolate and to parody, yet they are nearly always quirks of manner
or technical failures. The head may sometimes lead him astray, but
the heart seldom does. The core of his work is a compassionate
devotion to the lot of his fellow men, and an intense awareness of
the individuality of people which makes him, through all the gloom
and the sadness, very well worth reading.

Index

241